PLAINVILLE FIFTEEN YEARS LATER

PLAINVILLE
FIFTEEN YEARS LATER

by Art Gallaher, Jr.

1961

Columbia University Press · NEW YORK and LONDON

To DIXIE

Foreword

Plainville Fifteen Years Later is a welcome and excellent addition to the scant list of anthropological restudies. Here the restudy (and *new* study, since field problems and methods inevitably change) is of a Missouri farming community that I studied in 1939–40. "Plainville" was then "relatively isolated and . . . 'backward,'" and resisted many aspects of social change that attacked its traditional folkways. Much of the resistance centered on "scientific farming" (which not only assailed folk knowledge but also symbolized governmental interference with a way of life), and it extended to many other areas of "modernity."

In the sympathetic description and skillful analysis of Art Gallaher, Jr., the Plainvillers of today come alive to our eyes and ears—changed a little even in language during fifteen years; changed greatly in their economy, work habits, and attitudes toward money, leisure, and frugality; changed most in their acceptance of the principle of constant change, as induced by its "professional advocates": namely, the government agencies dealing with rural development and welfare and the mass communicators who deal with everyone everywhere, via press, radio, and television. In 1939–40 the voices against change were numerous and often angry; now they are fewer and more muted. (I cherish the wry lament of someone who says, "We never go visitin', always stayin' home glued to the idiot box [television].") Dr. Gallaher's book is an intensive analysis of the economic changes, and the accompanying changes in social structure and perceived values, in Plainville during the years from 1940 to 1955. For lack of good soil and other resources, Plainville is still a relatively poor community, but its people have moved closer to the larger American society in mechanization, consumption patterns, and—more extensively—consumption aspirations.

Yet, for all the changes, the Plainvillers described here are familiarly recognizable across the gap of time. Reading the present book is for me like reopening a conversation with old friends. They are "the same people" (some are in fact the same individuals), to whom much has happened in the interim; they seem to me changed far more in the accents and emphases of material life than in their deeply internalized modes of thinking and feeling. This means, of course, that human culture has continuity, in Plainville or anywhere. That the Plainville culture-in-continuity can be viewed without major discrepancies of factual data in two separate accounts—Dr. Gallaher's and mine—is a tribute to the basic techniques of social anthropology. However different in temperament, age, personal interests, or theoretical orientation, two anthropologists studying a given community by the systematic techniques of personal interviewing and participant observation will emerge with data that is in general consistent.

When I went to Plainville in 1939 few anthropologists had studied "contemporary" (that is, non-tribal) communities. Bell had published a few articles about rural Iowa; Miner had studied a French-Canadian rural parish; Powdermaker, Negro life in rural Mississippi; Arensberg and Kimball, the Irish countryman. To study one's own culture was considered by many to be an odd and even "unanthropological" pursuit. My own serious research problems had to emerge from the fieldwork itself, since there was little previous relevant anthropological experience.

Fifteen years later many excellent anthropological studies of contemporary communities had appeared. Their results had been discussed theoretically by anthropologists; anthropology, sociology, and psychology had contributed to each other in method and theory. Hence, Dr. Gallaher was able to enter upon his field research for the restudy of Plainville with specific hypotheses and problems, formulated beforehand with theoretical sophistication. This reflects a great advance in method. Another important methodological improvement is the greatly increased quantitative dimension of his research. By utilizing fully available statistical records (and by taking the trouble to gather considerable numerical data himself), he lessens error and increases his significant knowledge of the community; he does this without slighting the qualitative dimension. The result is a splendid scientific study of people —of people whose daily talk we seem to hear and whose lives we seem for a time to share.

CARL WITHERS
(JAMES WEST)

Acknowledgments

I OWE a debt of personal gratitude to Professors Edward H. Spicer and William H. Kelly, and to Mr. Carl Withers. I am particularly indebted to Professor Spicer for his encouragement and counsel throughout the period of research and during the preparation of the manuscript, and to Professor Kelly for much valuable aid toward understanding the material collected. I want to thank especially Mr. Withers for his detailed criticisms and suggestions about the manuscript.

The manuscript in various stages of preparation had the benefit of critical reading and helpful suggestions from Professors Edward Norbeck and Noel P. Gist, and Dr. Mary Ellen Goodman. My study has further benefited from unpublished manuscripts made available by Professor Milton Coughenour.

I gratefully acknowledge financial assistance from the Wenner-Gren Foundation for Anthropological Research.

Part of my field material was analyzed as a doctoral dissertation at the University of Arizona. I should like to thank Professor Emil W. Haury, Chairman, Department of Anthropology, at that institution, Professor Harry T. Getty, and the rest of the staff not already mentioned for their encouragement and support during my tenure there as a student and during my research. On this score, I should also like to thank Dr. Edward B. Danson.

I owe a special debt to my wife, Dixie C. Gallaher, for her constant encouragement and valuable assistance with the field work. To Miss Elisabeth L. Shoemaker of Columbia University Press I wish to express my thanks and appreciation for her valuable editorial assistance in preparing the manuscript for press.

A Note to Plainvillers

I WISH to thank all of you who gave your time, effort, and cooperation in the interest of the research reported in this book. I am doubly grateful to you because I am the second anthropologist within the span of a single generation whose request to consult with you about your community you have so graciously acknowledged.

Today, more than ever before, students seriously interested in American life, its problems and its variations, seek community laboratories in which to study and analyze carefully cultural forms and processes. You who live in communities chosen for study are the only ones who can provide the information needed for the kind of understanding sought by the social sciences. In this respect Plainville, Missouri, rightfully takes it place alongside Middletown, Indiana (also studied twice); Jonesville, Illinois (studied by another researcher as Elmtown); Wasco, California; Landaff, New Hampshire; Homestead, New Mexico; Yankee City, Massachusetts; Sublette, Kansas; Springdale, New York; and Irwin, Iowa, to mention only a few of many representative communities which have contributed to our understanding of rural and urban America.

I do not have to tell you that life in a small community under study is not the same as before a researcher arrives. You who live in such communities, who are intimately and emotionally involved in the fabric of daily life in them, are aware of the "strain" of being studied more than I or any other researcher can ever fully appreciate. It is understandable that you sometimes resent, certainly always find it difficult to accept, the relatively dispassionate, detached image of your community painted by one like myself who is not a permanent part of it. In this respect, I hope you can view Plainville at least partly as I have done—not as a unique community, but as one which represents certain features common to much of rural life in America today. With this premise in mind, I think you will agree that the kind of analysis attempted in this book can contribute to an understanding ultimately applicable to a wide segment of our society. The knowledge gained from your community and others will, we hope, shed some light on the processes that are rapidly transforming our institutions.

I am sure that some of you are not going to like the conclusions I have drawn about Plainville, but I believe you are aware that no analysis of community life can be completely pleasing and still be honest. Furthermore, I believe you will understand that nothing I have written is intended to cast ridicule on your community or anyone in it. In fact, I have the greatest respect for you, and I regard many of you as being among my closest personal friends.

ART GALLAHER, JR.

Contents

Tables

are Plainvillers adjusting to the rapidly diminishing isolation suggested by West? To what extent are they enjoying the improved level of living found in more industrialized farm communities? What needs do Plainvillers have in 1954–55 that they did not have in 1939, and by what means are they coping with them? What are the effects of rapid technological change on the class system reported in the first study? Were the conflicts observed by West sharpened or modified? What kind of leadership is emerging to cope with changing sociocultural conditions? What are the effects on the community of social planning directed by centralized authority? Most important, what are the processes of change, how are these influenced by outside authority, and what is the role of technology in them? Finally, what are the special conditions which influence most the acceptance or rejection of change?

Plainville was further suited to our research purposes because it is in a traditionally low-income farm area, and since it had been previously studied we had a good basis of comparison for our assessment of present life in a low-income family farm community. In this respect, Plainville offered an excellent limited universe in which to examine the cultural forces affecting life in such communities. Most of the families who live there, for example, are included in the one and one-half million low-income family farm units found in approximately one thousand counties in the United States today.[5] Woodland County, in which Plainville is located, and the counties like it have many features of a "cultural island," an underdeveloped area within the most prosperous and progressive agricultural economy in the world, and the farmers who live in such counties obviously constitute a growing group of underprivileged Americans existing on the periphery of modern industrialized farm life. In fact, these families, when viewed against the over-all structure of American society, are a political, economic, and social enigma. Their commitment to the soil is complicated by a shortage of good land, farms that are too small for mechanized farming, inadequate credit facilities, and often lack of management information and skill which might open wider opportunity. In addition, general environmental, economic, and social changes create difficulties and make adjustments necessary.

For one interested in directed culture change, though, it is significant that the family farmer in America does not face his problems alone, and has not done so since the 1930's, because he lives in a society which, through popular sentiment and political tradition, seems bent on his preservation. Many Americans, rural and urban, still cling to an image of family farms clustered about little villages, happy families seated at bountiful tables, farmers idling on wintry afternoons around a pot-bellied stove in the country store, and people living a simple, bucolic life with their few needs adequately met. That this image has a historical reality for some cannot be denied; that it is currently more mythical than real also cannot be denied.[6] Despite its mythical properties, though, the image continues to evoke nostalgia and idealistic associations—witness the attempts of those who seek national office to identify with the rural heritage. They commonly stump small towns and are photographed shaking hands in front of the general store (when one can be found).

This image and the awareness that the family farm tradition is valued so highly as an American heritage continue to give the family farmer a prominent place in our national political picture. As Bertrand (1958:204) observes,

When the vision is shattered or even marred, the fury of the protest is invariably great. A threat to the family farm is interpreted as far more than a menace to a property right. It is regarded as prejudicial to a way of life and thus intolerable. Such indignation has generated agrarian revolts that have found expression in political action.

Most such action, either by Congress or by established agencies such as the Department of Agriculture, seeks to protect the family farm tradition largely through innovative means.[7] For this reason a community like Plainville is an excellent one in which to study directed change. Again, in the case of Plainville, it is significant that the community had been previously studied and that the first researcher clearly indicated that much of the social reform then under way was introduced from "outside." In this respect, many hypotheses suggested by *Plainville, U.S.A.* served as guides during various stages of the restudy.

FIELD PROCEDURE

Problems involved in the restudy of a small, literate, community differ from those found in more conventional anthropological research. The people of Plainville, for example, quickly made known their knowledge of West and the first published report. Many remembered him with personal liking, but nearly all resented his book. I am convinced, however, that despite widespread conversational familiarity with the report few people have read it through. Those who have read it claim that, while essentially true, it emphasizes negative features of their culture. Many erroneously believe that West deliberately spotlighted them with ridicule,[8] that he poked fun at their backwardness, or that the book was written only for money.[9] The question Plainvillers most frequently asked us was "Why?" Why had they been studied in the first place? Why had the first book ever been published? Why had we selected their community for research? We tried to answer their questions accurately, but I am afraid that we were unable to communicate in a meaningful way to everyone the values supporting our research and the significance of it.

Our greatest problem was to establish a research role which would not identify us with the original research design and with West. This was not easy. We found, for example, that some people "naturally" identified us with the first researcher or assumed that I had come to check his findings. A few thought that I was going to investigate "scandals" mentioned in the first report. Other rumors identified me as a government agent "checking up" on special groups, such as old-age pensioners, farmers, "tax dodgers," or welfare recipients. These false role assignments quickly taught us the concern of Plainvillers over government interference in local matters. Fortunately, we could dispose of most false impressions by energetically reaffirming our research interests. As field work progressed, certain perceptive people who demonstrated good knowledge of communications in the community were periodically interviewed to assess my role as it was currently interpreted. This frequently permitted me to correct erroneous notions before they could be disseminated as rumors. The procedure is highly recommended for small communities such as Plainville, where rumors unchecked become fact and where the nature of the data developed is intimately tied to the image the community holds of the researcher. In Plainville, as in many other research settings, the image changes.

We explained as accurately as possible that we were not specifically concerned with checking the findings of West. I felt that this point should be stressed to minimize our chances of developing biased data. We made known, however, our interest in known or assumed discrepancies in his book. Our policy was, in fact, to exhibit neutrality regarding West's study. We stressed that our work was not a continuation of the original research project (which Plainvillers associate with Columbia University), that I was a graduate student in anthropology from the University of Arizona, and that our research was mainly for a Ph.D. dissertation. We emphasized our major interest as the analysis of economic and agricultural changes, especially those derived from government programs over the past fifteen years, and the determination of ways in which these and other changes had affected the lives of the people. Many people frankly admitted their uneasiness at being studied a second time, and some, unfortunately, were never convinced of our motives. For

Finally, many people provided personal papers, and I was permitted to examine diary accounts which, combined with interview materials, amount to life histories.

As much as possible, within the roles we established, my wife and I became functioning members of the community. My major role, of course, was that of research student. My wife taught in a one-room country school ten miles south of the village in an adjoining county. She spent most of her free time assisting with the research. We identified with the Christian Church but attended revivals and occasional services in other churches. I participated in the businessmen's organization, and occasional P.T.A. and county education meetings, became an assistant scout master, played basketball with the town team, served on the carnival committee for the March of Dimes, and took part in many other community functions during the year. Observations were regularly made at sports events, political meetings, and other special and everyday community activities. Neither my wife nor I participated in or became involved in any controversial situations.

Most of the data was obtained through formal and informal interviews. We met probably half the people in the community, and recorded information from 154 individuals representing 105 nuclear families. Intensive interviews were conducted over a period of several months with twenty-one people: seven women and fourteen men, who were selected on the basis of age, occupation, religion, and general social position in the community. Their ages range from twenty-six to seventy-eight. All religious denominations are represented, and there is one agnostic. The heads of households in the sample include three cattlemen, two dairymen, four businessmen, three laborers, two hill farmers, two general farmers, and a retired property owner. Three of the men are retired on pensions. Five are high status in the community, and four are extremely low status. Lower-status informants were by far the most difficult to approach. However, very intimate rapport was established and sustained with these people.

One serious methodological handicap is directly traceable to the first study. Many people objected to having notes taken in their presence, always with negative references to West's "little black book." Under these conditions the ideal interview was short, with my wife present to serve as a check on the data ultimately recorded. Disagreements with West's study, as these appeared in interviews, were checked as closely as possible. Some significant comparisons with his report appear in the concluding chapter.

Much valuable information was obtained from ex-residents of Plainville, seen either in the community, during their visits, or away from the village. Businessmen in surrounding towns and counties were interviewed to determine their attitudes regarding customers from Plainville. The only Extension agent available who had formerly worked in Woodland County was interviewed. Fortunately, James West visited friends in the community during the closing weeks of my research, and I had the opportunity to make his acquaintance and to discuss mutual problems.

Interviews with teachers and the school superintendent, and observations made by the latter, contributed greatly to the data on children of school age. Additional information was obtained from this age group through conversations at teenage loafing spots, at the scenes of sports activities, and during family visits. Three series of themes were obtained from junior and senior English classes on the topics "What I hope my future occupation will be, and why," "Community changes since my grandfather's time," and "Superstitions that I know."

One valuable body of data was destroyed a few months before field work began. This was the complete record of all activities and participants in the federal farm programs in the county. Federal regulations passed shortly before we entered the field permitted local offices to discard many records older than two years. The Woodland County office concerned destroyed a large volume of data covering more than twenty years. Some of this information was obtained for the county level, but not for individuals, by a laborious search of related records in the files of the state Agricultural Stabilization Conservation office.

2 The Setting

PLAINVILLE is a small farm community in Woodland County, Missouri, in a section of the state generally considered rich in natural beauty but poor in economic potential. The Woodland County countryside is dominated by rough, heavily timbered hills that rise highest, in rumpled masses, along the snake-like Apple River, which meanders among the hills rather uncertainly dividing the county into two parts. Away from the river, between north-south ridges of smaller hills, are three relatively level prairies, each surrounded by brush and timber. The larger of these, about twenty miles long and five miles wide, is called the Plainville, or "Twenty-Five Mile," Prairie.

Most Plainville farms today are on the prairie, where the top soil is relatively shallow, four to eight inches deep, and is not too fertile. The best farm lands are the small fields nestled on the thick alluvial deposits which occur infrequently along the river and some primary creeks. Least productive are the rocky hill lands, covering most of the county, with top soil less than four inches deep.

TABLE I. WOODLAND COUNTY SOIL TYPES [1]

Type	Percent of County Land
Crawford Gravelly (red limestone land)	8.30
Huntington Silt (bottom land)	6.23
Cherokee (prairie land)	20.07
Clarksville Gravelly (hill land)	49.83
Clarksville Stony Loam (rough timber land)	3.81
Lebanon Silt (post oak flat land)	11.76

There are four distinct seasons: spring, summer, fall, and winter. The growing season begins with the last killing freeze, around April 15, and continues to the first killing freeze, around October 15. During mid-winter (January) mean temperatures range from a minimum of twenty-two degrees (F) to a maximum of forty-four degrees (F), with readings below zero not uncommon. In sharp contrast, mid-summer (August) mean temperatures range from a minimum of sixty-seven degrees (F) to ninety-two degrees (F), with occasional extremes as high as 110 degrees (F).

Woodland County normally averages forty to forty-four inches of rainfall, most of which is evenly distributed through spring, summer, and fall. Until recently water for human consumption came from shallow wells. Good producers at twenty to fifty feet were common, and a "water witch" says that in the old days it was merely a question of "where a man wanted to sink his well." Stock were formerly watered from springs, running creeks, or natural ponds, some of which "never use to go dry." The region is now (1954–55) in its third year of severe drought, complicated by excessively hot summer months. Shallow wells are drying up, dependable springs are disappearing, and several "branches" have stopped running, causing a critical shortage of water. Farmers haul stock water from available sources, some people must borrow water for household use, and several families with modern plumbing are forced to revert to outdoor toilets. Several people are drilling deep wells, from 250 to 300 feet,[2] causing those with shallow wells to fear that these will drain off their meager supply.

Woodland County mineral resources, none of which are produced commercially, are barite, lead, and zinc. Barite possibly exists in commercial quantities, and mining firms occasionally express interest in acquiring local leases. Many older people believe "with all these rocks we're bound to have uranium."

Over half the county is covered by medium to heavy timber and underbrush, but only a small fraction of the county income is from lumber sales. Most of the bottom land hardwoods, walnut especially, were cut long ago, and existing varieties of oak and hickory are of poor commercial grade. Nevertheless, some of the latter are processed into rough siding at local sawmills. Several varieties of berries and some fruits, such as persimmons and pawpaws, grow wild, but none are important in local diet or commercial sales.

Edible varieties of fish are found in some streams, and raccoons, foxes, wolves, skunks, opossums, rabbits, squirrels, and deer run the timber. Few families, however, depend on fish or game as a source of food. Raccoon, for example, is eaten by a few but, with the fox, is primarily game for hound hunters. Wolves are trapped for bounty, but only two men spend much time at this pursuit. Skunks and opossums were formerly hunted for pelts, but today "it ain't worth the trouble to skin one." Rabbits and squirrels are hunted for dog and rifle sport, and a few people eat squirrels. Rabbits were formerly eaten, but now the risk of contracting infectious diseases is believed so great that few people will prepare them. Through the efforts of the state game commission, deer, which had been completely absent for several decades, are again plentiful in Woodland and adjoining counties. There is a brief deer-hunting season each fall, and several Plainville men and women participate. A few people fish and kill deer and other animals out of season to supplement food supplies. Plainvillers justify these illegal acts "if people need the food," and under such circumstances consider fish and game laws an imposition. However, those who wantonly kill wildlife, "just for the heck of it," are strongly condemned.

SETTLEMENT

Two separate waves of migrants from the east made the early settlement of Woodland County (West, 1945:4). The first of these, from the hills of Kentucky and Tennessee, arrived around 1830. They were frontiersmen and farmers who derived their food from hunting, gathering wild fruits and vegetables, and growing such minor farm crops as

corn and vegetables, such as potatoes, cabbage and onions. As the settlers increased crops of oats and rye and small crops of timothy and red top hay, and wheat began to be raised, but it was not fully understood by the farmers until the close of the Civil War how valuable the hay crops could be made (Wilson, 1907:25).

Farm lands were small bottom or hill fields, cleared of timber used for buildings, near springs or streams. Pioneer merchants accompanied the settlers, and small villages were established. Woodland County was surveyed in 1838, and by October of that year official land entries were being recorded. The county seat was platted in 1845 and the county was officially recognized by the state.

The second wave of immigrants came around 1860 but, unlike their predecessors, chose to settle on the prairies. The Plainville Prairie was "homesteaded" between 1860 and 1870, and in 1869 the village of Plainville was platted on the edge of the prairie. "We got the best town spot in all the county . . . the prairie to the west and south, and the timber in back of us, north and east." With prairie settlement there came modern farm technology and other traits associated with prairie life. Prairie living marked the appearance of a new way of life for Plainvillers, because prairie residents depended entirely on farming for subsistence. The breaking of the prairie was fully accomplished by 1890.

THE COMMUNITY

The community is defined as the area within the Plainville consolidated school district. This area extends eighteen miles in a north-south direction and about five miles in an east-west direction, and includes most of two of the county's nine townships. An estimated 275 nuclear families live in the community, plus many older people who live alone. These people all have one thing in common, the Plainville school. A few years ago they shared other social relationships—they traded, visited, and worshiped here—but today most of these activities transcend community limits as here defined. The village of Plainville is axial to the community. It is surrounded by neighborhoods, each identified by some present or former service agency.

Plainville is twenty-five miles north of Liberty, the nearest urban center. Liberty is a town of 3,500 people and the location of a small denominational college. About seventy-five miles south is Largetown, an urban area of 100,000 persons. Metropolis, with a population of 700,000, lies 120 miles north. Plainvillers do most of their "outside" shopping in these three communities, particularly Largetown, and all three towns have important recreational functions for Plainville youths and adults.

The hub of the village is the town square. It is covered with broad shade trees, and during the spring and summer months its green lawn is kept carefully mowed. There is a bandstand near the center, a town pump at one corner, and loafing benches along one side. A few tables were added in 1955 for the convenience of picnicking tourists from the new highway. Dwellings line one side of the square and business houses occupy the other three.

The business buildings are a contrast of frame and rough stone construction, a contrast of repair and deterioration. There have been few recent additions, and merchants operating in the old structures are under little pressure to modernize their stores. The most obvious change in the business section is a hard surfaced street leading off the highway, along the "busy side" of the square, to the high school. This was the "kickoff" project in a series of civic improvements undertaken in 1948 by the newly organized Plainville Commercial Club. It was financed through club dues and subscription by local merchants. "There was plenty of money around right after the war and we didn't have much trouble getting all the merchants behind something that was going to cost them a little cash." Today, however, interest in maintaining the pavement is so low that the town board has difficulty securing badly needed repairs.

Clustered about the nucleus of service establishments, arranged along shady graveled streets, are 131 dwellings. These are mostly occupied by businessmen, a few professionals, laborers, and people who are retired. Fanning out in all directions from the village, over prairie and hills, are the farms.

The impressions of a person entering Plainville are likely to vary with the time of day, week, or year. Through all of these times, however, one impression will persist—that of age. This feeling is engendered by the appearance of the business buildings and the large number of elderly people, sixty-five and above, who are readily observable.

The normal weekday cycle of activity is somewhat as follows: before nine o'clock village children wander up the streets to school, and businesses begin to open. Busses converge from all directions to deposit farm children at the school entrance. Merchants take advantage of the early hour to clean their establishments, arrange stock, and, perhaps, sweep front walks. Delivery trucks from urban centers arrive at groceries with perishables. A few farmers arrive for early morning shopping.

At 9:30 A.M. the first and largest of two daily mail deliveries arrives by truck. In addition to personal mail, the daily papers from Largetown and Metropolis are in this delivery. Within the next hour and a half someone from practically every family in the village, and from nearby farms, either walks or drives to the post office to check the mail. Many arrive early to visit with neighbors during the thirty minutes it takes the postmaster and his assistant to file the mail and open the general delivery windows. News of out-of-the-ordinary community events and of personalities at home and away is exchanged. If the weather is pleasant the crowd overflows the postal lobby and small visiting groups cluster in front of the building. The next mail, much smaller in volume and creating much less excitement, arrives at 1:30 in the afternoon.

Throughout the rest of the day farmers arrive to shop or loaf. Housewives may shop for groceries, and during the noon hour school children mill about the post office, stores, and pool hall. In pleasant weather male loafers "hold court" on benches in the square, but bad weather brings them and idle farmers into one or two stores that do not discourage loafing and into the pool hall. The pool hall opened in 1954 and in the opinion of many old-timers is a "God-send" for retired men with nothing to do but gossip with each other.

In contrast to former years, most firms do not stay open past seven or eight in the evening. Exceptions are those on the highway, where through traffic determines closing time. Aside from highway merchants there are three businessmen on the square who observe irregular evening hours. The pool hall, for instance, stays open if there are players, and one of the barbers, a farmer by day, sometimes opens his shop on weekdays in the evening. The other exception is an elderly storekeeper who lives in the back of his store. He is open for business, or loafing, until around 9 P.M. There is no movie house, and aside from school or church functions there is little organized evening activity. Most people stay home watching television or listening to radio.

On weekdays, then, the square is normally deserted in the evening. If the weather is warm a few older men sometimes sit on benches or on the curb under one of the street lights. Plainville, however, is no longer the "night town" of Woodland County, where formerly "there was always something going on."

Plainville sure seems dead to me now. I mean dead for people of our age and younger [informant aged thirty-two]. Kids use to flock here at night from all over the county. If you didn't get to Plainville on Saturday night you thought you had really missed something.

Saturday, traditionally the big trading day in rural America, is slightly more active in Plainville than other days. The village is sometimes crowded for short periods on Saturday afternoons, but people no longer stay into the evening, nor do they, as in former years, come back to town after chores for evening visiting. There is, however, some business, and partly because of this, and partly through tradition, local merchants keep their stores open on Saturday evenings.

Several factors contribute to declining Saturday trade. One of the most important is a change in shopping patterns. For example, some families trade mostly in Liberty or Largetown, and others, who shop in Plainville, prefer to run to town for daily needs instead of buying on one big trading day. Closely associated with this is the changing function of Plainville merchants as middlemen, a condition more fully discussed in the next chapter. Another factor, contributing to and accompanying the decline in Saturday trading, is a functional change in the relationship between shopping and social visiting. An elderly merchant makes this point:

Use to people come to town to trade and visit. People just got together on Saturday. . . . They brought their eggs and cream, and stuff they had to sell. They bought in our stores and they all talked. . . . People don't visit in town nowadays. They jump in their cars and run clear 'cross the county just to say "howdy" . . . and have some place to go.

Sunday is a day of rest, visiting, and church-going, except for highway businesses. All but two of these stay open. The elderly storekeeper previously mentioned also opens his general store for a short time in the afternoon. If the weather is pleasant male loafers gather in the square. Plainville youths drive about the village in their cars except during the basketball season, when boys sometimes spend the afternoon practicing in the high school gym. For the most part, though, the village square is deserted on the Sabbath.

The economic structure of Plainville is, and always has been, centered in a system of small, family-type farms. Early settlers came looking for new land and, as was previously mentioned, by 1890 all of the land had been claimed. Migration into this region of Missouri, except for small numbers, stopped, and emigration became the valve for siphoning off population increases.

During the early 1900s surplus youth emigrated from Plainville to new lands farther west. As the western land frontier closed, laborers from Plainville and other rural American communities looked elsewhere for economic opportunity. West (1945:25), writing of this period, notes: "The industrial expansion of the next thirty years absorbed many Plainville emigrants, especially as farm and ranch hands, miners, rough carpenters, and unskilled machine operators."

Then came the great depression of the 1930s, and for a few years more people came home than left. The population of the community rose slightly. This gain, however, dissolved during the 1940–45 war years. Many Plainvillers met the emergency by entering military service, others left for defense jobs in the cities, and some contributed to the war effort by staying on the farm. Following the war, from 1945 to about 1949, there was a brief period of prosperity—servicemen came home and some civilians returned from the city. They came hoping to buy a farm in the community or a business in the village. Many veterans enrolled in agriculture, vocational, or on-the-job training programs. Plainville, in fact, became the county center for G.I. agricultural classes.

The immediate postwar era is remembered as one of the most euphoric in Plainville's history. An elderly lady says of this period, "Seems like everybody in the community was happy. . . . Mostly I guess because the war was over and the boys were coming home." A young defense worker, then just back from Metropolis, remembers, "There was something going on all the time. We ain't had so many young people in this place since, and probably never will have." A merchant notes, with some nostalgia, "All you had to do was mention it and people took hold . . . like fixin' the streets. Everbody was livin' it up . . . everbody had money then and they was a-spendin' it."

Postwar prosperity was short lived. Many unable to find suitable farms or, if they owned farms, to make them pay during the postwar farm depression, or who, for other reasons, were dissatisfied with rural life again sought jobs in the cities. The G.I. farm classes graduated more men than could be absorbed on county farms, and it became a common joke that once veterans completed their training, "the day their checks was stopped, they high-tailed it to the city." Local agricultural authorities estimate that less than ten percent of the veterans from pre-1950 classes are today farming.

The 1940–50 decade, then, was one of movement in and out of the county, with final census tabulations (1950) revealing a net population loss of seventeen percent. The two townships included in Plainville, though, lost only twelve percent, while the village proper actually gained eleven percent.

TABLE II. COMPARATIVE POPULATIONS FOR WOODLAND COUNTY, COMMUNITY, AND VILLAGE OF PLAINVILLE: 1930–1940–1950 [3]

Area	1930	1940	1950	1930–40 Percent of Increase	1940–50 Percent of Increase
County	6,430	6,506	5,387	1.2	−17.2
Community	1,573	1,692	1,488	7.6	−12.0
Village	237	269	299	13.8	11.1

During this decade there were approximately one third more births than deaths recorded in the county.

TABLE III. WOODLAND COUNTY BIRTH AND
DEATH RATES: 1940–49 [4]

Year	Births	Deaths
1940	99	65
1941	105	64
1942	93	75
1943	92	75
1944	86	57
1945	71	46
1946	71	42
1947	108	53
1948	96	65
1949	102	64
Total	923	606

By 1950 the population density of Woodland County was 13.1 persons per square mile. Of the 5,387 people recorded in the 1950 federal census, twenty-six percent (743 females and 647 males) were nonfarmers and seventy-four percent (1,887 females and 2,110 males) farmers. Table IV reveals greater loss in the farm than in the nonfarm group.

TABLE IV. WOODLAND COUNTY POPULATION
CHANGES, FARM AND NONFARM [5]

Area	1940	1950	Percent of Decrease, 1940–50
Farm	5,027	3,997	−20.5
Nonfarm	1,479	1,390	− 6.0

It is significant that Plainville's village population increased as the farm population declined. This is attributed to the recent pattern in which older farmers, especially widows, retire to the village in such numbers as to more than offset the number of youths who emigrate to cities. This leads some to complain that the village is rapidly becoming an "old folk's town." Thirty-three percent of the 304 people living there are over sixty, and the trend is toward an even greater imbalance in the future. This aging trend is not, however, as some Plainvillers assume, limited to the village

—older age levels are steadily comprising a greater percentage of the county population.

TABLE V. COMPARATIVE AGE LEVELS,
WOODLAND COUNTY, 1940–1950 [6]

Age Level	Percent of Population		Percent of Increase
	1940	1950	1940–50
Under 5 years	8.0	8.8	0.8
5–9	8.3	8.4	0.1
10–14	9.7	8.5	−1.2
15–19	10.3	7.1	−3.2
20–24	7.0	4.3	−2.7
25–29	6.4	5.6	−0.8
30–34	6.2	5.9	−0.3
35–39	6.4	5.9	−0.5
40–44	6.2	6.6	.4
45–49	5.3	6.6	1.3
50–54	5.5	6.3	.8
55–59	5.5	5.6	.1
60–64	4.3	5.8	1.5
65–69	3.9	5.7	1.8
70–74	3.3	3.7	.4
75 and over	3.7	5.0	1.3

The few recent immigrants to Woodland County have come for business or retirement reasons or, in the case of farmers, to buy relatively cheap farms. Within the past six years (1949–55) several "outsiders," farmers and stockmen from drought-stricken neighboring states, have bought large blocks of Woodland County land.

COMMUNICATIONS

One of the most significant changes in communications is a national, cross-country highway, completed in 1940, which passes through the edge of the village and places Plainville on the main street of a busy artery of national traffic. The effects of such a highway upon a relatively isolated community, such as Plainville was in 1939, are difficult to assess.

An immediate effect was to make roughly one fourth of the village businesses directly dependent on "outsiders" who travel the highway. These firms are attuned to such business and regulate their activities and ethics accordingly. They maintain longer hours, advertise with neon signs, and cater to tourists and travelers. The latter are expected to pay more than local customers, particularly for automotive goods and services, and, in fact, they do—two cents more per gallon for gasoline, and those unfortunate enough to have mechanical difficulties are charged more for repair services than hometowners. One café operator on the highway is strongly criticized for charging Plainvillers tourist prices, ten cents, for coffee and Cokes. A few people feel so strongly about this breach of etiquette that they refuse to patronize the café, and some, rather than give in, drive five miles to Discovery for their coffee.

The main highway increases contacts with outsiders and reminds Plainvillers that a few days' driving time takes them anywhere in the whole country. With its constant flow of traffic the highway is a prominent symbol of rapidly diminishing isolation. An ex-Plainviller back for a visit made the following observation:

People have gotten out and around the country. . . . The days of the thirty- and forty-year-old "rube" [7] are just about past. These boys go to the army, or they take out down the highway here. . . . They aren't backward like they use to be. . . . These people don't even think like they did when I lived here.

A network of state and county roads connects the village with outlying neighborhoods. Heavy rains and winter snows used to slow traffic on these arteries to a virtual standstill. This was, however, considered a normal, temporary problem in man's constant interaction with the elements. Even in good weather the roads were rough and uncomfortable, but then there were few occasions for trips outside the county. Visiting was confined to neighbors and relatives, children walked to

makes. These are admired and are not considered ostentatious if the owner can afford them. However, one who buys an automobile "just for show" is criticized. "His car don't impress me none." Of the eighty-one vehicles in the village in 1955, seven were 1955 models, twenty-five were of 1950–54 vintage, thirty-seven were made between 1940 and 1949, ten were 1930–39 models, and two were models older than 1930. There are thirty-eight Fords, twenty-five Chevrolets, three each of Nash and Mercury, and two each of Plymouth, Dodge, Cadillac, Buick, jeep, and Pontiac. Older automobiles are owned mostly by elderly people who have little occasion to travel outside the community. Younger generations aspire to later models. "Most of them high school boys would give their eye teeth to own a car . . . we've had several around here quit high school so's they could git one." One disgruntled father tells of purchasing a car for his son "just to keep him in school that last year. He wanted to quit and go to the city and buy him a car and tear around and raise hell before he went to the army." Plainvillers commonly joke that young people who go to the city to work "bust theirselves buyin' a new car" to bring home "and show it off." They consider the automobile a prominent symbol of economic achievement, and evaluate it as such long after the ex-Plainviller has concluded his visit and returned to the city.

It is easy for those without cars to "hitch" rides to nearby villages or to travel, for a small fee, to Stanton and Discovery with the mail carrier. Women who shop in Liberty and Largetown often travel in groups of two or more, and men frequently do the same. If something from another community is wanted, a friend or neighbor making the trip will procure it. A spirit of neighborly assistance often surrounds trips to the city, and obliging individuals frequently spend more time shopping for friends than for themselves. One man, who formerly drove a milk truck from Plainville to Largetown, developed such a favorable reputation for his accommodating manner that this became an important factor in his election to a county office. When he announced, "people remembered" and "folks felt an obligation." "Why, he'd drive clear across Largetown to pick up some little package for you."

About the same percentage of farm families as of villagers owns and operates automobiles. Pickups, however, are favored by many farmers, both for pleasure travel and for utility transportation. The number of farmers who own pickups increased by thirty percent between 1940 and 1955.

The nearest railroad comes through Stanton, fifteen miles west. The line now carries only freight. Older people, however, reminisce with some nostalgia of their trips to Stanton, "not too many years ago," to ride the train a short distance (to another village) "just to see what it was like." Most Plainville freight, particularly goods for merchants, now arrives by truck. An innovation in line with the changed shopping patterns is regularly scheduled "country" deliveries by urban department stores. Local merchants, on the other hand, do not consider delivery a part of business policy. There are a few exceptions, but these are special cases and are thought of as friendly favors. The feed store operator, for instance, delivers feed and fertilizer to some customers, and two grocerymen deliver to elderly pensioners who have no transportation.

Radios are the most widely accepted, and most frequently used, communicative device for linking Plainvillers with their region of the state, the state itself, and the nation as a whole. West (1945:15–16) wrote that radios were "considered almost a necessity. Over half the townspeople and nearly half the farmers own them." Today, every village family owns a radio of some kind, and few farm homes are without this entertainment and news medium. The availability of electricity is a major factor in the increase of radios among farmers. "Them old battery sets cost a lot to operate. . . . We do a lot better on REA."

Plainvillers listen to a variety of network and regional radio shows, but prefer those featuring "hillbilly" and folk

music, news, and market and weather reports. Regional stations loose a continuous barrage of rural consumer-oriented
advertising. Network programs, on the other hand, sponsor a
wider range of products. The acceptance of these, among
other things, identifies Plainvillers with values common to
much of American society outside their region. Newscasts and
weather reports are "musts." One popular weather forecaster
on a Largetown station intersperses his weather reports with
regional folklore, personal experiences, and folksy dialogue.
He has a big audience in the community, and is frequently
quoted and referred to in conversations. In a series of interviews with Plainville farmers to determine what they thought
would be the most effective media for disseminating innovations among them, several individuals stressed the potential of
this well-known radio personality. As one progressive farmer
observed, "The Extension people orta use him to sell their
stuff . . . everbody listens to old Smith . . . and a helluva
bunch of 'em believe everything he says."

A more recent innovation is television. The first TV set
appeared in 1950, and the owner recalls that his small living
room was crowded with curious neighbors "every night for
a week." At this stage reception was very poor. "The snow
was so bad, made yore eyes water," and many thought
"There's too many bugs in it . . . never be any good for us
people way out here in the country." Others said it would
always be too expensive for "common folks." By the end of
the year, however, TV had caught on. Soon another village
family and three or four farm families had bought sets, and
the 1950 general census reported forty in the entire county.
In 1955 forty percent of the village families and fifteen percent of all farm families owned sets. Most of the community
accepts television, and but for the expense involved many
more families would own a set. This innovation, however,
and the complex of traits associated with it, is expensive.
Plainville is in a reception fringe area, and owners must buy

expensive aerials, gadgets for rotating these, and power boosters if they wish to tune in distant stations.

There are some severe critics of television. The most rabid are certain Holiness and Baptist people who criticize most liquor and tobacco advertising, "them scanty clothes," and other types of "worldly sins." Defenders of TV argue that those who object most strongly are frequently exposed to "wordly sins" through radio advertising, and point out that "some of them same people use to complain about the rest of us playing radios." Critics, however, do not consider auditory advertising as potentially "bad" as the visual type. There are some, set owners included, who object to television on grounds other than moral. These critics lament that television disrupts visiting patterns. "People that own a set just suppose you come to watch a program when you go to visit, and so they turn it on," or "We never go visitin', always stayin' home glued to the 'idiot box.' " Most people are aware, however, that television is only one of many innovations that disturb traditional visiting arrangements. Some, in fact, believe TV is beneficial because "now people stay home together more'n they use to." This "stay at home" influence of television, however, is criticized by organization leaders who are convinced that it explains poor attendance at meetings of the P.T.A., Extension and home economics clubs, Commercial Club, scouts, and other groups.

Television fans favor hillbilly music, news, weather (the radio weather caster previously mentioned also appears on TV), sports (particularly wrestling), and variety and adventure programs. Special events, such as the baseball world series, championship boxing matches, and major political speeches, find non-owners visiting friends who own sets. This is reminiscent of the era mentioned by West (1945:16), when men congregated in stores to listen to similar events on radio. Interest in sports, incidentally, as in past years, is heightened by friendly betting pools. Visiting groups discuss television programming more than radio, and many people, particularly old-timers, marvel that their television screens bring them things which they "never dreamed were real."

In Plainville, as in most of rural America, the telephone is an important communications fixture. Here, as in many small communities, there is a colorful body of folklore surrounding a group of elderly women who it is believed continually listen in on party lines. Jokes about these women are an integral part of Plainville humor. The satisfaction derived from weaving humorous anecdotes about them is probably much greater than is justified by their behavior. The tell-tale "click" of the eavesdropper is heard, or imagined, often enough, however, that people hesitate to discuss confidential or important business over the phone.

Party line eavesdroppers or not, "jangling" the telephone call bell symbolizes the most effective means of rapidly disseminating local information. A network of phone lines connects eighty-four of the village's 131 households, eighteen businesses, and 130 farmers (farmers own and maintain their own equipment), to a central "switch office." The phone company is owned by a widow who, because she maintains discreet and dependable silence, commands respect from the entire community. "She's bound to know all that's goin' on . . . so much goes through the 'switch.' . . . But she don't talk to anyone about other people's business." Whenever someone wishes to send a telegram the telephone operator calls the message to the depot in Stanton or, during the night, to Liberty.

The most widely read newspaper, and the most important link connecting ex-residents with "home," is the weekly Discovery *Beacon,* which has been published each Thursday since 1885. It features a special section reporting visits, births, deaths, community happenings, and religious items, for each Woodland County community. "It's a week by week account. . . . Ain't always right. . . . Sometimes you do things you don't even find out about till the *Beacon* comes out." Despite occasional inaccuracies, many Plainvillers compete for recognition in the paper, and all anxiously await their weekly copy. The Plainville section is quickly digested and rehashed, and news about other communities is then read with considerable interest.

Another prominent *Beacon* feature is a full-page farm section with articles by the Extension agent and news releases from state and federal farm organizations. This page is carefully and critically examined by farmers, particularly the articles written by the agent. His column is used by friend and critic alike as one of the criteria for assessment of the agent's proficiency when viewed against the expectations which people have of him.

The favorite daily paper, with fifty-four village subscribers and a third as many in the country, is still the Largetown *Bee*. The *Bee* arrives by mail six mornings a week, and on Sunday morning is delivered by a high school boy. *Bee* news coverage is regional, with considerable space devoted to agriculture. Another daily, the Metropolis *Sun* is not so regional or state conscious, and gives much better coverage to national and world events. Both papers feature a mass of urban advertising, much of which includes rural consumers by extending mail-order privileges for specified goods. This type of merchandising competes with the traditional mail-order houses and their catalogs, which, however, still exist and are widely used by Plainvillers.

In addition to newspapers, most farmers subscribe to one of several weekly farm papers, and some take one or more monthly farm journals. The journals vary in interest, from general agricultural coverage to special breed, farmer's organization, or marketing magazines. Many farmers also buy, or receive free of charge, educational pamphlets distributed by the agricultural extension office.

A very few families subscribe to *Life, Time,* or some other weekly news magazine. The drug store has a well-stocked news stand, including a few copies each of *Life, Look,* and

The Saturday Evening Post, all of which normally sell. A wider variety of national news magazines is not stocked because "most of the people who would buy those subscribe to them anyway." Other magazines carried include *Ladies' Home Journal, Better Homes and Gardens, Sports Afield, Field and Stream, True, Argosy, Real, National Geographic,* "hit song" publications, *Reader's Digest, Coronet,* and a wide selection of comic books, "confession," "confidential," and "romance" magazines, and "western stories." "Confessions" and "westerns" are popular sellers. The drug store also stocks a large number of paperbound novels covering a wide range of subject matter. Since these are bought in "package deals," the owner cannot buy selectively and much of the material does not sell.

The Plainville school subscribes to *Reader's Digest* and *Successful Farming,* both used in classroom instruction. The school receives several free magazines, such as *The Ford Times* and *Friends.* The superintendent subscribes to *Time* and *Look,* and makes his copies available to the students, and another teacher does the same with her copy of *Life.* A few years ago the school subscribed to *Life,* but it was discontinued when several parents objected to liquor advertising and "them naked women in it." However, no one currently objects to the teachers' making their magazines available to the children, though liquor ads and scantily clad females are still present. The matter was discussed at one P.T.A. meeting, but no action was taken. The superintendent sometimes buys *Popular Mechanics, The Saturday Evening Post,* and *Seventeen* for school use.

A few Plainville women belong to book clubs and some trade books with each other. There is a small library in the village, begun during WPA days, which opens on Saturday mornings for several customers. However, few people show much interest in maintaining or increasing the library inventory.[8]

In addition to all the other means of communication, the

post office ("the only business in town that's run right") and rural free delivery should be mentioned. A few years ago postal substations were operated in neighborhood general stores but, much to the consternation of neighborhood residents, these were recently consolidated into the village post office. A discussion of the significance of the consolidation, and others, on the functional demise of local neighborhoods is reserved for a later section.

3 The Economy of Plainville

THE ECONOMIC ORGANIZATION of Plainville, indeed of the entire county, rests on a large core of farm families and a smaller group of entrepreneurs and specialists who depend directly on the farmers for their livelihood. Since the 1930s a third significant group has arisen, consisting of people dependent on government sources—old age assistance, welfare, and other programs—for most of their income.

In 1939 and 1940, at the time of the first study, the Plainville agricultural system consisted mainly of small, family type, low income, farm units. It was a system which functioned optimally under conditions of relative isolation.[1] There was a low level of agricultural professionalism, the felt need for accumulated surplus convertible to cash was minimal, and subsistence farming was valued by many as a way of life.[2] Since then, however, most of these conditions have changed, bringing accompanying changes in practically all areas of economic behavior. For example, Plainville farmers and nonfarmers now have more actual cash to spend than ever before. This, in turn, has led to a new standard of living, accelerated the shift from subsistence to cash-type living among farmers, and has permitted more people to enjoy a higher level of achievement within their present notion of ideal living standards.

Despite improved economic conditions, the people of Woodland County and Plainville still have relatively low incomes. For example, during 1949, one of the better years of production and income in the county's history, 1,505 farm and nonfarm families and unrelated individuals reported a median income of only $852 to the federal census.[3] Unfortunately, census data for 1939 are not comparable. However, financial data reported by West and derived from other sources clearly indicate that Plainvillers had far less to spend in 1939 than in 1949,[4] although their 1949 median income compares unfavorably with the $2,619 figure reported for the nation as a whole in that year.[5] However, when we consider that many Plainvillers, particularly farmers, still produce part of their food, the contrast is not so great as first appears, since the buying power of such families is greater than that of an urban family with a similar income.

The ideal living standard of the younger generation varies considerably from that of their parents. Their notion of a desirable life emerges from their concern over efficiency, especially in ways of making a living, and from an interest in material comfort, particularly as reflected in current consumption patterns. Both of these interests involve operational and living expenses far exceeding, as some elderly Plainvillers say, "the wildest expectations" of prior generations. These interests also conflict sharply with prominent values held by older people, such as, for example, frugality. This does not mean that older individuals universally reject the standard of living considered ideal by their children. They do, however, reject many labor-saving conveniences as "wasteful" or "silly," or as "things which are really not necessary."

More than anything else, older people deplore the seeming indifference to indebtedness of young Plainvillers. A woman of seventy-five expresses the sentiments of her generation thus: "Only a few years ago people bought only what they could pay for. . . . Maybe they wanted other things, but they didn't buy if they couldn't pay cash. . . . [Today] youngsters buy most anything they want and give no thought to the future." Her daughter, about forty, defends her generation with: "You might as well enjoy life by being in debt as to do without and be miserable like most of our older people done when they were our age." The older woman expresses a system of values which emphasizes hard work and frugality as prerequisites for independence in old age. She,

like others of her generation, feels justified in criticizing her
children for being "too free with money they ain't got."
These are the Plainvillers who, even though prosperous beyond precedent during recent years, vividly recall losing all
during the drought and depression of the 1930s. Convinced
that they possess the valuable experience which comes only
from having lived a full life, they feel obligated to caution
"youngsters" to "put away some of that easy money."

This, however, is not the type of advice that "youngsters"
appreciate. Young Plainvillers scoff at the economic conservatism of their elders. They are not afraid of going "head over
heels in debt." For example, two young farm couples in a
group interview, both deeply in debt but managing to continue a high level of living and meet their monthly obligations through long-term installments, expressed the sentiments of their generation by saying that had they saved the
money to pay cash for their cars, modernize their homes and
farms, and specialize their farm operations, "we woulda been
too old to enjoy it." These couples remember that their
parents had little need for cash incomes, "and we wouldn't
neither if we lived like our folks lived . . . which we don't
intend to do." They, like others of their contemporaries,
severely criticize young people who are more conservative
than themselves, and almost always attribute such conservatism to parental influences. "Just look at Bill, he's a good
worker and could be one of the best farmers in this county
. . . but he come home from the army and he ain't done
nothin' since but foller his old man around." Criticisms of
this nature are, however, relatively rare. More often one
hears children compared to parents, or parents criticized by
children. For example, a young, progressive farmer, convinced that ultimately man's technological developments will
master nature, says of his father:

He done all right in his lifetime, but he lost his butt once't in
the depression and he ain't been willin' to spend a nickel since.
Won't buy even half the machinery he needs. He wants me to

have everything but he'd crap in the snow before he'd build an indoor "john," and he's got the money to build a good one, too.

Some young Plainvillers, in fact, attribute all local economic ills to the conservatism of their elders:

The trouble with the whole darned county is we got too many old people in it. . . . These old-timers around here won't change their ways for nothin'. . . . They won't git modern in the house . . . always the last to catch onto somethin' new. . . . Try to do somethin' for the town, and ever old person in it starts countin' their money.

It is fairly obvious that not too many young people orient their economic behavior toward the accumulation of land and surplus cash as many of their parents did. Rather, they are more concerned with their income potential at a given point in time. This permits them to attain a desirable level of living without ready cash to meet long-term obligations; it permits them, through installment purchasing and long-term mortgages, to maintain a level of living only dreamed of by their parents when the latter were "starting out." In short, the younger generation supports the philosophy of "pay as you go." Their primary concern is with the present, and some of them facetiously rationalize their lack of concern for economic independence in old age with: "The government will take care of you when you get old." This jest is indicative of the diminishing isolation which has shifted certain forms of power and economic decision making to extra-community centers, some as far removed as the state or national capitals. Government programs since the 1930s, including old age assistance, public health, welfare, farm security, conservation, Extension, acreage controls and allotments, and parity, have had their effects on the present generation.

Many underlying factors have contributed to changes in the economy of Plainville since West's study. Two of the most important aspects of economic behavior are consumption patterns and ways of making a living. Change in either of these, of course, is accompanied by, and at the same time initiates, change in the other. For example, under favorable conditions of technological change new money income is available to the members of a society, and this creates more alternatives in goods and services. Expansion of goods and services on the other hand tends to affect the ways of making a living found in a society. Both of these areas of economic behavior may, of course, also be affected by other influences.

MAKING A LIVING: THE AGRICULTURAL SYSTEM

American farmers since the 1930s have entered an era in which agriculture has become increasingly identified with the federal government. Let us now direct our attention briefly to the government agencies which have affected Plainville farming.

THE GOVERNMENT AND AGRICULTURE

Probably the most significant innovation has been the establishment of federal agencies in the county for the sole purpose of assisting or regulating farm production. The innovative role, explicit or implicit, assumed by these agencies during the period covered by our research cannot be overemphasized. In fact, their local representatives function as intermediaries between specialists who make discoveries, social planners who design farm programs, and Plainville farmers. These representatives consciously and unconsciously direct changes in the customs and beliefs of the latter. Their task is not now, nor has it ever been, an easy one.

One of the first and most aggressive of the federal agencies to appear in Woodland County was the Agricultural Adjustment Administration (AAA). The AAA was born of national drought and depression during the 1930s, a decade when rural America, along with most of the nation, urgently needed economic assistance. It appeared in Plainville during an acute emergency, and here, as elsewhere, assumed a regulative role. By 1940, theoretical baseline for the present study, the philosophy underlying AAA had emerged as follows:

Basic in the New Deal's farm policy has been an attempt at outright government control of agricultural production and marketing for the purpose of raising prices and the buying power of farmers. Information and advice have given way to positive inducements and compulsions as the chief instrument for influencing farmers' decisions (Schmidt, 1941:121).

Government intervention in the highly individualistic occupation of farming, initially conceived as a short-term solution to an extraordinary situation, was still present in 1955, but under a different agency name. Thus, in 1945 the original AAA became the Production and Marketing Administration (PMA); under the Eisenhower administration it became Agricultural Stabilization Conservation (ASC).

In the eyes of Plainvillers, programs emanating from this office dwarf all other government farm gestures. Their dominant interest in ASC, however, has always resulted from and centered in the regulatory features of the many and varied "adjustment" programs. Outside regulation is, and always has been, resented by Plainville farmers, most of whom like to think of themselves as "individualists." Thus, we find that many people in this predominantly Republican community stigmatize regulatory features of ASC with the label "Democrat." In fact, "Democrat" and "New Deal" are synonymous, and criticisms of parity or acreage restrictions, or the more general complaint that "the gov'ment's meddlin' too much in the private affairs of us farmers," are invariably linked to one or the other.

Most farmers who criticize ASC nonetheless cooperate because of cash incentives. Negativism is further tempered by the general acceptance of a major feature of ASC, the Agricultural Conservation Program (ACP). Support for the ACP has gradually crystallized as farmers have come to recognize the need for soil-rebuilding and conservation practices. This amounts to positive acceptance of part of the major philosophy underlying the long-range plan of federal innovative agencies. However, this program is tied to price support and production controls, theoretically not a part of the permanent philosophy underlying the agricultural movement, a tieup resented by most Plainvillers.

Possibly the most energetic of all change-producing agencies in Woodland County during the past two decades has been the Agricultural Extension Service. The administration and subsidy of this service are a joint effort of the United States Department of Agriculture, the State Agricultural College, county government, and a local sponsoring organization, the Extension Association. The latter organization boasts only 418 members throughout the entire county and, considering that many families hold dual memberships (husband and wife being listed separately), involves only about 200 families, not all of whom are farmers. Many members are businessmen or other interested persons.

The Extension Service in Woodland County is an innovative agency which diffuses among farm families the latest useful and practical information on agriculture and home economics. Local service policy is formulated by the Extension agent who, theoretically, acts upon the advice of an Extension board composed of representatives from each of the county's nine townships. Members of the board presumably suggest special problems for the year, and the agent is then, according to Plainvillers, supposed to communicate, through demonstration and other techniques, new methods and procedures for solving these problems.

Cooperation with Extension programming is always voluntary, and for this reason is conditioned by principles different from those governing many other agencies in the county. The Extension agent as head of the program does not have formal sanctions to insure that his recommendations are followed or, for that matter, even tried. To a very large extent his power and influence depend on his ability to establish a large group of friends and supporters who will be predisposed to heed his advice. Analysis of the development of Extension in Woodland County reveals, for example, that the number of supporters has, at different times in the past, been conditioned by one or more of the following variables: meaning and function of the organization as perceived by potential clients; recognized need for change; and, because of the intimate type of interaction between specialist and client, agent personality.

The first full-time Extension agent opened an office in 1938. He immediately encountered several significant problems, some of which still have a bearing on Extension work. Due to a set of unfortunate circumstances surrounding the establishment of the office it was initially confused with the then extremely unpopular AAA, and consequently represented, for many Plainvillers, "just one more damned program of the Democrats." This confusion came about because the Extension agent had to use the same office as that occupied by the AAA. "The money for office space was supposed to have been appropriated by the county, but none was appropriated." [6] The function of the new organization was further confused when the agent had to spend part of his time working with AAA, propagandizing programs of the latter, although aware that the county was "radically Republican" and that "Extension was too closely identified with AAA and the Democratic party." [7] The confusion was intensified when the only "leading farmers" in the county who could be enlisted to propagandize Extension turned out to be well-known county Democrats. As the first agent recalls:

Unfortunately our early leaders were political leaders, and Democrats on top of that. We spent an awful lot of time overcoming resistance to the organization . . . not so much to what we were trying to sell, although there was some of that, too, but to the Extension setup itself.

Successful establishment of Extension was further complicated by a general resistance to "scientific" agriculture. West, for example, observed this resistance among all but a few local farmers, noting that:

For the average farmer a new habit or trait must "get into the tradition" through acceptance by neighbors before he ceases resenting it enough to try it. . . . By most farmers . . . "scientific" farming practices are only accepted one by one, as they trickle down into the ancient tradition (West, 1945:223–24).

Again, the first agent recalls: "The people had their own preferred methods and just took the attitude that 'you have nothing to offer us'." Such resistance was very real in 1939 and 1940, and served as one of the primary factors conditioning interaction between farmers and Extension personnel.

Two major barriers, then, immediately blocked the successful innovation of Agricultural Extension in Woodland County. However, as we have already indicated, the first agent was aware of these and undertook a rigorous educational program to eliminate both. To achieve this goal he resorted to personal contacts "to sell the individual man." He considered this approach "an absolute must. . . . I had to personally contact every man I could." The success of his strategy is reflected in the following retrospective comments of Plainville informants:

We use to give old Perkins hell, but now when I look back on it, he was one of the best. He always was comin' by to visit and talk. . . . I didn't always agree with what he was sayin', but now when I call back on it, he done all right; perty good, in fact.

Old Perkins was the first one [Extension agent] we had and I figger he was 'bout the best ever. Never had to worry 'bout findin' him, he was always comin' by and talkin' up somethin' new. He like to work hisself to death sellin' some of us hardheads, me included. . . . He was humpin' all the time. Some of these other fellers been a little lazy that way.

They orta train these danged agents to git along with people 'stead of so much agriculture. They gotta git out and circulate, like Perkins done. . . . Some we've had since him ain't done that so good. You gotta go look 'em up.

Most Plainvillers, then, have come to personify the Extension Service to such a degree that the agent gains acceptance of changes only after having first won acceptance as a person. This is particularly evident in the tendency of many people more often to express irritation with the agent's personal traits and mannerisms than to praise or denounce his professional qualities.

Another federal agency effecting considerable change in the Plainville farm economy is the Farmers Home Administration (FHA), an agency of the U.S. Department of Agriculture, which was established in 1946 as an outgrowth of the earlier Farm Security Administration (FSA). It provides long-term loans, some for as long as forty years, with interest rates pegged at around 4½ percent, for purchasing family farm units, for building or repairing farm structures, and for development and operation. Loans are made only for farms on which the borrower lives and works, and the farm must be large and productive enough when purchased, enlarged, or developed, to enable the borrower to earn a good living, pay operating expenses, taxes, and insurance, and meet other obligations while amortizing the loan. The basic philosophy underlying the program is that a farm family should be able to devote full time to an economically productive farm unit, which will provide a satisfactory standard of living.

Several factors determine an applicant's eligibility for a FHA loan, but the prime requisite is that he shall not have been able to obtain reasonable credit from other sources. An applicant submits his request to the county FHA supervisor, who in turn is advised by a committee of three Woodland County farmers regarding the applicant's qualifications. The criteria used by the committee in making its recommendations are character, experience, managerial ability, industry, and financial resources. Upon approval of his loan, an applicant then develops, with the assistance of the county FHA supervisor, a program of approved methods for farm and home management. The supervisor's primary role is educational; he works with his client to establish a sound farm and home management system that will assure repayment of the obligation on schedule.

The FHA program, then, offers the cash incentive to "get a start" on a family-type farm, combined with an educational program loaded with innovative possibilities. In general, as Longmore describes it, the FHA planning and supervision takes the following form:

1. Long-range farm and home plan is developed by the farm family with the aid of the county FHA supervisor, showing cropping system, farm practices, health and sanitation, garden, canning, housing, clothing, surroundings and education.

2. Annual farm and home plans are developed with the aid of the FHA supervisor covering details with respect to specific undertakings and with respect to the management of financial affairs which it is impractical to incorporate in a long-time plan.

3. The farm family keeps accounts in FHA family record books.

4. The FHA supervisor visits farms of borrowers during the year to confer and advise with farmers about cropping systems, rotations, varieties, fertilizer applications, pest control, livestock management, and the like.

5. County supervisor meets with the borrower for annual checkout, involving an examination of the borrower's family record book for completeness and accuracy, analyzing the year's business, and completing farm and home plans for the coming year (Longmore, 1953:150–51).

LAND AND THE FARM

All but a few Plainville farmers live on the land they till.[8] In fact, the land is dotted with farm houses located a quarter to a half mile apart and, except for a few "timber" homes, usually near, or at least visible from, the road. "Use to be a feller traveled only a few minutes without wavin' or maybe stoppin' to talk with somebody he knowed. . . . Why, our nearest neighbors was just shoutin' distance away." Today, however, there are many rapidly deteriorating unoccupied dwellings, mute evidence of some of the more significant changes in Plainville farm life.

One important change, for example, is a trend toward larger individual land holdings—from an average of 151 acres in 1945 to the present (1954) 217 acre average.[9] It is significant that the only acreage classes to gain during this period were those exceeding 500 acres. All others declined. (See Table VI.) The decline in some of the smaller classes

TABLE VI. WOODLAND COUNTY FARMS
BY ACREAGE CLASS [10]

	Number of Farms				
Acreage Class	*1945*	*Percent of Total*	*1954*	*Percent of Total*	*Percent Increase over 1945*
Under 100	617	40.3	327	32.3	− 47
100–139	265	17.3	123	12.1	− 54
140–179	198	13.0	127	12.5	− 36
180–219	136	8.8	108	10.8	− 21
220–259	93	6.0	76	7.5	− 18
260–499	191	12.4	180	17.8	− 6
500–999	28	1.8	65	6.4	+170
1,000 and over	4	.3	14	1.4	+250
Total	1,532		1,012		− 37

could have resulted from the removal of some 12,500 acres from agricultural production since 1945.[11] However, for all practical purposes we can assume that most of the decrease in total farms was achieved by consolidating smaller units into larger ones.

A major factor underlying the decline of small farms has been a rising level of living based on new consumption patterns which depend on cash expenditures. Thus, as Plainvillers have become increasingly dependent upon cash to satisfy certain needs which have continued to expand, they have come to value farming more as a business enterprise than as a way of life. This value shift has had significant repercussions in the agricultural system. First and foremost, it has been accompanied by, and has been partially the result of, mechanization, itself so closely associated with the present generation's values of "efficiency" that many farmers have "over-mechanized"; secondly, there has been a definite trend toward beef and dairy specialization as a means of realizing greater and more dependable cash income; finally, it has facilitated receptivity to scientific practices for controlling and bettering the soil.

Implicit in the above trends is the recognized need for larger farm units as a first requisite for a more satisfying standard of living. Thus, farmers who mechanize and specialize want and need more land and are trying to purchase it, while farmers with holdings too small to provide their desired level of living, who are unable to secure larger holdings, are selling or leasing their property and emigrating to salaried jobs in urban communities and other states. Cattlemen and dairymen who remain are trying to expand and are competing not only with each other, but also with a few individuals who are trying to buy land for investment purposes. This highly competitive situation is largely the result of favorable economic conditions which, combined with the fact that land is, as always, a scarce commodity, tend to raise prices out of proportion to actual worth.

The real value of land, as already indicated, depends mostly on location. Cleared prairie and bottom land is in great demand but is seldom for sale. Hill and timber land, on the other hand, is more often available but holds little appeal for prospective buyers. Good prairie land brings from $60.00 to $90.00 per acre, with bottom land, seldom for sale, considerably higher. One owner of some rough, timbered hill land, good only for poor pasture, is asking $20.00 per acre for the roughest of his property, and $40.00 per acre for that located nearer the road with a good spring on it. His neighbor, a cattleman, who would like to buy the property, considers these prices "outrageous." "Why, that old ridge-runner knows blamed well that land ain't worth that. . . . That's the way fellers do, hold you up . . . scared that somebody is gonna git a little ahead." The "ridge-runner", informed that his price was considered too high, retorted:

There's always some big feller just waitin' to gobble the little man up. . . . What's goin' to happen to all them people ["little land owners"] if just a few fellers take over? They been goin' to the city, but hell's bells, I don't see how they can keep on takin' care of everbody up there.

Unusual climatic and economic conditions sometimes soften the land market. For example, this region is now (1954–55) in its third year of severe drought, which on top of an already strained agriculture market, offers added incentive for some families to leave the farm. During the research period, for example, there were forty-six general farm sales in Woodland County, eight of which were in Plainville. In most cases owners disposed of stock, machinery, household goods, and miscellaneous items. A few sold land, although more leased it. Most of those "selling out" gave their reasons on sale bill notices, and the ones most often advanced were "drought," "job elsewhere," "going to the city," "leaving the farm," "leaving the state," and "poor health."

Every Plainville farmer wants ultimately to own his farm. However, since few can pay cash, most farmers at one time or another secure long-term mortgages to finance their farms.

TABLE VII. WOODLAND COUNTY FARMS
BY OWNERSHIP CLASS [12]

| | Percentage of Total Farmers | | |
Year	Full Owners	Part Owners	Tenants
1940	47.4	16.0	36.5
1945	65.0	8.3	26.7
1950	62.8	19.7	17.5
1954	56.1	25.1	18.4

Loans are normally obtained from relatives, private lenders, banks, or from the Farmers Home Administration. Most borrowers, however, prefer to obtain money within the immediate family, because under these conditions interest is minimal or not charged at all. However, "you gotta be real careful in dealin' with relations . . . sometimes that's the worst loan a feller can make." Individual lenders charge from six to eight percent interest, and a similar rate is charged by nearby banks. The cheapest interest rate, except for that charged by relatives, is the 4½ percent charged by the FHA. The FHA insures loans for ninety percent of the value of the farm.

In 1955 the maximum loan value set for Woodland County farms (by FHA) was $15,000. This figure presumably was the amount required to purchase a "family-type farm" of good enough quality to provide a satisfactory standard of living for the owner and his family. The figure arrived at by the county FHA committee is submitted to the state FHA committee, and is ultimately approved by the Land Economics Department of the College of Agriculture of the State University. The drastic changes in the maximum FHA loan limits since 1950 support the earlier hypothesis that larger farm units are necessary to achieve the present desired level of living. Thus, we find that the maximum Woodland County loan limit insured by FHA in 1950 was $7,500, just half what it was in 1955. Requests for further increases are an imminent possibility. These increases are not to enable the farmer to pay more per acre for his land, but to enable him to purchase, enlarge, or develop a larger and more efficient farm.

SOILS AND CROPS

West (1945:221) wrote that one of the objectives of the agricultural movement in 1939 and 1940 was toward "shifting land from soil-depleting crops to leguminous pasture or hay, and simultaneously shifting cash incomes from crop sales to sales of livestock and poultry and their products." I agree that innovative agencies were, at that time, attempting to change the cropping practices of Plainville farmers. Table VIII, however, indicates that farmers did not depend on crop sales as a major source of income.

The program in question, initially sponsored by AAA, was designed to shift land away from soil-depleting crops to those that would replenish the soil. Extension became involved,

TABLE VIII. SOURCE OF INCOME,
WOODLAND COUNTY FARMERS [13]

Source	Percent of Total Income (Farm)			
	1940	*1945*	*1950*	*1954*
Livestock products	58.2	49.9	56.1	57.8
Poultry products	21.9	26.1	15.7	8.3
Dairy products	11.2	18.7	22.2	33.1
All crops	8.7	5.3	6.0	—

however, because of its program to produce more and better feed for livestock and poultry which, along with their products, were already the major source of cash. This became one phase of a larger Extension program aimed at increasing income by specializing beef, dairy, and poultry production. Other phases of this important program stressed improved quality, care, and disease control. These features will be discussed shortly.

The programs of federal agencies greatly altered land-use patterns in Woodland County between 1939 and 1954. One significant change was a decline from 60,000 acres of cropland harvested in 1939 to 42,500 acres in 1954. During this period the number of acres planted in corn dropped from 18,000 to 12,000, and approximately the same percentage (30%) of decline occurred in wheat and oats acreage. This was accompanied by a corresponding increase in the land turned to pasture or planted in soybeans and lespedeza. For example, the number of acres in soybeans increased from 554 in 1939 to 1,425 in 1954. Lespedeza, already widely accepted in 1939 (West, 1945:223) with 10,500 acres under cultivation, reached its highest point in 1944 when 20,000 acres were planted. There were 15,000 acres in 1949, but because of severe drought planting dropped to a low of 700 acres in 1954. There was a slight rise in alfalfa production during this period, and with the increasing trend toward dairy specialization there is new interest in this high grade legume. Alfalfa requires good soil, and several dairymen are working bottom fields up to necessary specifications for growing this high quality hay. Twenty-six Woodland County farmers planted 118 acres of alfalfa in 1940, but sixty-eight planted 460 acres in 1954.

Despite acreage cuts, Plainville farmers now produce more grain, discounting uncontrollable weather, than at any previous time in their farming history. For example, in 1940 Woodland County farmers harvested 239,871 bushels of oats from 11,394 acres, or twenty-one bushels per acre. In 1954, even with a drought, they realized 258,714 bushels from only 7,239 acres, or thirty-six bushels per acre. The increase in wheat yield is just as dramatic. This improved productivity is linked to an important innovation—the use of commercial fertilizers.

Commercial fertilizers were introduced by the AAA which, during its early phases, stressed the use of lime and phosphates. Plainvillers accepted these [14] with some initial resistance (West, 1945:223), but by the end of the Second World War this had dissolved. They have since expanded their inventory to include high analysis potassium, nitrogen, and phosphate compounds.

I once said I'd prosecute a man who'd put lime on my place. I know better now. . . . I use all the fertilizers. Biggest change we had in farmin' in this country is fer us fellers to realize you gotta put somethin' into the soil. Gotta work it good. . . . Naturally, these things cost money, but we git more fer crops. . . . You know, Art, a farmer can't put his money ahead of his soil. If he does he's ruined. . . . Big trouble in this county is we took too much from the soil fer too long a time. I was just as bad as the next man, but I been showed just like a lotta others been showed.[15]

The acceptance of this innovation is underscored by the fact that in 1954 sixty-five percent of all Woodland County farmers bought commercial fertilizers, spending an average of $215 per farm. Considering the severe drought, this figure is high. However, with normal weather some progressive farmers budget as much as $600 to $1,200 for fertilizer. One young farmer, for example, spent "well over $3,600" for materials which he applied to sixty-five acres of small grains and grasses over a five-year span ("and even then my soil ain't up to specifications"). Another man spent as much this year (1955) to fertilize a corn crop as he otherwise could expect to earn from the crop. He says: "Sure it costs, costs like hell. But my increase in perduction offsets my fertilizer costs, and at the same time I'm buildin' up my soil."

Plainvillers are, through the efforts of innovative agencies, overeducated in the *use* of fertilizers and undereducated in the methods for their *proper* use. They accept, for example, the main practice in an innovative configuration, the application of commercial materials, but do not accord the same degree of acceptance to two complementary traits, soil testing and follow-through applications.

Extension personnel have tried since 1948 to gain general acceptance of soil testing. This program provides low cost (ninety cents per analysis) technical service which enables farmers to determine the exact kinds and amounts of fertilizer needed on their land. This insures maximum treatment for the soil, and the farmer profits by adding only needed materials. The economic logic is so obvious that planners have spent much less time on education in this program than they did in getting fertilizers accepted. For example, the Extension agent's 1950 annual report shows only sixty soil tests that year, although several hundred farmers bought commercial fertilizers. The number jumped to 230 tests in 1954, mainly because ASC now requires all farmers who participate in its soil-rebuilding programs to secure soil analyses from the county agent. This slight coercion may finally insure acceptance of soil testing.

Implicit in soil rebuilding is the follow-through, particularly the use of nitrogen, which is necessary to maintain optimum fertility. Farmers who neglect to follow through fail to secure the maximum benefit from their investment. Such neglect is rationalized by most men as "too expensive," or more often, by the assertion that weather conditions are too unpredictable.

The trend to beef and dairy specialization since 1939 has defined a major problem for Plainville farmers—the need to produce more feed at home and to purchase less from outside markets. Feed costs, revealed in Table IX, are high, and because of this profits are lowered.

TABLE IX. FEED EXPENDITURES FOR WOODLAND COUNTY FARMERS [16]

Year	Income from Livestock and Poultry and Their Products	Feed Expenditures for Livestock and Poultry	Percent of Income Spent for Feed
1954	$1,830,282	$584,632	31.4
1949	2,240,198	572,423	30.0
1944	1,709,848	650,000	36.2
1939	600,000	94,000	15.6

One attempt by ASC and Extension to ameliorate local feed conditions is the "improved pasture program." This innovation seeks to improve pasture when grazing is poorest, during the fall and winter months. Acceptance of the program thus far is conditioned by three variables, each of which emphasizes significant problems in the local acceptance of scientific agriculture.

The first variable involves the communication of meanings and intentions by the innovative agency to the potential acceptors. The improved pasture program, for example, was introduced to Plainville farmers as a "permanent pasture program," with little or no effort to clarify the key term "permanent." It was assumed that farmers knew the program would provide fall and winter pasture which, combined with spring and summer pasture, would make grazing lands "permanently" available throughout the year. This assumption proved erroneous. Several leading farmers interpreted "permanent" to mean perennial grasses which could provide serviceable grazing twelve months of the year, but because of their skepticism rejected the innovation from the beginning. Others, who made the same assumption but were less skeptical, were well involved before learning that the program provided only fall and winter grass. Some of them reacted negatively, inferring that the innovation had been deliberately misrepresented. Much confusion was eliminated by changing the program title to "improved pasture," but only after a negative base had been established.

A second variable conditioning the acceptance of the "improved pasture" program relates to cost. Establishing "improved pasture" is expensive, and for this reason met with some resistance. Labor excluded, soil preparation and seed cost from $40.00 to $45.00 per acre. Besides the initial outlay, a farmer should spend $10.00 to $15.00 per acre annually to maintain the pasture at optimum strength. Many consider such costs prohibitive when measured against potential return and uncertain weather, and therefore view the innovation as unrealistic. This is, incidentally, a major complaint directed against innovative agencies, particularly Extension. Bob Hawkins, a prominent dairyman, states it thus:

I been callin' them guys [Extension] out to my place fer years . . . and ever time they always recommend somethin' too expensive. You fellers know when a man is drownin' and asks fer help, he needs help. I just don't think they realize what the situation is. They got some fine ideas, but there is too much money involved. We got to work with what we got . . . and that includes this pasture program.

Carl Lindsey, who agreed with Mr. Hawkins that innovative agencies are not realistic, added: "Iffen I had the money to buy all them fertilizers and everthing the Extension people and the ASC bunch want me to, I wouldn't have to farm no more . . . I'd be well fixed."

Despite the early semantic confusion and high cost, the improved pasture program was on its way to general acceptance when the drought struck in 1952. (See Table X.) Because of the drought participants, some with sizable in-

TABLE X. WOODLAND COUNTY PARTICIPANTS,
IMPROVED PASTURE PROGRAM [17]

Year	Number of Acres	Number of Participants
1949	299	50
1950	224	19
1951	900	122
1952	908	146
1953	311	70
1954	196	37

vestments, did not realize their expectations. Max Crandall, a cattleman who needs pasture badly, observed that many people, including himself, were frustrated by the weather.

I prepared the soil and planted about ten acres of orchard grass and fescue. . . . Cost me about $55.00 an acre. . . . I got it in and it was doin' right good, and this God damn drought caught me. I still got my soil fertility, but that's all. My pocketbook's a lot lighter.

One persistent dairyman lost "over $250" per year in a three-year attempt to establish "improved pasture" on "just nine lousy acres . . . and I need that pasture bad . . . got to cut down on my hay bill."

Thwarted by natural events, frustrated by loss of money, some farmers turned their hostility against the main innovative agency, Extension. A few early acceptors insist that Extension oversold them; others say that Extension is not as aware of local conditions, weather and otherwise, as it should be before making recommendations; and some criticize the agents: "Them fellers got to git good cooperation on them programs to make their reports to the higher-ups look good."

The partial failure of this program because of uncertain weather focuses on a prime concern of Plainvillers attempting scientific farming: "You can spend $100 an acre, but if the *weather* ain't right, it don't do a bit of good." Their concern rests on a conception of nature and the land tempered by over a hundred cumulative years of realistic experiences. The oral tradition of Plainville is rich in stories of coping with the land and natural elements. Good and bad crop years, tried and proved practices, droughts and floods, all are vividly recalled from the past, and serve constantly as the background against which to compare and evaluate the present. Likewise, modern methods for working the land stand out in bold relief against those of yesteryears.

Scientific practices introduced by government agencies convey to Plainvillers man's potential control over the land, and in so doing give them new respect for it. There is, however, always the weather, and when Plainvillers ponder man's relationship to this element the present blurs against the past. This bothers farmers ("No matter what you do, you got to have the right weather for it"), and makes them question the gamble of cash outlays for fertilizers and other expensive programs if weather controls are lacking. This does not mean that Plainvillers possess no technology to control some of the effects of weather. Terracing and contouring, for example, help to reduce erosion; pond and reservoir construction gives more efficient water management; and some drought-resistant crops have been accepted. However, there is a level beyond which present technology permits no control. That Plainvillers are aware of this empirical level does not mean that the issue is resolved, but rather that, for some, other explanations must be invoked. Thus, a declining few occasionally use magical practices (see also West, 1945:11), such as planting by the moon or "them almanac signs" (zodiac), or hiring a "water witch" [18] to find ground water. And there are some who place their faith in prayer. In fact, there is occasional agitation for a special "old-time" community-wide prayer meeting to fight the drought, but so far nothing has materialized beyond occasional references in public prayers. Criticism of this proposal by less orthodox individuals makes it unlikely that such a meeting could involve the entire community.

A growing number of Plainvillers are content to place their faith in a continually expanding technology that eventually will overcome the vicissitudes of nature. Their hope emerges in constant, favorable comparison between today's methods and those of yesterday, and through an active interest in rational-empirical methods developed elsewhere but not yet in local use. For example, during the drought there was talk of the possibility and feasibility of irrigation, though few seriously considered it for themselves.[19] There was a lot of interest in the rainmaking experiments conducted in several western states, but no one considered even the remote possibility of local experiments.[20] Nevertheless, the Plainviller's knowledge of such developments supports his faith in man's potential further to subdue land and weather. This faith was set in motion by the sudden influx of great numbers of technical traits, enough of which were accepted to create an expectation of change in this area of Plainville culture.

The Plainvillers' expectation of technological change, by no means confined to farming methods, is accompanied by dependence upon a few sources of innovative authority, mostly government-sponsored agencies. The role expectations by which Plainvillers define Extension are an excellent illustration—people view the function of Extension almost solely as that of "introducing new ideas." The agent's failure to recognize this role expectation often leads to conflict between his office and potential clients. Thus, an agent with nothing new in the offing is criticized by Plainville farmers for not fulfilling his role:

There's no point in having an agent if he isn't on the ball. The people at the university and places like that are coming up with something new all the time. . . . Doesn't mean we'll go along with what they say, chances are we won't, but it's the agent's job to feed it to us. Otherwise . . . no need to have an agent.

FARM MECHANIZATION AND RELATED PROBLEMS

Immediately following the Second World War, there was a rapid transition from manpower and horsepower to motorpower on Plainville farms. This transition is now complete to the extent that a farmer following a team of horses or mules, a common sight a few years ago, is rarely seen today. A few farmers still prefer to work animals, but most horse and mule owners keep them more out of sentiment than for work, or, in the case of horses, keep one or two riding animals.[21]

All us Blackburns use to live up north here . . . and we was all knowed as mule men. My old gran'daddy had the best mules in this county, and kept 'em till he died. I intend to keep mine till I die, just like my old gran'daddy done. I like mules. Like havin' 'em around. Them I got now is seven years old, and I been offered $500, but I just cain't sell 'em. Don't use 'em . . . just cain't sell 'em.

Plainvillers have mechanized many farm tasks. Enthusiasm for machines is so great, in fact, that some technical areas are over-mechanized. We can examine this problem by looking at the focal trait in the complex of farm machinery, the tractor, principal power machine for most farm tasks. Rapid acceptance of tractors is indicated by their presence on sixty percent of all Woodland County farms in 1954–55 as compared to only seven percent in 1939.[22] This rate of acceptance assumes added importance when viewed against the background of diminishing cropland acreage for the whole county, down thirty percent in fifteen years, and the small number of acres individually cultivated by most farmers. For example, of all the farms reporting cropland harvested in 1954 eighty-nine percent report less than fifty acres.[23] With these small acreages, machines stand idle in farmyards much more than they are used in the fields.[24] Furthermore, these idle tractors, costing between $1,200 and $2,000, are easily the most expensive implement on most farms. Thus, examination of the number, size, and cost of the tractors, the amount and kind of work they do, and the time required for this work reveals that Plainvillers own more tractors than they need for the amount of land they farm.

Underlying the current mechanization trend is the acceptance of a new style of farming. The farmer now defines
his role mainly as manipulator of machines designed to do
what formerly were irksome, time-consuming agricultural
tasks. This new role involves a redefinition of farm labor and
the acceptance of new criteria for assessing industriousness.
Thus, men who a few years ago gained prestige by working
long hours at hard physical labor are remembered today as
"slaves" to hard work and long hours, and if one of them still
manifests these qualities he is ridiculed as "behind the
times." Industriousness is now measured by the speed and
ease of labor performance, which is achieved by an implement complex built around the tractor. Because of the diversified cropping system in Plainville this frequently leads
to technological elaboration. For example, traditional machines such as the plow, disc, harrow, and corn planter, to
name only a few, have long been adapted to tractor power.
In addition to these, more expensive equipment, such as
combines, field forage harvesters, hay balers, corn pickers,
and manure spreaders, have been accepted. Again, when
viewed against the background of objective *work* and *economic needs,* it is obvious that Plainvillers own too many
of these machines. For example, between 1949 and 1954
the number of combines increased from fifty-one to eighty-
one, corn pickers from fifteen to forty-seven, and pickup-
type hay balers from twenty-two to eighty-two.

The elaboration of farm machinery in Plainville involves
variables other than redefinition of the farmer's role. Why,
for example, does Ray Jones buy a large tractor when a
smaller, more economical unit would be adequate? Why
does his neighbor Steve Luck buy a combine when he has
less than fifty acres of grain? These dysfunctional consumer
patterns are not exactly new: West (1945:10) [25] mentions
them, but I believe they are more prevalent today than they
were when he was in the community. Their increase is related to many factors, including greater acceptance of mod-

ern machinery, the nature of Plainville farming, and the large number of alternatives in price, size, quality, and function which confront the purchaser. The interaction of these variables presents a frustrating picture to most Plainville farmers who, though convinced that mechanization is the way to farm, own limited, often diversified, cropland acreages. One result is that an increasing number of farmers buy machines for which they have limited use.

Owners of unnecessary machines must face primarily the problem of retiring interest and principal, and secondarily that of added maintenance and operating costs.[26] This has led to a class of specialists made up of some (not all) of the owners of expensive equipment, particularly combines, hay balers, and ensilage cutters. They rent their machines and services to neighbors who cannot yet afford the outlay for equipment of their own. In 1954, for example, Woodland County farmers spent $89,000 for machinery hire, considerably more than the $52,000 paid for this service only five years before. In 1940 this expense was negligible. During the same fifteen-year period the amount for hired labor increased from $19,000 in 1940 to $62,000 in 1954,[27] an increase explained more by the use of additional labor than by the improvement of wages for farm work.

The Plainviller's desire to own machinery is further supported by a strong emphasis upon individualism. Individualism is so highly valued that close relatives may duplicate major and expensive equipment. Farmers, in fact, agree unanimously that "it's best for every man to own his own equipment." Furthermore, they believe that cooperative machinery buying and work scheduling are not feasible.[28] As one young farmer expresses it:

People got their own idees . . . And they like to be their own boss. Soon as I git the money I'm buyin' me a combine. [He has about twenty-five acres of grain.] May have to git a used one like Steve Luck done, but hit'll be mine. When I git ready to combine I want hit done right now . . . don't like to depend

on some other feller to do hit fer me. Shore, hit'll be costly, but hit'll be worth it.

The relationship between mechanization and individualism is further apparent in certain group-oriented social changes. Acceptance of the combine, for example, caused threshing bees to disappear, and there is little need for haying parties if one owns or hires a baling machine. Exchange labor, common a few years ago, rarely occurs nowadays. Close friends or relatives sometimes exchange labor, but usually "there is no need for trading out work," because "with the right equipment a man can get it all done by hisself." Then, too, "fellers don't have time to swap work . . . they do their own." Or, "they'd be scared t'other feller wouldn't give back as much as they put out."

Finally, it is obvious that some Plainville farmers want new and expensive machines for prestige reasons. Equipment is an important symbol of achievement in the competitive agricultural system, and its possession is a major criterion in the evaluation of individual success. As a measure of social worth its importance stems from the fact that most people are secretive regarding their incomes. Since incomes are a topic for speculation and gossip among neighbors, the amount is inferred by reckoning from expenditures. Inasmuch as a significant part of the farmer's budget is allotted to machinery and its upkeep, judgments of neighbor upon neighbor invariably stress the quantity, size, and expense of equipment, all known variables.

SPECIALIZATION [29]

The first full-time Extension agent came to Woodland County in 1938. In his first annual report he emphasized the need for specialization:

In order to conserve the natural soil resources, maintain and increase farm income, and work toward a better land use, a program for the county is being planned to encourage a breeding and feeding program for livestock, dairy, and poultry, that will increase the income and utilize the land to the best advantage.

This program will aim to build up the livestock carrying capacity of the farms of the county, and at the same time increase the quality and health, as well as the number of livestock (Agent's Annual Report, 1938).

Thus, an agricultural reform program was launched which had significant repercussions in the Plainville farm system. Not only is there a developing trend toward farm specialties, notably dairying, but Plainvillers now accept many innovations designed to achieve quality production in these specialties. Acceptance of these is accompanied by, and partially the outgrowth of, a growing attitude among the farmers that "the time is coming [some say it is already here] when a man is going to have to be the best to stay in business"— "in a country like ours, where you can't get too big [because of land scarcity], you got to depend almost entirely on quality."

Dairying. A major change in the Plainville agricultural system is a steady increase in the number of farmers who earn over half their income from milk sales—up from seven percent in 1945 to thirty-three percent in 1954.[30]

Specialized dairying was introduced to Plainville in 1916 by an enterprising farmer who imported a herd of Holsteins from Wisconsin—as old-timers remember it, "twenty-two cows and a registered bull . . . each cow in a separate crate of her own." The only market at this time was for sweet cream. The first dairyman's son recalls, "We separated it off into five-gallon cans, hauled them to Stanton to load on the train, and shipped them to Metropolis." The surplus milk was "hogged," that is, used to fatten feeder pigs for market. A few years later another farmer bought some registered cows and specialized in dairying. Not, however, until 1927 did these men secure a market for whole milk, and then transportation problems were so great they could not effectively exploit it. They hauled their milk to Prairietown, seventy-five miles away, from which it was shipped to St.

Louis and other cities. The two pioneers received a break
in the early 1930s when a small cheese plant was built in
Discovery and two more were established in neighboring
counties. The plants, however, were not successful. Drought
and depression forced dissolution of the "big herds," and
by 1936 the dairy specialists were out of business.

As Plainville emerged from the economic chaos of drought
and depression, attention once more focused on specialized
dairying. This coincided with the arrival of the first full-
time Extension agent, who perceived the major and immediate task of Extension as

bringing more cash into the area. . . . Through this cash there
should result a better standard of living. . . . The people needed
more purchasing power to get the things needed to raise their
standard of living and make life a little more enjoyable. The
triple A people were concentrating on soil rebuilding practices,
and we figured that we should concentrate more on herd development . . . particularly beef and dairy cattle in the area.

Further interest in specialized dairying was stimulated by
two simultaneous, important, and related innovations. In
1937 and 1938 several major milk firms built cheese and
milk products plants in nearby counties, creating a regional
market for whole milk. This development was followed in
1939 by milk pickup routes. These two advantages, plus
Extension encouragement, spurred interest in dairy production, and by 1940 fifty-one Woodland County farmers
were selling whole milk. Few had at this time, however,
specialized their farms for large-scale production. This came
with high dairy prices during the Second World War. By
1945 specialized dairying was firmly established, with seven
percent of all Woodland County farmers earning over half
their income, and better than thirty percent of the remainder
supplementing their income, from whole milk sales. During
this period (1940–45) the number of milk cows in the county
increased from 4,331 to 6,157, gallons of milk sold jumped
from 42,879 to 988,116, and income from dairy products

climbed from $74,198 to $338,329. By 1954 the sale of dairy products in Woodland County amounted to $696,989.[31]

The success of a dairy specialist depends on his ability to develop efficient but quality production. He must have good, high grade stock and an adequate feeding and bookkeeping system. The importance of these factors is emphasized by state agricultural experts who estimate that "normally twenty to thirty percent of the milking herd must be replaced each year." Therefore, maximum efficiency is possible only by eliminating poor producers and replacing them with heifers of good breeding. First and foremost, a successful dairyman recognizes the need for good sires.

The dairy program of the Extension Service emphasized from the start that quality animals are developed only by rigid culling and breeding controls. This emphasis led to the purchase of many registered bulls in the county, and at one time some farmers even considered "bull clubs." However, because of the Plainviller's stress on individualism, bull cooperatives were never successful.

In 1946, under favorable sponsorship of the State Farmers Association, artificial insemination was initiated. The innovation received strong support from Extension and other agencies, but initial acceptance by farmers was tempered by several objections. Farmers accustomed to paying neighbors a "bull fee" of "fifty cents to a dollar," "maybe getting it done free," considered the $6.00 per cow insemination fee outlandish. Many, in fact, still complain of the expense, and one prominent dairyman believes "maybe the government orta pay part of the cost." [32] Others were skeptical about methods and results, but the favorable production records obtained by initial acceptors soon disposed of their fears. This does not mean, however, that every dairyman accepts the innovation or that criticism is lacking. For, despite the continued success of artificially inseminated herds, the practice is declining. Some initial acceptors who are discontinuing the innovation claim that sources supplying the "dope" do not always use quality bulls. The most vehement critics, though, are dairymen who increased production with the method, but who fallaciously assumed, or were led to believe, that they could expect increases in succeeding generations. When the increases did not appear the rationalization, for many, was "inferior dope."

A dairyman's success also depends, among other things, on his ability and willingness to control expenses. One way of doing this is to produce most of the feed for his herd. Because of the drought this problem was very serious during our stay in Plainville. One dairyman, for example, with a herd of twenty cows, earned $3,000 from milk sales in 1954, but spent over $1,000 for feed.[33] With normal weather conditions ("when I grow more feed at home") he would spend about half this amount, which means that his yearly profit should be at least $500 more than it is. However, even with normal weather most dairymen lower their profits by buying some feeds which they could produce themselves.

Dairymen must pay close attention to culling and feeding practices, and this means perfecting managerial ability. Their specialty, more than any other type of farming, is adaptable to rigid bookkeeping. The farmer, through daily contact with the unit of production, can measure animal efficiency by comparing unit output against feed intake. Thus, by carefully testing individual animals he can keep close control over these two variables. He can, for example, alter feed proportions or quantity, and determine whether production will improve, remain the same, or fall off. With proper records he can maintain an efficient herd by culling "boarder" animals ("You can have one old cow who isn't putting out, eating up the profit on a couple good cows right beside her"). The grade A dairyman, however, who is mechanized, with milking machines and refrigeration systems, may never see the milk from individual cows, and consequently has no way of even roughly estimating unit output. He must, therefore, buy mechanical testing devices or hire someone to do the testing for him.

In November, 1944, the Woodland County Dairy Herd Improvement Association was organized.[34] This organization provides a trained tester to regularly test member herds and help the owners to keep accurate records. The service costs $5.50 per month for the first ten cows, and fifteen cents for each additional animal. Despite the economic advantages, particularly for owners of a large herd, DHIA has never been well accepted. In 1954, for example, although 337 farms reported dairy sales as their major source of income, only ten farmers were enrolled in the program. The overwhelming rejection of DHIA is astounding, considering the reasons given by Plainvillers for not participating. Many offer expense as an excuse, and for the owner of a small, substandard herd this is understandable. For others, however, the money saved by testing would more than offset the expense involved. Some participate only if they like the tester or are pleased with their test results. These men sometimes attribute poor results to the tester's biases. As one disgruntled man explains:

Them fellers come in to test yore milk. . . . You pay 'em for it, and they make mistakes all over the place [inference that mistakes are purposeful]. Before Max Stanton got the job my herd was on top in the county . . . my tests dropped soon as he started. The Jersey men just can't stand to see a Holstein man out in front of them.

This kind of criticism emphasizes a prominent feature in the Plainviller's stereotype of a successful dairyman—ownership of quality, high-test animals. And, judging from the amount of boasting done by dairymen, owning good cows confers prestige. This is quite apparent in the image which many people have of the DHIA program. They associate it with high quality animals, and only with leading dairymen. Some men see the program as one of the rewards of success, not a means for achieving it. "Why should I test with this scrub stock I got? I'd be ashamed for anyone to see a test on my stock. Soon as I get my herd built up, I'll start."

Another prominent feature in the Plainville stereotype of dairy success is grade A production. The grade A market is the most recent, and easily the most significant, development contributing to local professionalism in the dairy industry. Grade A production began in 1948 when representatives of city milk firms came to Woodland County to recruit suppliers. Within a few months six grade A plants were under construction, and by 1951 the number increased to eleven. In 1955 there were forty grade A producers in the county, twelve in Plainville.

A grade A dairyman must accept a complex of technical and social innovations designed to insure hygiene. The barn is mechanically designed to transfer milk from cow [35] to refrigerated container under maximum sanitary conditions. The farmer agrees to rigid specifications for sterilization, handling, and care of equipment and building. He must also consider his own personal cleanliness. All of these conditions involve direct submission to external controls which dictate minimum levels for quality production. In this case the symbol of authority is the inspector who represents the company buying milk. He regularly inspects the grade A producer's plant. To some Plainvillers, this "snooping" is obviously irritating: "I got all the equipment and I know how they want it done. I don't always agree, but I know how they want it. We been drinkin' this milk for years and nobody's died from it yet. Can't figger out why them city dairies has got to be so finicky."

For their extra investment in equipment, and for acquiescing to externally imposed production standards, grade A dairymen receive a bonus which in 1955 amounted to seventy cents per one hundred pounds of milk.[36] Some farmers believe this is not enough for "all the fuss and bother," and choose to stick with the grade C market.[37] Most dairymen, however, believe their future is intimately linked to quality production, and consequently there is a steady movement in that direction. The transition from grade C to grade A status costs from $3,000 to $6,000, including the price of the special milking barn. An investment this large normally requires a loan, so most men seek finance arrangements which permit them to apply the income differential between grade C and grade A milk to their obligation. Under these conditions it is three to five years before the loan is retired and the dairyman realizes any economic advantage from his investment. In the meantime, though, his prestige rewards are quite apparent. The grade A barn stands as a symbol of prestige and individual achievement; he is now a "big operator." Inasmuch as several grade A setups in the county are valued in excess of $25,000, the term is appropriate. Furthermore, since many big operators know that modern technology enables them efficiently to handle more cows and make more money, they are planning to become even bigger operators.

Several factors underlie the present trend toward dairy specialization, but two are particularly outstanding. These are (1) a greater need for cash, and (2) a need for a steady source of income. The first of these is important because most Plainvillers need additional money to enlarge their present standard of living, and many need additional cash to maintain their present level of living. In their attempts to solve these problems Plainvillers are turning to installment buying for major purchases and to long-term mortgages, often government supported, for real estate transactions. Thus, most families need a dependable monthly income to meet their obligations. Dairying offers this, and consequently appeals both to farmers and to the businesmen who depend on them. Many businessmen, in fact, believe that "dairying has saved this county." Though a little extreme, their contention does have merit. It is obvious, for example, that many dairymen are economically secure, and that many farmers not classified as dairymen, but who own two, three, or four milk cows, are benefiting from an improved milk market.

Changes related to dairying are not entirely confined to economic behavior. There are, in fact, some interesting social changes arising from the dairy complex. A few years ago, for example, men and boys did the heavier work involving cows, such as herding and feeding them, women and girls took care of the milk, and both sexes frequently shared in the actual milking. Money earned from cream and butter sales, however, belonged to the women. West (1945:47) wrote: "With it they pay for all 'boughten food,' plain clothing, and other frequent small expenses of 'running the home' —which is the woman's domain. These products pay for a family's normal 'living'." West (1945:46) also observed that the traditional division of labor mentioned above was altered first by acceptance of the cream separator, "a 'heavy' machine," because "women are thought to have 'no head' for machinery, and most tasks involving machines are appropriated by men."

Today, new behavior patterns are developing around the modern, highly specialized dairy. For dairying, more than other kinds of farming, makes rigid, monotonous demands of farm families. They milk twice daily, seven days a week, every day of the year, and for big operators the monotony is compounded by mechanization. Grade A producers, especially, must operate, clean, and care for equipment in a precise way during and after each milking. Because of this they emphasize speed.[38] Thus, for maximum efficiency the milking procedure requires a small, well-organized team, in this case the family, working as a production unit. Wife and children work the electric milkers, store the milk, keep records and, in general, assist with all but the very heavy tasks. There is, then, a greater spirit of cooperation in successful dairy families than is found in other farm roles. Under no conditions, however, should a wife play a greater role than her husband in any phase of dairying, including the care of milk and equipment. There is, in fact, only one known case in the community where this occurs, and the man is severely criticized for permitting it.

Specialized dairying obviously eliminates butter and cream monies spent at the discretion of the farmwife. Milk money makes up all negotiable revenue in many families, and consequently most husbands and wives democratically share in the decisions on how to spend it. This, plus the division of labor previously discussed, suggests the hypothesis that decision-making roles are more democratically structured in dairy families than in other farm families in the community.

Finally, Plainville dairymen, more than other farmers, are sensitive to market conditions. They sell their product daily, not seasonally, and their specialty makes constant cash demands upon them. The serious dairyman feels he should keep informed on market trends and should, if possible, exert some influence over them. This concern with the market also makes dairymen, probably more than other farmers, sensitive to federal and state legislation regarding their product, and certainly motivates the big operators to contribute to national promotional organizations, such as the American Dairy Association. Interest in the latter led to the first annual Woodland County Dairy Festival in 1955, the local counterpart of the American Dairy Association's campaign to recognize a national dairy month. The well-attended festival was held in Discovery, and featured high school band music, sack and terrapin races, milk-drinking and beauty contests, and speeches. Association posters were prominently displayed in stores throughout the county, and for three weeks preceding the event major milk-products manufacturers bought large courtesy ads in the *Beacon*.

Livestock Production. The federal farm census reports from 1939 through 1954 show that the sale of livestock, exclusive of dairy and poultry products, accounts for around sixty percent of all the farm income in Woodland County. Livestock farming in this area is practically synonymous with the production of feeder beef. A few farmers raise sheep and hogs, but the number is, and always has been, slight.

Until recent years, beef animals raised in Plainville were of poor quality, because of ineffective culling and breeding practices. A few cattlemen owned registered Hereford herds as early as the mid-1920s, and bred feeder stock from these, but most farmers were not actively concerned with improving their stock until about 1938. Again, interest in quality coincided with the establishment of Extension in the county.

Certain developments before the arrival of Woodland County's first full-time Extension agent made Plainville farmers ready for livestock innovations. The AAA stock surplus reduction program, plus other government programs for culling diseased cattle, had eliminated much of the "scrub," or "Arkansawyer," stock; [39] Plainvillers were optimistically recovering from the drought and depression; and regional and national livestock prices were on their way up.

The first Extension agent launched an aggressive program to achieve two objectives: (1) to minimize herd losses from disease and parasites, and (2) to improve the quality of beef cattle through better feeding and breeding controls. The livestock program was a success from the start. For example, within two years [40] 131 farmers [41] vaccinated their animals against blackleg, 1,144 farmers tested 14,600 animals [42] for Bang's disease,[43] feeding practices were improved by sowing more small grains for fall and winter pastures, and seventy-five pure-bred bulls were bought by county farmers. This initial and vigorous interest in registered animals, which continued through the years, is easily the most significant development in Plainville livestock farming. Within this interest there are two obvious trends, specialization in Hereford and Angus breeds.

Registered Angus herds in Plainville are a recent innovation. A few farmers sold feeder animals sired by registered bulls during the early 1930s, and in 1938–39 one of them started the first registered herd. His two sons quickly and successfully followed his lead, and in a few years other farmers became interested. There are now (1955) seventeen registered Angus herds in Woodland County, seven of them in Plainville. Norvel Ballou, a prominent Plainville Angus dealer, says this is too many: "if we only had three or four that would be plenty, and the cattle would be worth more."

Angus cattlemen are organized into a county association which sponsors an annual banquet and sale. The sale ties the local organization to the State Angus Breeders' Association. A representative from the latter group, for example, supervises the sale, and the state association receives one percent of all the money derived from it. The county group is also linked to the National Angus Breeders' Association by a breed journal which each member gets with his annual $5.00 dues. Local members can request national and state representatives to help them buy or sell registered bulls, and may call them for advice about any special problem which develops in the Angus business. Members of the local organization are aware of, and accept, the fact that part of their dues is used for promotional funds. Acceptance by Angus breeders of this normative pattern, a vital one in functionally specific associations based on specialized interests, proceeds from premises similar to those already mentioned for dairymen who support the American Dairy Association.

The greatest expansion in the number of registered Herefords occurred roughly during the same period as that of the Angus. Hereford breeders, however, have been longer established, and in greater numbers, than their Angus competitors. Most Hereford stockmen subscribe to a breed journal, and in other ways keep abreast of the latest developments in their specialty. But since they feel their breed is well accepted by consumers, they believe they have no need for an organizational and promotional setup.

Besides the "big stockmen," owners of large registered or feeder herds, there are many Plainville farmers who are "small stockmen." [44] These are men who own a small number of animals, either registered or feeder, but who do not specialize their farms to full-time proportions.

A few Plainville farmers specialize in feeder or registered hogs and sheep. One Plainville man, in fact, is known as the best "hog man" for several counties around. However, he, like most pork producers, combines hog raising with cattle raising. The number of men who specialize in hog production has declined as farmers have shifted croplands from corn to other grains.

The Plainvillers' vigorous interest in registered cattle has had some negative consequences. It is apparent that the widespread acceptance of registered stock is, among other things, an attempt to improve the quality of local herds. Plainvillers believe, on the basis of common-sense generalizations, traditional knowledge, and the educational efforts of innovative agencies, that one obvious way to do this is through improved breeding practices. Some believe this so strongly that "registered" has become a synonym for quality. This has led to the registration of many inferior animals purely because they are from eligible blood lines. This condition is further complicated by overanxious buyers who insist upon registration papers, and is perpetuated by a few unscrupulous breeders who take advantage of the market by "overselling" buyers on registered stock.

One simple fact stands out above all others: the local and regional market for registered cattle is near, or at, the saturation point. This fact was driven home to some cattlemen who attended a prominently advertised Hereford dispersal sale on a Plainville farm. One animal was bought by a Woodland

County farmer; all others that sold went to buyers from outside the county. This kind of market creates problems for some cattlemen because the quality of their registered herds is not good enough to compete in an outside market. At the same time, the difference between registered and feeder animal prices which local buyers will pay has dropped so low that some cattlemen question whether registered stock are worth their trouble. Jim Owens, a leading Hereford breeder, complains:

Not more than four or five years ago I could get around fifty or sixty dollars more per head for my registered stock than for my grade stuff. Now I'm lucky if I get ten to fifteen dollars more. It costs two dollars to register a cow . . . and it ain't worth it! I'm tired foolin' with buyers comin' to my place and bein' so darn finicky . . . "this one's got too much white, the horns ain't right," and just such bellyachin' as that. I still breed registered stock, but I don't bother to register my calves.

The most serious problem facing Plainville stockmen is not that of too many registered animals. During the 1940s beef prices, money for expansion, good pasture, and land scarcity, combined to produce general overstocking of available land resources. By 1950 there were 3,816 animals above the acreage-animal ratio advocated by the State College of Agriculture [45] for Woodland County, and during the next four years the excess climbed to 4,717 animals.[46] This surplus assumes added significance when we consider that during these four years prices steadily declined. By 1954 the drought had further complicated the overstocking problem, forcing farmers to convert 4,000 cropland acres to pasture.[47] Still, the acreage-animal ratio was not adjusted, and water facilities remained woefully inadequate.

The Extension-ASC improved pasture program should help somewhat, and water conservation programs, particularly stock ponds, will also help. Farm experts, however, question that these measures are adequate. They believe, as do some farmers, that a few good weather and marketing years will only accelerate overstocking and further deplete local resources. They base their assumption on two points. First, many economically secure farmers want to expand their land and cattle holdings. However, since beef and dairy specialization is making land, always a scarce commodity, harder to obtain, some of them will further crowd their land with additional stock. Secondly, there are farmers who cannot afford to buy more land but who, when weather and market conditions are favorable, overstock their resources nearly to the breaking point, gambling on maximum weather and market conditions to see them through. These are marginal cattlemen who can easily be put out of business by a slight market decline or minor weather reverse.

The number of livestock specialists in Woodland County dropped from 375 in 1950 to 257 in 1954. Some of these men turned to dairying, thus increasing the number of operators from 295 to 337. Some left the farm, and still others concentrated more on general farming. The following composite interview with a middle-aged couple expresses the sentiments of several Plainvillers who have failed as cattlemen.

When we came back to the farm [late 1949], we were going to raise cattle. We went beef and lost our shirts that first year. Here is where we realized that it [present-day farming] was a cash business . . . we had more bills coming in ever month, and we didn't have a cent of money coming in. We bought our cattle high and we were forced to sell low. . . . In the meantime we spent ever bit of our bank account meeting monthly bills for electricity, payments on equipment, the place and everthing. We only tried cattle for a year . . . realized we didn't have the money to see us between beef sales [here they switched to dairying]. I believe you got to specialize to make money; got to be good at something. If you're in the cattle business you got to do it big. You got to do it big in the dairy business too, but in it you got a check coming in ever two weeks or so. It gives you something to operate on. You just don't have that in the beef business. It's a long time between checks.

This couple, if they stay on the farm, will ultimately invest enough in their dairy enterprise to buy a reasonably good beef setup.[48] However, dairy farming is more easily developed than stock farming from a small economic base, and since their capital resources are limited their choice is a logical one. Like most of their farm neighbors and business friends,[49] though, they value highly the role responsibility of the "stockman" because it involves a minimum of rigid daily and seasonal demands.[50] "You don't have to work from morning till night like you do in dairying" or "work all day in the fields, then spend several hours just doing the chores when you come in." Max Crandall, a cattleman, phrases it thus:

Beef is just a lot better farmin' than milk. I tell you, Art, them fellers that got them dairy herds really have to keep busy, milkin' and all that. And I just don't think they got a good enough market here for what they got invested and the trouble they have to go to.

Above all else, Plainvillers associate wealth and leisure with successful cattlemen. They, more than any of the other farmers, are glamourized through oral tradition as "the big winners" or "the big losers." Plainvillers know that large herds mean big investments, and that returns on the investment, whether gains or losses, can be spectacular. A cattleman, for example, has many occasions while buying and selling to manipulate large sums of money—his investment is a dynamic one when contrasted to the big dairyman, who may have as much invested but whose returns dribble in each month. A cattleman may not make any more money in a year's time than a successful dairyman, but he makes it all at once and, in Plainville thinking, does less of a different kind of work to make it. Another ex-cattleman turned dairyman says:

I'd get back into the beef business in a minute if it'd pay me off regular enough. . . . You got to have capital enough to run you for six months or a year. I hope to someday retire with a cattle spread. Beef cattle are lots easier than these milk cows. You just turn 'em out to pasture and let 'em go. You got to baby them dairy cows.

Cattlemen, then, enjoy a more favorable occupational status rank in Plainville's prestige system than do any of the other farm specialty groups. Aside from the values attached to the role of cattleman, high rank derives from the fact that his status is synonymous with individual achievement in the economic system. This stems from an assumption made by many Plainvillers that one can become a real cattleman only after being successful in another phase of farming.

Poultry. During the early 1940s a favorable wartime market and an energetic Extension program interested many Plainvillers in poultry farming. The Extension agent during this period emphasized poultry production as a means of earning supplementary income.[51] He was instrumental in getting several hundred improved poultry buildings constructed, and scientific feeding and culling practices were widely disseminated and accepted. Poultry production, however, has always been a minor specialty on Plainville farms, comparable in no way to livestock and dairying. It did not constitute a full-time operation in 1954–55 for any known farm family. Furthermore, Plainvillers do not differentiate any group of poultry producers as "big operators."

One factor underlying the minor role of poultry in the local economic picture is the traditional notion of Plainvillers that poultry sales are only supplementary to other farm income. Depending on the nature of the farm, poultry sales may make the difference between losing money, breaking even, or showing a profit for the year, but still poultry is considered a marginal enterprise. In this connection, the management and care of poultry, even of very large flocks, are still the responsibility of women, although money earned from poultry is not always "woman's money" as it once was. Many families nowadays consider such income an integral part of over-all farm revenue—not money exclusively budgeted by the farm wife.

Plainville interest in poultry reached its climax around 1945, when fifteen percent of all Woodland County farmers earned over half their income from poultry products. Since then, however, interest declined to a point where less than three percent earned that much in 1954, and the number of chickens on Woodland County farms dropped by more than fifty percent.[52] This accompanied an inverse economic development, not entirely unique to poultry production, marked by falling income but steadily rising operating and living costs. Several families who made annual chicken and egg profits of $1,000 and over during the mid-forties say they lost money steadily between 1950 and 1954. Bob Hawkins, a dairyman whose wife is known as an excellent poultry manager, is more precise: "We went out of the poultry business last year. We had seven hundred pullets and we lost almost $500. . . . Just couldn't make it with the drought and poor market." One index of the deteriorating poultry market is the price of eggs. Plainville farm wives averaged twenty-eight cents per dozen for eggs in 1954 as contrasted to thirty-seven cents per dozen in 1950. Feed costs have increased by an inverse amount.

Plainvillers' lack of interest in poultry was apparent in their response to a county-wide meeting I attended, which featured a talk by an expert from the State Extension Service. The County Extension Office, sponsor of the program, publicized it through local news releases and 800 letters mailed to farmers over the county. The meeting, held in the Plainville school, attracted only twenty-three people, six of them not farmers. Only ten farm families came, none of whom earn the major part of their income from poultry and egg sales. Those who came heard what they already knew: that the egg market is "glutted" by overproduction, there is always a need for better birds to produce better quality eggs, and there is a need for local and regional "quality" markets. Much of the talk didn't make sense to those present. They know, for example, that the few people who do sell to "quality" markets complain that the added expense of special storage facilities, culling their flocks, and the time required to clean and grade the eggs is hardly commensurate with the small bonus they receive. As one premium producer commented: "I sold $1,200 worth of eggs last year . . . but with the drought and poor market I cleared less than $400 for my work. I was selling premium, too. Carl wants to build a new chicken house next year, but I'm fightin' it."

Plainville women who sell premium grade eggs must depend on out-of-state buyers who regularly come by with trucks. They get about five cents per dozen above the "current receipt" local market. Some progressive poultry producers advocate state marketing laws to regulate egg grading and quality, but many more are apathetic. Such laws exist in adjoining states and do support minimum prices well above those found locally.[53]

One promising innovation in Plainville's poultry economy occurred in 1952, when three people tried large-scale turkey production.[54] Profits were so good during the first two years —$1.25 to $2.00 per bird—that several farmers became interested. However, by 1954 several complications developed —a market slump, drought, and rising feed costs—and producers were lucky to break even: consequently interest waned.

MAKING A LIVING: THE SERVICE CENTER

The village of Plainville is exclusively a local service center. It owes its existence to the continued productivity of surrounding farms and to the large number of elderly people, mostly retired farmers, who live there. The number and kinds of services available to these two consumer groups, and to the other Plainvillers, have changed little since 1939–40.[55] In fact, most changes involve nothing more than shifts in proprietors and the movement of some businesses from the village square to the highway.

There are thirty-six service institutions, listed below, which satisfy some, though by no means all, of the community's needs. They provide total economic support for thirty-seven families and partial support for twenty-one others.

Barbershops (2)
Beauty shop
Beer hall
Blacksmith
Cafés (2)
Churches (4)
   Baptist
   Christian
   Holiness
   Methodist
Drug store
Feed store
Ford agency and service station
Funeral home
Garage
General stores (2)

Groceries (2)
Hardware
Library
Liquor store
Meat market
Osteopath
Pool hall
Post office
Rest home
School
Service stations (2)
Service station and garage
Shoe repair
Skating rink
Telephone office
Tourist court

Three of these businesses, skating rink, rest home, and pool hall, were new in 1954. Inasmuch as the latter two are innovations, their acceptance warrants some consideration.

The owner of the pool hall, although not from Plainville, anticipated difficulty in gaining acceptance of his type of business. Therefore, before opening it he interviewed the town board and talked with leading businessmen. Preliminary interviews at these levels revealed some resistance from one or two older men and from "some of the good Baptists." However, his initial contacts encouraged him to carry the project through. Several men, in fact, agreed with him that "some of the better people in town should go in there and get the place off to a good start . . . keep a rough crowd from taking over."

The pool hall was moderately successful from the start,

mainly because it provided a good loafing place for Plainville men. West (1945:99–107) wrote that loafing groups were a traditional part of Plainville's social structure in 1939, and that businesses encouraged loafing by making benches and chairs available. Most merchants, however, have removed these facilities and in other ways have made known that they do not appreciate this pastime.[56] One store owner who formerly encouraged loafers says: "I got tired having a store full of nothing. They did nothing but spit [57] on the floor . . . never bought a thing. I took my benches out several years ago . . . it was bad for business having loafers hanging around."

Before the poor hall opened, only one business provided an atmosphere which loafers consider suitable—"a place where fellers can go and talk . . . and say what they want to." The pool room immediately filled this void. Many are convinced that it would not have gained ready acceptance had there been "loafin' places like we use to have." The following comments are abstracted from a loafing-group "bull session" around the pool room stove one snowy February evening:

This is one place in town that don't discourage loafin'. . . . Men in this town just didn't have a good loafin' place till the pool hall started up. . . . A good thing fer the community . . . gives a feller a place to go and be with men. There was a lot [of criticism] at first, but it's sorta died down. . . . But you just wait, some of these women will start raisin' hell when their men start stayin' up here too much. . . . We ain't heered the last from some of these preachers . . . and some of these narrow-minded church-goers, neither.

As one of the loafers observed, criticism of the pool hall did diminish somewhat after its opening. Some, however, still complain of the business and the owner. The pool room is called "a hall of sin" and "a boar's nest" (an obvious reference to its being a male loafing place), and the owner, like those who own the beer bar and the liquor store, is accused of "leading them young boys astray" and "having a bad influence on the menfolks." Certain Baptist and Holiness church members are the most obvious and vehement critics, and occasionally negative references to the pool hall creep into the services of these churches.

The other new business in the community which has attracted considerable attention is the "rest home." Several Plainvillers have lived in a "home" in Stanton, so this type of business is not entirely new. The rest home is operated by a practical nurse who rents a big house and owns hospital-type beds and other equipment for taking care of older people. Her customers are old age pensioners, most of whom require only room and board. Fees for these services "takes about all a feller's pension check," but most people believe "it's worth ever bit of it takin' care of them old people."

There is favorable reaction to the rest home from all age levels throughout the community because now Plainville's older people can live in a "home" nearer their relatives and friends. This, however, is not the only basis for acceptance. A more fundamental reason, tied to functional changes in Plainville kinship, is redefinition of role responsibilities by children toward aged parents, and concomitant redefinition by the latter of the role rights which they expect in social relationships with their children. In short, since the inception of old age assistance many children no longer feel economically responsible for aged parents,[58] and many of the latter feel the program gives them a measure of independence not otherwise attainable. In most families the norms now permit, and may even encourage, a pensioner to live in the "rest home," or children may suggest to an elderly parent that he should live there, and in either case the older person does not feel that he is being abandoned or is a burden to younger relatives.[59] An elderly man living in the "rest home" sums it up nicely:

I don't have to live up there, but I like it. I'm aroun' people like myself [60] . . . got a good place to eat and sleep, and my kin can come visit me when they want to.[61] Takes about all I git in a month, but got enough left over fer a few seegars. . . . Ain't good fer old people to be under foot of their kids . . . gits on everbody's nerves.

Not all elderly people, however, sanction the rest home. A seventy-five-year-old man listened to the statement of his friend just quoted and commented, "I wouldn't live there if they drug me in by the heels." [62]

Over half of Plainville's business and professional men are outsiders who have moved there since 1939. With the exception of two businessmen who grew up in Plainville, outsiders are generally believed to own better paying "propositions" than the home folks. Actual incomes of business and professional men are not known because most of them do not divulge this information. There are, however, several men generally believed by Plainvillers to excel in business. They are the owner of a service station-café-motel combination, owners of a general store, the operator of a highway service station, owners of the liquor store-café combination, the owner of the Ford agency-farm implement-garage combination, the owner of the grocery-feed store combination, the undertaker, and the doctor.[63] Net incomes are known for only four of those mentioned, and in 1954 these ranged from slightly under $500 per month to around $1,000. Most people are convinced that the undertaker and the doctor are the best-paid men in the community.[64] As one elderly man laughingly says: "With all us old people livin' here, they can't miss . . . specially the undertaker."

No estimate is ventured regarding other business incomes in Plainville, because, as mentioned previously, most of the merchants are quite secretive about their gross and net incomes. In 1948, locally considered one of the better business years since 1940, the average Woodland County retail business reported gross sales of $27,630,[65] a marked increase over the $5,300 reported by West (1945:23) for 1939. This does not mean, however, that all Plainville merchants average this gross, or even that the majority of them do. In fact, several admit that they barely get along, and there are some who are known to be in serious economic difficulty.

Factors contributing to the poor success of most Plainville businessmen are varied and complex. Some men simply do not have the necessary business acumen. On the other hand, there are certain management problems common to all, such as defining a realistic credit policy in the face of rapid social and economic change. Demands for credit are not new to Plainville merchants, who have long been plagued by them. Furthermore, in a crisis such as a drought these demands are intensified and the merchant is sometimes pressured into economic procedures which are not desirable under even the best conditions. One grocer, for example, has let many people become indebted to him "several hundred dollars" each. His simple explanation is: "They got to live. . . . They can't be turned away." His dilemma is how to define realistic credit policies when economic relationships with customers are based on intimate kinds of social interaction. The dilemma is always there when times are bad, and it appears too often when times are good, even when one's own economic security is threatened. A former businessman, who went bankrupt in Plainville when economic conditions were most favorable, succinctly states:

I had a good business going right after the war . . . except for the credit. I let some fellows get in to me when they had the money to pay their bills. No excuse for it then. When times got a little harder I had to let some people get in over their heads. What can you do? You know them people—who's got sickness, and things like that. I just couldn't last. I took a real beating. Some got in so deep they wouldn't come around . . . musta been ashamed. What little money they could spend they went somewhere else to spend.

The last complaint, incidentally, is echoed by most Plainville merchants.

Credit problems are further complicated by changes in the economic responsibilities of merchants to their suppliers, matters which are not common knowledge to most of their customers. A few years ago, for example, most wholesalers granted merchants liberal billing allowances, but nowadays they more and more often demand cash on delivery. An interview with one firm supplying products to Plainville summarizes the wholesaler's views:

> Use to I could string along with my customers . . . but things are too tight now. Take old Kenneth Pickens, one of my customers in Plainville. I don't dare make a delivery there without getting my money. Use to I could give him thirty days, but I can't do it anymore. Business is bad and I know it. We all got to manage pretty good to come out these days.

It would be a serious mistake to assume that all, or even most, of the businessman's economic ills are traceable to poor management. This explanation is too simple and completely ignores the important and far-reaching influences of changes in the function of the service center. The village no longer is *the* trading center where (1) many of the farmer's products are sold, and (2) most of his buying is done. The middleman role of village merchants declined as farmers started specializing. Plainville farmers, for example, formerly milked their cows, separated the cream, which they sometimes churned into butter, and then sold or traded it to local merchants who passed it on to processors. Today, however, a Plainville dairyman or general farmer with two or three cows sells whole milk [66] through contractual agreement to major milk companies. None of the cash involved passes through the hands of local merchant middlemen. The same is true of the more successful poultry producers, who sell directly to wholesale buyers. Beef producers have for many years, of course, depended mostly on outside markets.

Farmers, therefore, no longer feel a symbiotic relationship

between themselves as sellers and the service center as a marketing place. Along with other Plainvillers, they define their roles mainly as consumers. The problem, then, is one of functional consistency between the needs of consumers and the extent to which these are met by local service institutions. When viewed in this way most Plainville consumer needs are not, and cannot be, under existing conditions satisfied locally. Plainville's changing standard of living has expanded since 1939–40 to include a great variety, quantitative and qualitative, of comfort and labor-saving devices common to urban and more technically advanced rural areas. Plainville farms and homes are being mechanized and modernized, and decisions involving major purchases begin with the premise that brand, quality, style, and price alternatives must be considered. Plainville consumers are aware, just as their city cousins are, of variety in the vast supply of material goods continually produced by American industry. They are constantly exposed to urban newspaper, radio, and television advertising. These media play an important role in directing consumer preference toward items available only in city stores; more importantly, they provide a handy guide by which Plainvillers can evaluate merchandising policies, products, and prices available locally. Plainvillers shop and compare, and regardless of the comparative unit used local merchants invariably suffer. This is true of hard consumer items such as appliances and machinery, most of which cannot be bought in Plainville, and also of soft goods, particularly foods. In fact, an increasing number of Plainvillers buy most of their groceries in Liberty and Largetown. They justify one or two shopping trips to "the city" each month by contrasting supermarket selection and prices (advertised in the Largetown *Bee*) with those found in local stores. These contrasts lead to one conclusion—"Plainville is the highest damned place in the state"—and convince Plainvillers that local merchants are "getting fat off them high prices."

It is true that merchants have not updated their methods

to keep pace with their customers' expanding needs for goods and services. The reasons, however, are simple: Plainville businessmen do not have the physical and economic resources to take advantage of appliance and machinery markets, nor can they, for the same reasons, compete with the range of quality, price, and variety featured by city stores. One obvious result is that more of their customers travel to the city to buy all kinds of goods. Furthermore, city stores send appliance and furniture salesmen into Plainville, offering such inducements as free delivery and extended time payments. This is tough competition. In fact, Plainville businessmen find urban stores more of a threat than mail-order houses ever were. This does not mean that catalogs have disappeared. Enough people still buy from them that older merchants occasionally still make caustic references to mail-order firms: "People don't buy as much from the catalogs as they use to. They'd ruther go to town. There's still a bunch here, though, who buy a lotta stuff from 'em. We damned well got some here who'd room and board with Sears an' Roebuck if they could."

In short, business and professional men in Plainville face a dilemma for which they have no solution. They cannot supply the alternatives in goods, services, and prices which their customers demand; consequently there is a growing fear that they cannot long stay in business if they do not sell more of the limited goods which they can supply. Potential customers, on the other hand, say that they cannot afford Plainville prices and cannot depend on local merchants and professional people to satisfy their needs and wants. This impasse foments considerable latent hostility between the two groups, and on occasion leads to open criticism.[68]

While Plainville merchants are aware of their limitations, they are also aware that they stock many items required by all families. They believe that people should feel obligated to buy these in their home town "out of loyalty to the community." This notion of community loyalty, obviously based on self-interest, is not shared by others, who say it is a dollars and cents matter with them, and that their loyalty to Plainville does not extend to their pocketbooks. Tom Officer, a prominent Plainville merchant, bitterly observes: "All we can sell a lot of these people are minor items they forgot to buy in the city . . . and I can't stay in business that way." He criticizes customers as "horse traders" who will not pay reasonable prices for goods and services, but who always insist on "jewing" him down. Mr. Officer and other merchants complain that farmers and villagers drive sixty miles to the city to buy some items which they can supply for only a little more. They forget, or are not aware, that people enjoy going to the city, and that the interest in finding bargains may well be an extension of the traditional trading complex in this region (West, 1945:20).

A small minority of Plainville consumers seriously questions the need for a service center except as a place for "old age pensioners to live in." Most of their arguments appear in the following composite interview with one of Plainville's most successful farmers:

The small village is on the way out. It has served its usefulness, and these people might just as well get ready for it. They can't possibly hope to compete with the larger stores in the cities. Small business just can't hope to keep up with the big chain stores and the like. . . . Why should I patronize some guy like Reece Hart in his general store, or some of these groceries, when I can go to Liberty and have a better selection and cheaper prices? . . . When I need repairs on my equipment, I can't get the job done in one of these little villages . . . I got to go someplace where they know something about it. . . . They are mostly places for old folks to retire. . . . Sure, we got schools and churches there, too, but not enough people to support either of them.

Many Plainvillers are quick to enumerate and criticize the deficiencies of their community, and almost eager to compare it unfavorably with others. This is a marked change from prewar days. Then there was community pride; people thought of Plainville as "our community" and boasted of its superiority as a county leader in business and education.

Against a background of rapid change, Plainville merchants have found that established techniques for attracting consumer interest are inadequate and that traditional leadership roles cannot create new ones. A few years ago certain men, because of family background, personal qualities, business achievement, or political authority, were recognized leaders who assumed the initiative for organizing activities like Saturday "drawings" (people put tickets obtained from merchants in a box and those lucky enough to have their tickets drawn receive a prize) or entertainment in the square, both sure-fire community attractions, and used personal influence to secure school bonds, road improvements, and other benefits, to make Plainville the "best" and "liveliest" community in the county. Their role was simplified by the economic interdependence of farmer and villager, and because the social, religious, and educational interests of both groups were community centered. Today, however, this type of personalized leadership is rejected by many, and one who attempts to assume this role is criticized. This is partly explained by some of the economic changes already mentioned. Businessmen, for example, are more competitive than formerly, and many of them fully admit that whenever one of their number is too aggressive, say in the Commercial Club, they individually question and analyze his motives. The business community is not, however, entirely without leadership. Rather, leadership has shifted away from specific individuals to a formal organization, the Commercial Club. A more complete analysis of the success and failure of the club is reserved for a later section. Here we can say that its leadership effectiveness has steadily declined since its founding, and has now reached the point where it functions for little more than social purposes.

The only attempt by Plainville merchants to revive local

business in 1954–55 was an irrational, badly outmoded, and very unsuccessful Saturday afternoon drawing. The reasons why drawings are no longer successful have already been mentioned. One factor, however, growing from improved communications, deserves special mention. Several Plainvillers attend the local drawing and immediately drive to Stanton, and then to Discovery, for other drawings. This multiple participation tends to split buying power which normally might be concentrated only in Plainville.

Twelve public school teachers comprise the largest single professional group in Plainville. All but four of them are from Woodland County, a fact which leads some to conclude, and perhaps rightly so, that "our schools would fold up if we didn't have some of these home-grown girls with a little college work." This generalization is particularly true of the elementary school, which is staffed only by local women, most of whom are willing to work for relatively poor salaries because, among other reasons, they do not rely on their income for their total support.[69] Their annual salary, $2,070,[70] is substantially lower than those of secondary teachers [71] who earn the following: superintendent, $4,000; vocational agriculture teacher, $3,600; coach-social science teacher, $3,100; home economics-science teacher, $2,700; commerce teacher, $2,700; and music-English teacher, $2,250.[72] Opinion as to the adequacy of teachers' salaries varies with the educational and financial positions of individual Plainvillers. Those with low incomes or poor educational background generally believe that "teachers git more than they're worth," whereas others feel that teachers' salaries should be better.

The only full-time religious specialist in Plainville is the minister of the Christian Church. He lives in a rent-free parsonage in Plainville, from which he travels, and ministers, to a five-church circuit over the county. His salary for this demanding position is $3,000 per year, paid by the five churches. The Baptist minister, who is a long-time resident of Plainville, gets "in the neighborhood of $60.00" for preaching two Sundays per month. He is also a part-time carpenter, and is the elected county representative to the state legislature.[73] The Holiness minister, who farms in an adjoining county, provides his congregation with the only complete schedule of religious services in the community. He preaches two sermons every Sunday, and is rewarded rather uncertainly for his labor from the collection plate.[74] The present Methodist minister does not live in Plainville, and appears only one Sunday each month to hold morning and evening worship.

The best salaried positions available are those of postmaster and rural mail carrier. Starting pay for these jobs, available only when an incumbent dies or retires, is around $3,600 per year. In 1954 the rural carrier died and the postmaster retired shortly thereafter, setting in motion a current of excitement throughout the whole community. The retired postmaster jokingly told me that if he had known his retirement was going to excite so many people he would have done it long ago "because this is more fun than a barrel of monkeys." Several interested men and women prepared for several months to take the civil service examinations,[75] and the three who were most successful then had to compete for the all-important endorsement by local politicians. The economic security of a permanent civil service appointment, plus knowledge of the numerical and temporal scarcity of the postal positions, contributes immensely to their desirability, and to the prestige of individuals who hold them.

Besides the business and professional people already mentioned, several men and women who live in the village are wage earners. Five men work for the state highway department, a like number work as truck drivers for themselves or for the quarry that supplies lime to farmers, and some others are best classified as laborers and handymen. They do construction work for seventy-five cents to $1.00 per hour, and farm labor for similar wages with, perhaps, a meal included. Several men live and work in Metropolis, coming home to see their families on weekends. Most of them started working there during the Second World War and stayed on in industrial or construction jobs after the war. In this respect it is significant that thirty-nine percent of the county's farmers did off-farm work in 1954, and that of this number seventeen percent spent more than 100 days in non-farm jobs. Most of them work on construction jobs, as highway laborers, or as truck drivers, but some own and operate village businesses. The significance of off-farm income should not be underestimated, because in 1954 twenty-six percent of all Woodland County farmers earned more this way than on their farms.[76]

There are few taboos against Plainville women working outside the home. Most businessmen's wives assist them, and four Plainville women are heads of business firms. One of these holds a justifiable reputation as one of the most astute business figures in the community. For the most part, however, there are few local or county opportunities for women who want to work. Six Plainville women clerk in local stores or work in court house offices in Discovery, and four others perform domestic services for very reasonable charges. One woman, for example, lives with and cares for two elderly people, and charges only $15.00 per week. Another gets $2.00 to $3.00 per day for washing, ironing, cleaning, canning, and similar tasks; one does washings for $1.25 per bushel basket of clothes; and still another is a seamstress.

"LIVING OUT OF THE POST OFFICE"

No discussion of making a living in Plainville is complete without consideration of the impact of government-derived money upon the community. It is becoming increasingly apparent that this is a vital factor in the economic life of the people. Not only are varied government programs the sole source of money for many individuals and families, but they funnel into Plainville and Woodland County a significantly large percentage of the actual cash available for circulation.

Two major sources of the money which ultimately circulates in the Plainville economic system are agriculture and the government. A few people obtain funds from other sources, such as working in urban industry, but the amount is insignificant in the over-all economic picture. Most of the potential circulable cash in Woodland County comes from agricultural sales, which in 1954 amounted to $1,830,283.[77] During the same year the Woodland County welfare office paid out $305,355, and the Agricultural Stabilization Conservation program spent $33,553. In addition, many people receive money from social security, G.I. training, military disability, and civil service. Administrators of some government programs live in the county, and several other people who qualify one way or another as survivor's beneficiaries also receive government funds. Considering all sources, it is estimated that over twenty percent of the total money circulated in Woodland County in 1954 came from federal programs. As Plainvillers say, "There's a lot of people here living out of the post office."

Most Plainville businessmen know that "all them people living outa the post office is a big help to this town." Grocery store owners are particularly aware that a large number of their customers, old age pensioners, depend entirely on government money for their maintenance. There were, for example, 155 people in Plainville in 1954–55, eighty-four in the village alone, who received old age assistance checks averaging $51.00 per person per month,[78] and there were twenty-five more people in the community who received other types of welfare assistance. Thus, Plainville merchants, mainly grocerymen, could expect around $10,000 per month from these sources alone. This figure assumes added significance if we consider that most of these people are not economically mobile, and therefore spend most of their money in Plainville, and that most of their income must be spent just to get by. Available figures show that welfare recipients in all categories received well over $100,000 in 1954. This is a vital and steady source of income for local merchants.

PATTERNS OF CONSUMPTION

The following discussion of consumption patterns is not intended as a complete analysis of Plainville consumer behavior. A good deal, in fact, has already been said indirectly about this phase of the Plainville economy in the discussion of ways of making a living. This is inevitable because of the functional interdependence between these two areas of economic behavior. What follows, then, is a description of some of the more important consumption patterns not already referred to, which are, nevertheless, important to the economy of Plainville.

HOUSES AND FURNISHINGS

One indication of a rising level of living in Plainville is the construction of new dwellings, and remodeling, repairing, painting, and adding to older houses. Plainvillers attribute these material improvements, so obvious throughout the community, to better economic conditions: "People didn't use to have the money to fix up their places . . . but most of us got to makin' a little more, 'specially durin' the war, and we took more interest." Or, "Those pension checks have improved the looks of some of these towns. I notice where occasionally some of the old people will paint and pretty up their houses. . . ." More, however, is involved than economic improvement—values of desirable living standards have changed.

There are a few stone and brick houses in Plainville, and still a few log dwellings, considered oddities today, but most houses are of frame construction. Some of the latter, however, have been covered with imitation brick cloth or asbestos shingles. Probably a third of the houses in Plainville are called "little houses," one to three rooms; a few "big houses," some two-story, have more than six rooms; but most dwellings are "average" size, with four to six rooms.[79]

Older homes have large front porches, and on hot summer afternoons and evenings elderly people sit on them to "cool off," visit, and watch passersby. An elderly friend of mine laughingly says that she can sit in a rocking chair on her porch, and from this vantage point find out everything happening in the village. She keeps a pitcher of iced tea handy, as she says, to "snare" those with whom she wishes to share her news. Younger people, who build the newer homes, do not consider large front porches fashionable, and as one elderly gentleman sadly lamented during an interview on his porch, "Young people don't seem to enjoy jus' sittin' like us old people done all our lives . . . they got to be runnin' here and there. They jus' can't seem to settle long enough to enjoy sittin' on a porch and jus' talkin'."

Some houses have basements but most people consider them too damp to be practical. All dwellings have a front and back yard, and since well-kept front lawns are a source of pride, power equipment is appearing in the yard tools of villager and farmer alike. Many people plant flowers in their yards, and some landscape them with shrubbery from city nurseries. One owner of a new home, in fact, contracted with a Liberty nursery to landscape his front yard for him. Many people think the plants are beautiful, but criticize the family as ostentatious for having had them planted by a nurseryman. This farm home, incidentally, modern and functional in design, is considered by most Plainvillers as the ultimate in beauty and comfort. There is lively interest and speculation about the cost ("It must be the most expensive home ever built here"), quality of materials, and construction. The owner and his wife occupy high-prestige positions, and are considered among "the best workers in the community" ("They deserve a house like that"), but people never cease to ask, "How in the world can they afford to build such a fancy place?" Shortly after the home was completed and newly furnished, scarcely before the family moved in, rumors were rife that they were already delinquent in "their payments" and firms were making repossessions. The rumors were false but functional—several Plainvillers volunteered that they were started by "people who were jealous."

Garages are considered much more essential today than formerly, and when present are built at the side or rear of the house. Outdoor privies are always located at the rear of the back yard, and some families build small storage buildings behind their houses. Passing out of the back yard of farm homes one finds outbuildings for housing animals and storing feeds, and, perhaps, a new grade A dairy barn. Machinery and equipment are stored in the open, near the barn, or in the case of more well-to-do farmers, in a machine shed. Gardens, property of the women, are located at the side, or rear, of the house.

The seventeenth annual United States Census of Housing reveals that of the 2,000 farm and nonfarm homes in Woodland County in 1950, over 1,200 were built before 1919. Fifteen new farm houses have been built within a five-mile radius of the village of Plainville since 1940, most of them after 1948, and between 1940 and 1950 twenty-four houses were added to the village, most of them after 1946.

Building costs are up in Plainville, as elsewhere, but local labor is still cheap, and some building materials can be bought cheaper in the county than in cities. Two conditions have caused sharp increases in the cost of certain lots and village property. First, the great number of elderly people who live there, and those who plan to retire to town, have created an unusual demand for houses near the square. "The old people like to live as close in as they can get . . . close to the stores." Secondly, business shifts toward the new highway since 1940 have made lots and property adjoining it the most desirable business sites in the village.

Plainvillers believe that every family should own a home, and that preferably "a man oughta have the money ready when he buys or builds." An investment this large, however, usually requires a mortgage, which most owners seek to amortize as quickly as possible. Table XI shows that a substantial number of Woodland County farm and nonfarm owners managed to do this between 1940 and 1950, locally considered stable economic years.

TABLE XI. OWNER-OCCUPIED DWELLINGS
IN WOODLAND COUNTY [80]

Year	Number Reporting	Percent of Total Owner-occupied	Percent of Owner-occupied Dwellings Mortgaged
1940	1,886	57.3	23.4
1950	1,766	72.9	10.9

The median value of Woodland County nonfarm dwellings reported to the U.S. Bureau of the Census in 1950 was $2,318. This figure applies to Plainville, although the trend now is toward more expensive construction, generally in the $3,000 to $7,000 class. A few homes cost more than this, and certainly many are cheaper. The more expensive, newly built, single-story compact units, well insulated, and preferably with modern plumbing, contrast sharply with the older one-and-a-half-story houses. They are evidence of significant social and economic changes which affect the lives of Plainvillers. People in Plainville today appreciate a good, comfortable home, well stocked with labor-saving appliances and gadgets similar to those found in urban middle-class neighborhoods. Such a home symbolizes a desirable standard of living and represents the owner's economic achievement.

A major factor providing better Plainville living standards is more available electric power.[81] West reported that in 1940 "two thirds of the houses in town 'have lights.' The rest, like nearly all the farm houses, are lighted by kerosene lamps" (1945:13). The situation in 1955 was drastically different—all houses in town had electricity, and the few farm homes without it soon will have it through REA expansion.

In fact, the increase in electrical service to farmers is dramatic. The U.S. Agricultural Census for 1940 reported electricity on only 7.2 percent of all Woodland County farms. The same source reports electricity on 11.2 percent of all farms in 1945, followed by a sharp rise to 59.7 percent in 1950. By 1954, 91 percent of all county farms were serviced by electrical power.

The kitchen and its many appliances symbolize the importance which modern Plainvillers assign to electricity. Practically every kitchen includes some of the following: refrigerator, washer, dryer, home freezer, mixer, toaster, coffeemaker, electric range, hot water heater, and iron. The ideal kitchen includes all of them, but housewives consider a refrigerator most important and necessary. The seventeenth annual U.S. Census, 1950, reports that this appliance is owned by fifty percent of all Woodland County farmers and by more than sixty percent of all nonfarmers. Certainly, few people in the village are without an electric "ice box," and anyone who expresses dislike for this convenience is thought too "tight," or backward, to buy it. Lack of money, in fact, is no longer a justification for not owning this "necessity," because it can always be bought "on time." Since 1950 home freezers have steadily gained popularity. An estimated thirty percent of all Plainville families own them and, in addition, many farmers and villagers rent locker space in the Discovery frozen locker plant.

One appliance dealer in an adjoining county has sold "over two hundred" refrigerators and home freezers in Woodland County, mostly in Plainville, since 1945. Most units are financed, but "we seldom get a repossession. People seem to do about anything to keep their refrigerators . . . just won't part with them." One salesman from Liberty loads refrigerators on his pickup and drives through the community in search of customers. He contends that "these are tradin' people," and he will "take anything" in trade on a new refrigerator.

Most families own an electric or gasoline powered washing machine. A few women travel to Liberty and Stanton to use "help-ur-self" laundries, and some with washers dry their clothing there during bad weather.

West reports that there were three modern bathrooms in Plainville in 1940. By 1955 there were twenty-five in the village, exclusive of highway service stations, with about the same number in farm homes. Many families who feel they cannot afford modern bathrooms install running water for kitchen use, and some anticipate the future by setting aside a room, or planning to add one someday, for an indoor bath. The "inside toilet" is not, however, universally acceptable to Plainvillers, because some say that it gives them an uncomfortable feeling when they have to use one. One man with a modern bathroom is amused by some of his friends who feel this way: "I'll show 'em where it is, and some'll hem-haw around. . . . Some will insist on usin' the outdoor toilet, and some will use the indoor. When they use the indoor, they usually come out lookin' sorta silly 'cause they done their business in the house."

The cost of buying and installing fixtures, particularly septic tanks (professional servicing of these is an added cost), and, in most cases, of drilling a deeper well to provide water, deters many who want modern bathrooms. This is particularly true now (1954–55) because of the drought. Most new wells are between 250 and 400 feet, and drilling charges are $1.50 per foot for the first 100 feet, and $2.00 for each additional foot. These costs, plus well casing, electric pump, and weatherproof (against freezing) pump house, run as high as $1,000 to $2,000, depending on the type of equipment used. This expense, incidentally, is almost a certainty for those who build grade A dairy barns. There are many dairymen, in fact, with modern plumbing in their barns who cannot yet afford such equipment for their homes. This point was very effectively made during an interview with a grade A dairyman one snowy winter afternoon. He excused himself to go to his outdoor toilet with the following comment:

"Them damned cows got it better'n I have. . . . I gotta wade snow to get to my toilet. There orta be an inspector to inspect people's houses . . . maybe then we'd all see to it that we could afford an inside toilet." Another expense for those who modernize their homes is a hot water tank. Most people install electric units, and at village utility rates this adds between $1.50 and $3.50 per month to the electric bill. REA rates paid by farmers, however, are somewhat lower.

One of the most recent innovations to affect Plainville life is the substitution of commercial heating and cooking fuels for wood. As late as 1950, according to federal census reports, over eighty percent of all Woodland County homes were heated by wood. Plainville was no exception. Since then, however, fuel oil, and to a lesser extent propane gas and coal, have gained widespread use. The major reasons for shifting to oil are that it is more convenient and easier to use than wood or coal. It sells, delivered to the customer, for thirteen cents per gallon. The amount used varies with the weather, condition and size of house, and warmth desired. A family of five, living in a typical five-room, noninsulated house, spent $148 for fuel during the winter of our research ("even then we couldn't keep our place warm"); a young couple spent "over $65.00 just to keep two big rooms warm"; and an elderly female pensioner laments: "It takes ever extry bit of my pension to buy oil." However, she also says, "I wouldn't do without it now I tried it. The man just comes and fills my barrel and I don't have no fuss or mess to clean." Like many others, though, she has never taken down her wood-burning stove, and she admits that "once in awhile I build a fire in it so's I can get real warm. . . . Seems a wood fire just puts out more heat than oil does."

Actually, not more than twenty village families used wood as a major source of heat in 1954–55.[82] This was enough, however, that spirals of smoke were visible on cold days, and when fires were banked for the night a smell of oak or hickory smoke settled over the village. The town people who burn wood find it hard to buy. It sells, sawed and delivered, from $3.50 to $4.50 per rick, but, as an elderly hill farmer retired to the village explains: "Most wood I bought this winter's been so darn green it ain't worth foolin' with . . . and besides, the price they want is turrible. Next winter I aim to burn fuel oil. Ain't nobody much sellin' wood nowadays . . . not many as wants to work the timber like use to." Several wood-users share his sentiments. They all complain of the poor quality and high prices, whereas the few men who still work the timber complain of the lack of customers. Incidentally, more farmers than villagers still use wood, but they cut their own. Before leaving the matter of heating homes, we need to mention that central heating units show promise of increased popularity and acceptance.

The shift away from wood as a cooking fuel is pronounced. As recently as 1950 federal census reports show that over fifty percent of all Woodland County families used wood for cooking. However, no one in the village of Plainville cooked with wood in 1954–55, and the number of farm women who still use this source of cooking heat is rapidly declining. Appliance dealers in Woodland and adjoining counties report that sales of wood ranges are drastically down, but that there is an increased demand for gas and electric stoves. The availability of REA makes electric ranges more attractive to farm wives, whereas villagers, who must pay more for electricity, prefer ranges adaptable to propane gas.

Most Plainville homes are divided into a living room, a kitchen, and one or more bedrooms. Depending upon house size and the likes or dislikes of the owner there may be a dining room. Some houses have only two rooms, and in these the living room doubles as a bedroom. Floors are covered with linoleum or rugs or left bare. The most popular covering in terms of cost, cleanliness, and attractiveness, is linoleum. In fact, in many older homes with rough wood flooring it is absolutely necessary for warmth. Rugs are particularly preferred in the living room, and these sometimes are attractively handmade, braided rugs. Walls in older homes are usually papered, but it is more fashionable to paint them in newer houses. Calendars, framed pictures of friends or relatives, religious scenes, and framed scenic colored prints customarily decorate walls.

Stylistically, Plainville home furnishings range from home-made to modern, with quality, of course, related to the owner's finances. Most people prefer overstuffed living room divans and chairs. Many higher economic status families own pianos, prestige items that stand in the living room, usually topped by photographs of friends and relatives. In addition to these furnishings, there is the usual complement of tables, lamps, radio and, perhaps, phonograph and television, the last of which, when present, tends to dominate furniture arrangements. Windows are covered with curtains, window shades, or draperies, and some of the newer homes, and a few of the older ones, have venetian blinds. Bedroom furniture varies with the likes or dislikes and the finances of the family. Older homes conspicuously lack closet space, forcing modern families to buy ready-made wardrobe units, but all newer houses have bedroom closets and ample built-in kitchen cabinets. Many older kitchens have been remodeled to include built-in storage facilities.

Twenty-five percent of the villagers rent their homes, usually from Plainville property owners. Small two and three room, nonmodern houses rent from $5.00 to $20.00 per month. A modern three to five room house (and there are only four for rent) rents from $30.00 to $45.00 per month.

FOOD

Plainvillers normally eat three big meals daily: breakfast in the morning, dinner at noon, and supper in the evening. Pork, bacon, and chicken have long been the most common meats on Plainville tables, but as the level of living improves more people are eating greater quantities of beef. A wide

variety of vegetables is eaten, the most popular being potatoes, corn, green peas, and several types of beans, and dairy
foods (milk, butter, and cottage cheese) are a vital part of the
diet. Common mealtime drinks are coffee, milk, or cocoa in
the winter, and iced tea, milk, or some commercial sweet
drink in the summer. Desserts are popular, particularly cakes,
pies, cobblers, and home-canned fruits, and more than one
of these may commonly be served at a meal. Jello and ice
cream are considered very good desserts, and as a popular
pastime on summer evenings several families will gather to
eat home-made ice cream. Most foods are liberally seasoned
and there is always ample quantity. In fact, an outsider receives the impression that Plainvillers love to eat, and to eat
a lot.

Eating is primary at most social gatherings, and at times,
for those present, takes precedence over the overt reasons for
their having come together. Plainvillers' concern with food,
and the sheer pleasure of consuming it, is manifest in the
amount of talk devoted to the topic. Out of their conversations certain men are consistently identified as "big eaters,"
and certain women as "top cooks." Women are particularly
proud of their ability to "set a good table," and they are
especially proud to be identified at church or community
suppers with special dishes.

There is a mild bustle of activity in early spring as most
farmers, and probably three fourths of the villagers, prepare
and plant garden plots. A former Woodland County home
agent [83] estimates that by her garden labor the Plainville
farm wife saves her family $350 to $400 per year; the amount
is slightly less for village families whose gardens are smaller.
A good garden can supply fresh vegetables during the growing season, and a canned surplus for winter consumption. Not
everyone, however, cans food, so grocery stores now stock
fresh vegetables in the winter, but find it is not profitable to
stock them during the garden season. A farm wife who does
not can, but buys all her food from the store, is criticized as

lazy or citified, and is said to be "living pretty high." Farm experts believe that economy, rather than well-balanced diet, is still the main incentive for Plainville housewives to can food. They say that too many jars are filled with preserves, jellies, and jams, and not enough with vegetables. A recent innovation may offer some improvement—many women now freeze fresh vegetables and fruits rather than can them. This eliminates much of the work and risk in food preservation, and is preferred by those who can afford a home freezer. Home freezing introduces a new complex of traits which the Plainville housewife must adjust to, but these are not so radically different as to develop technical resistance.

Practically all farmers produce their own poultry and dairy products for home consumption. Not too many years ago most villagers did the same, but "town people just don't own chickens and cows like they used to." [84] Instead, they buy milk and eggs from farmers or, more often, from local grocery stores. Some older people do not keep cows, nor do they plant gardens, through the fear that what they produce will be deducted from their pensions. They are, of course, sensitive to even minor deductions in their small checks. This is one of many overt manifestations of the concern which some feel for government regulation and control over areas of behavior where such interference has traditionally been taboo. As one elderly pensioner sarcastically puts it: "When you git on the pension you cain't do nothin' but just sit down. Somebody'll come nosin' aroun', and then yore check'll be cut . . . and I cain't have that."

Most farmers still fatten hogs, and occasionally a beef, for home use, and several village families regularly buy a hog or beef from local farmers. Seldom, however, is meat processed at home. Farmer and villager alike have the animals butchered by one or two part-time specialists, and then store the meat in their freezer or in the Discovery locker plant. They take hams to small packing plants in neighboring counties or to one or two local specialists for curing. Many families buy meat from a small market in the village, owned and operated by the wife of one of the custom butchering specialists,[85] or buy it in city supermarkets. Interestingly enough, a few ex-Plainvillers who now work in nearby cities come "home" once or twice a month to buy dairy and poultry products from relatives or friends at cheap home prices. This is a minor source of revenue for a few farm families.

There are only two or three families, and a like number of bachelors, who depend to any extent on fish and wild game as supplementary food. Plainville men do a lot of hunting and fishing, and more often than not the game is cleaned and eaten, but these activities are recreational and are undertaken with little thought of adding to the family larder. Most people deprecate dependence on wildlife as a major source of food. "Why, anybody can get out and make enough money today [to provide for minimum essentials]."

CLOTHING

Aside from businessmen, who wear khaki or dress trousers and sport shirts, Plainville men wear bib overalls, khaki or denim trousers, and work shirts and shoes as everyday dress. They wear caps or hats winter and summer, and during cold weather wear heavy coats and sweaters. For "better" occasions dress trousers or clean khaki, with sport shirt, are appropriate. Plainville men wear suits to funerals, or occasionally to church and school functions. West (1945:39) wrote, "A man's suit lasts many years, because it is worn only rarely." Men complain that they feel uncomfortable in a suit, particularly neckties which "choke a feller down." A trip to Largetown or Metropolis, depending on the type of business involved, may require attire other than work clothing.

Everyday apparel for women consists of a cotton dress or, perhaps, a discarded "dress-up" garment. For church, school functions, or shopping trips to the city, women dress in fashions similar to those of urbanites. They are more style conscious than their husbands, and a few are singled out as particularly stylish dressers. Most married women are not ostentatious, and few dress so as to deliberately emphasize the financial status of their husbands. This is not true of their daughters.

The apparel of junior high and high school girls, more than that of any other group in the community, symbolizes parental economic status. Girls from economically secure families are clearly differentiated, in both style and cost of clothing, from those with poorer parents. They are extremely fashion conscious, wear the latest hairdos, and maintain the quality and style of urban teenagers in dress and appearance. With the assistance of devoted mothers they are the epitome of local fashion and parental indulgence. These girls are ready acceptors of style innovations, and more than any other group in the community are attuned to magazines, catalogs, and other media which effectively disseminate these innovations. They are both admired and envied by their peers and by adult women as well.

Plainville women make many clothes, such as dresses, blouses, and skirts, for themselves and their daughters. Girls are especially fond of skirts and blouses for school wear, customarily with a sweater or jacket for cool days. Coats are commonly cloth, although a few women own furs. Hats are seldom worn, except by some to church or funerals, but head scarves are common for all females. Adult women usually wear hose for winter warmth, but school girls wear anklets and low-heeled shoes. Nylon hose and high-heeled pumps, or low-heeled dress shoes, are worn for more formal occasions. Some of the junior high and high school girls ignore the taboo against shorts-clad women appearing in public. A few young married women wear shorts in their homes, and occasionally one will risk the criticism of older men and women by apppearing so clad in the village. Girls of pre-school age wear dresses.

High school boys prefer blue jeans or wool slacks, sport shirts, and leather jackets for school wear. Most of them own a suit for special occcasions, but the attitude prevails that it is "sissy" to get too dressed up. Boys of preschool age wear shorts, blue jeans, overalls, or long trousers, often in imitation of adult males. Parents state that it is much less trouble and expense to dress a boy than a girl, and the characteristic dress of the two groups clearly indicates this to be true.

The dress of Holiness people varies enough to warrant some mention. Women of this sect should not wear short sleeves, low-necked dresses, jewelry, or makeup, nor should they cut their hair. Most older women conform to these taboos against "worldliness," but some middle-aged women and the few teenagers in the congregation do not. The major clothing taboo for Holiness men is the necktie which, somehow, has "worldly" connotations. This taboo, however, is not as strong as in former years, and some Holiness men are occasionally seen wearing ties. The Holiness group, as do many Baptists, objects to makeup and to girls playing basketball in shorts. Most of the community consider Holiness and Baptist views regarding dress as "odd," "strange," "silly," "crazy," or "just their ways."

HUNTING AND FISHING

Hunting and fishing are two activities which owe their economic importance not to the contribution which they make to subsistence, but rather to the amount of time and money spent on them. These activities are mostly sport and recreation—an obvious fact considering that the sum spent in pursuing them far exceeds any monetary value that might be assigned to the game taken.

The money invested in hunting and fishing gear by some men amounts to several hundred dollars.[86] Many own more than one outboard motor, and some own two boats; all sportsmen own multiple pieces of equipment, such as two or more guns or several sets of fishing tackle, and the well outfitted huntsman or fisherman owns many items of special clothing. Some men derive great satisfaction merely from the ownership and care of their equipment. There is pride in having just the right gun or fishing reel, and in keeping gear in top condition for any occasion which might arise, and there is prestige in owning a large inventory of equipment. It is symbolic of the owner's economic status in the community. There is a definite element of conspicuous consumption in the economic behavior of many Plainville sportsmen. In addition to their equipment investment they spend much time and money traveling to well-known fishing and hunting areas. In fact, these activities are second only to visiting relatives as an excuse for high prestige families to vacation in other states or in other sections of Missouri.[87]

Furthermore, many Plainville men are motivated to spend time, money, and effort, to compete for the prestige of excelling as a huntsman or fisherman.[88] The following comments abstracted from interviews with a particularly perceptive man are revealing:

I don't enjoy fishin' any more . . . nowadays it's work, and perty danged costly. . . . Some of these fellers work at fishin' like they gotta do better'n the next man. That ain't what I call fun. . . . These fellers laugh at my old fishin' pole . . . they figure they gotta have somethin' big and fancy nowadays. . . . Hell! I wouldn't enjoy eatin' a fish that took maybe fifteen or twenty dollars to catch. . . . Ain't like it use to be . . . it costs money nowadays just to have fun . . . and what use to be fun, like fishin', ain't so much that way any more. . . . If you make a big perduction outa goin' fishin' and then don't catch nothin', you're a real failure. One of them fellers catches a big one and he's all up and down Main Street with it . . . carries the danged thing aroun' till it stinks. If he don't catch nothin', lotta times you won't know he's been . . . 'less he made a big trip out of it.

Several men in the community hunt fox and 'coon with hounds, and others own bird dogs for quail hunting. Five or six men add to their incomes by spending part of their time training and selling dogs, and one man specializes in breeding and training quality hounds, which he sells throughout the United States and in several foreign countries. A good hound

4 Social Organization

THE PRINCIPLES of alignment which underlie social units in Plainville are varied and complex. There are some units which rest on kinship, age, and sex; others are based on specific interests, local or nonlocal, such as religion, occupation, and politics. People are members of neighborhoods, lodges, clubs, and schools, and they belong to formal and informal cliques and voluntary associations. Through all of these social units they relate to each other and, to some extent, to people outside Plainville. In this chapter, then, and the one that follows on religion, we are concerned with those forms of social organization for the direction and control of individual and group behavior in the community, and with some of the changes which have occurred in the social organization of Plainville since 1939–40.

THE AGE-SEX STRUCTURE

In Plainville, as in all human societies, the most fundamental social division is between the two sexes. Children are expected to demonstrate at an early age personality traits attributed to their sex, and throughout the remainder of their lives are accorded differential treatment and are expected to conform to the interests and duties that are theirs by virtue of sex and age statuses. As West (1945:176) points out, "It seems to be the purpose of the society to establish very early separate sets of of behavior habits for boys and girls—habits which have to do with clothing, work, morality, and personality. . . ."

One of the most clear-cut delineations between the sexes is the economic division of labor within the nuclear family. By the time they enter school children have been taught by parents, and have learned through observation, to differentiate between the economic roles considered appropriate to each of the sexes. Thus, small boys follow their fathers very early, learning minor chores they can perform, particularly outside the house, while little girls "tag after" mothers and learn to do dishes, make beds, clean house, and perform various other female tasks. Both may make "nuisances of theirselves" by attempting roles for which they are inadequate, but most Plainville parents, convinced that role assignments in minor economic matters are a necessary part of constructive child training, endure this "nuisance." The present generation of parents, however, is not so far committed to this socializing principle as their parents were. They generally believe that children should assist only with chores or field work that are not too arduous for a child's physical capabilities and do not interfere too much with school attendance, home study,[1] and ample recreation time. Young parents often say: "I can't see having my boy [or girl] work like I had to. . . . Why, I was doing a man's [or woman's] work when I wasn't much more than ten or twelve." Still, the same parents are likely to brag: "I got a young son who can plow like a man." [2] By the time sons and daughters are high school age and older, they are expected to do some work during the year, even though they regularly attend school. In this respect, it is much easier for farm parents than for village families to find chores and other jobs for their children, particularly the kinds of tasks normally assigned to young boys. Girls, on the other hand, whether they live in the village or in the country, have pretty much the same duties.[3]

Plainville wives have the responsibility of caring for children, cooking, sewing, laundering, canning, keeping house, and contributing to the non-money, and in some cases the money, income of the family by doing most of the work connected with gardening and poultry. Plainville men are fathers and breadwinners who have the major responsibility of furnishing economic support for their families.

There are, however, some situations which require mutual participation by men and women, and certain special conditions in which it is possible for members of one sex to assume a role normally identified with the other. For example, women should not work in the fields, but "in a real tight pinch, like maybe during a harvest," or "if work gets piled up on your man," it is permissible, and even desirable,[4] for a wife to assist her husband.[5] Men sometimes, "in a tight spot," assist with the care of children, particularly boys, but almost never help with the cooking and, if a wife or daughter is present, never do housework. On the other hand, certain phases of some economic activities encourage the mutual participation and cooperation of both sexes. Thus, as previously indicated, it is common for husband, wife, and children of both sexes to work as a team in the milking operation on specialized dairy farms. Similarly, men break ground for gardens, considered heavy work, and frequently assist their wives, during the cool of evening, with the weeding.

Out of the economic division of labor there emerges in most younger families a fairly equal balance in economic power between the two sexes.[6] The decisions preceding major purchases [7] for farm and home are, in these families, democratically resolved by husband and wife, both of whom are aware of the family's total financial picture. This contrasts sharply with older-aged families, more patriarchal in structure, where the husband, at least overtly, controls the economic decision-making process.[8] Our interview materials reveal that some young and middle-aged couples discuss even minor expenses such as the grocery bill, and according to several merchants "almost as many men as women do the buying, nowadays."

Plainvillers recognize the following age-determined categories: "babies," "kids," "teenagers," "young people," "married people," and "old people" (see West, 1945:108–14). "Babies" are ordinarily pre-walking infants, but once they start to walk are called "little kids," and are now expected to have more interest in a good time than in anything else. Parents and older siblings believe so strongly that little boys "just naturally" want to play with other little boys, and that little girls "just naturally" want to associate only with little girls, that a conscious effort is made to influence them in these directions. At an early age, for example, strong distinctions are emphasized in patterns of dress and in patterns of behavior,[9] particularly behavior designed to inculcate a sense of economic usefulness in children. Thus, Plainvillers believe that small girls not only are more adept at household tasks, but that they prefer them.[10] Small boys, on the other hand, prefer outdoor work, and are more rugged and individualistic than girls. They are considered "cute," and are a source of pride to parents, when they act "growed up" and "manly," use "slangy" talk like their fathers, and behave in other ways considered immodest or "not proper" for little girls.

At six years of age "little kids" begin school, and for the next several years are identified as "grade school kids." "The school is the first important formal disciplinary institution which the child enters outside his own home" (West, 1945:188). Not only that, but this marks the first time that "the child is drawn partially away from his mother's apron strings and begins long periods of contact with more children than he has [heretofore] been accustomed to" (West, 1945:189). Many parents view their child's first day in school with mixed emotions. They recognize this as an important status change for the child, and wish that it could be delayed, somehow, a little longer. A young mother, her son now only three years old, adequately makes this point by projecting the event: "I don't know what I'll do when he goes to school. . . . It'll kill me to see him go off all day." Another reveals a further dimension of the problem when she says: "I just can't bear to have somebody else correcting him." Entering school, then, is an occasion which symbolizes to parents that

After graduation from high school, or during their late teens if they do not attend school, teenagers become "young folks." They should not become "married folks" until sometime between high school graduation and their late twenties, because it is not until then that they "pretty much make their own way." Because of this, much criticism surrounds the infrequent marriages between high school students, or, for that matter, marriages in which even one of the partners, usually the girl, is still in school.[15] "Young folks" not married by their middle or late thirties are ascribed old maid or bachelor status, terms which, incidentally, are sometimes applied to widows or widowers who have not remarried.

The adolescent period is terminated for most Plainvillers by a rather early marriage ("soon after high school"). Girls from high-status families sometimes are married in church, and may have appropriate showers and receptions, but such ceremonies are exceptions. Most marriage services are performed by a minister or justice of the peace. It is customary for the couple to take a short trip to an adjoining state or, more often, to some Missouri resort region or city. The honeymoon over, young folks assume the status of "married folks," and are now expected to stop "running around" as much as when they were "going together," and to confine their social interaction to married couples near their own age, or, perhaps, parents and siblings. When they have children their status changes considerably, and they are now known as the such and such family. Some distinction is made between "young," "middle-age," and "old" "married folks" and "families," and functionally this has some importance—middle-aged families are viewed as the solid core of the community. They are considered the most interested in schools and community development, and the most attached [16] to Plainville. What is more important, they are the recognized primary productive group. One measure of their importance is the competition among the four churches to attract them to their congregations. A leading Baptist church worker accurately states the issue when he says: "These are the people that make the church grow. . . . They have the children and the money."

"Old folks" are people sixty-five and above, particularly those whose children are married and away from home, and those who, because of age, no longer compete in the economic system. They are expected to show vital interest in politics ("They gotta have something to complain about"), to be extremely conservative with their money, and hence against most community improvements, and, in general, to be content just to loaf and gossip all day. It is an age level which is steadily acquiring new members, and one which elicits paradoxical behavior from the members of other age levels. Parents, for example, teach their children respect for older people, particularly relatives, and at the same time they equate the foibles of the aged with the childishness of the very young (see also West, 1945:59). This leads to conflicting notions among children regarding proper behavior toward the aged. One result is that some of the old people who manifest eccentricities, such as "yelling and fussing" at children who they assume, sometimes erroneously, are intentionally bothering them, become targets for torment by youthful pranksters. An elderly woman, for example, hard of hearing and with failing eyesight, continually complains to the county sheriff that children, and even grownups, are bothering her. Her fears are more imagined than real, but nevertheless cause her to behave in a way that encourages some people to conform to her expectations of them. Thus, young boys sometimes do throw stones at her house, spin their automobile wheels on the gravel in front of her dwelling, knock on her door and run, and in other ways elicit from her behavior which they find amusing.

This kind of torment is not without its serious consequences. It has negative psychological implications for the older person involved, and carried to extremes may provoke the persecuted individual to retaliate physically. In the case just cited, the county sheriff removed the firing pin from the woman's shotgun, fearing that she might shoot at real or imagined tormentors. Many parents, in fact, warn their children to "leave old Becky alone . . . she might hurt you."

This is not an isolated case; there are others more serious. There is the elderly man who, after a long history of trouble with Plainville boys, became so exasperated that he fired a rifle bullet into the radiator of a pickup carrying several youths whom he accused of "halloweening" [17] him. The father of the boy driving the vehicle was quite upset and threatened to prosecute the elderly man, but, in the end, took no action. Plainville opinion divided along generation lines. Older people thought the man was "in his rights" shooting at the boys; younger and middle-aged parents were shocked that he should do such a thing, and some felt he should be arrested.

Another elderly man, much pestered by youngsters, boasts that he has a club ready for any boy whom he can catch "trickin' my car" or "messin' around in my wood pile." Two youths who "trick" the man's car by honking the horn and turning on the lights at night, and "mess around" in his wood pile, by toppling over the neatly stacked ricks in which the old man takes pride, were asked why they do this. They do it because "he raises so much hell about it," and "he accuses us of botherin' him whether we do it or not."

Opposed to the behavior mentioned above is an ideal pattern of respect for old people, so strong that it is sometimes manifest in overt community expression. The observance of Mother's Day and Father's Day in Plainville churches, for example, recognizes not only those parents who are most prolific or, perhaps, youngest, but also the oldest who are present. Furthermore, during holiday periods—Christmas, Thanksgiving, and Easter—many individuals and church groups feel obligated to visit the "rest home" with refreshments and entertainment "to cheer up the old people a little." The greatest expression of the ideal, however, oc-

curred during our stay in the community, when several leading citizens initiated a community-wide picnic to honor the
aged. Old and young alike assembled in the square one
pleasant Sunday afternoon to share food, enjoy planned entertainment, and accord recognition, symbolized by small
prizes, to the oldest man and woman and the oldest married
couple present. The affair was well attended and generally
considered successful, but was boycotted by some of Plainville's senior citizens. One elderly man, asked why he wasn't
there, replied:

I wouldn't go over to the squar that day . . . not with all them
old people over there. I'm sebnty-two myself, and I don't ask nobody fer special treatment. Best thing some of them people
could do fer me is keep their kids in at night . . . they run up
and down here yellin' and tearin' aroun' my house till all hours.

Some of his peers express similar feelings—they question the
sincerity of a picnic held solely in their honor!

West (1945:113) wrote: "A Plainviller's passage from one
stage of life into a later stage is marked by various events,
acts, rituals, or ceremonies and by conventionalized sentiments and verbal statements." A child is born, and the first
big event in his life is entering school. The next high point,
symbolized by a formal ceremony and presentation of a diploma, is graduation from the eighth grade. Four years later
he receives a second diploma, more important than the first,
signifying completion of his high school career and, for most,
the end of formal education. Both graduation ceremonies are
attended by most of the community. In between the time he
graduates from the eighth grade and the time he enters high
school the child normally is baptized into one of the churches.
The next formal step is marriage, dignified by ceremony,
license, and, more often than not, a "shivaree" by friends.
This is followed by the birth of children and the many years
devoted to them until they leave home and establish families
of their own. The status of grandparent may result, but in
any case the Plainviller is soon "old," maybe "on the pen-

sion," and is, perhaps, widowed. Finally comes death, climaxed by a "decent" and "fitting" burial.

FAMILY AND KINSHIP

The major unit of social structure in Plainville, as in all Western communities, is the nuclear family, defined as a married couple and its dependents, usually children, in which the crucial bond is the one between husband and wife. Ego customarily refers to this basic kin unit as "my [his, her, your, their] family," and derives from it essential patterns of residence, economic cooperation, and reproduction. Extensions of the nuclear family are variable, depending on the particular unit, but in most cases include at least ego's parents, adult siblings, grandparents, aunts and uncles, nieces and nephews, and cousins. The extended kin group, sometimes referred to as "family," but more often called "kinfolks" or "relatives," includes a special category of "in-laws."

Upon marriage a husband and wife establish, if at all possible, neo-local residence and, as I have already indicated, divide labor within the nuclear family. Head of the family is the husband and father, although he seldom exercises absolute authority; most major decisions are arrived at jointly by both spouses. Both are expected to exhibit mutual respect and familial support in all matters involving one or the other. Thus, a wife should be submissive (sexually), but a "good" husband refrains from making demands upon her "when she doesn't feel like it," "at least two months" before a child is born, and for a similar period after a birth. In matters of sex both partners are expected to maintain fidelity throughout marriage, and neither should "look with favor" upon another man or woman (see also West, 1945:60). The sharp tongues of neighbors immediately react to known, or assumed, violations of this norm.

Not many years ago a newly married couple thought it best to have children as quickly as possible. We found, however, that most young people now want to live together "long enough to get to know each other," or to wait "until we can afford them," or "until we get a little something ahead," before having children. Furthermore, many young couples want only as many children as "we can do right by," and a small number, to the consternation of their parents ("Every family should have at least one or two, maybe more"), do not want any at all. Large families, "from six or eight to maybe twelve or fifteen," uncommon for many years (West, 1945:165), are associated with low status, "them that don't know better," and are almost always identified with poverty. Two or three large, but very low-status, families are stereotypic examples of the negative consequences implicit in a "house full of kids." The father of one of these families, during an interview, criticized a married son who does not want children, "leastways, not more'n one." The father believes that every home should have "six or eight. . . . We had that many that lived and done right by them." He believes that young parents don't want "the 'sponsibility" for "feedin', clothin', and schoolin' " children. He is convinced that he was a good father, which, to him, means "a good pervider," and is not particularly concerned that none of his children went to high school: "They didn't want to go." At least three of them, however, are known to lament their lack of education, and attribute it to the fact that "we didn't know no better when we was growin' up." The boy whom the father criticizes says: "I'll be damned if I'll have a house fulla kids that I cain't care fer." He, like an increasing number of Plainvillers in all status levels, is planning his family by spacing or limiting it to the number of children which he and his wife [18] feel they can afford. All adult Plainvillers are aware of simple commercial contraceptives, and apparently these are widely used.[19]

Ideally, a wife should be happy whenever she suspects or learns that she is pregnant. Her husband is told right away, but relatives and friends should not be informed until the couple is "sure," "probably after two or three periods" have gone by. Plainvillers find it amusing if an extra-proud prospective father breaks the news before then. After it is revealed, friends of the mother-to-be may surprise her with a baby shower, particularly if it is her first child. Most people assume that older children will welcome the arrival of a younger sibling; nevertheless some parents try to prepare them for the event.

Few pregnant women are embarrassed nowadays at being seen in public (see West, 1945:166). Young wives say that pregnancy is "natural," "it's obvious," and nothing is gained by trying to conceal it. Most of them, and most of the middle-aged women, scoff at much of the folklore about prenatal influences. Some, however, still believe that a mother's diet can mark her child, that one has a "strawberry mark" because his mother craved strawberries while she was carrying him (see West, 1945:166), or that a pregnant woman's craving for strawberries, or some other food, predisposes her child particularly to like the food.

Today, more than ever before, there is practical concern for a pregnant woman's health, and most people feel a very real medical concern. Prenatal and childbirth care are areas in which innovative agencies, such as Extension and Public Health, are most successful in creating health awareness. Most women, for example, consider it unthinkable nowadays to give birth without a doctor's assistance. "Why, lots of farmers have vets with their cattle, why not have a doctor with a woman?" Only "very backward," extremely low status women do not consult a physician. Most prospective mothers contact a physician as soon as they realize they are pregnant. Many higher-status women consult obstetricians in Largetown [20] and Liberty, and most of them spend a week to ten days in a Largetown hospital during and following delivery. Other women are delivered in hospitals nearer home, and some have their babies in the local osteopath's office. Women who choose the latter course come to the

office whenever their pains are "right," stay there a few hours
after delivery,[21] and return home to spend four or five days
in bed recuperating. During their convalescence relatives
or friends come in to help with young children, care for the
house, and cook meals. Some women still prefer to have
their children at home, but with a doctor in attendance.
However, as Table XII indicates, their number is steadily declining. Few births attended only by midwives or "granny
women" now occur.

TABLE XII. WOODLAND COUNTY BIRTHS
BY ATTENDANCE, 1938–52 [22]

Year	Total Births	Physician in Hospital	Physician Not in Hospital	Midwife	Other
1938	103	2	89	5	7
1939	96	3	87	3	3
1940	99	6	85	3	3
1941	105	11	84	3	7
1942	93	10	81	0	2
1943	92	25	67	0	0
1944	86	25	58	0	3
1945	71	23	48	0	0
1946	71	22	49	0	0
1947	108	59	47	1	0
1948	96	51	45	0	0
1949	102	69	33	0	0
1950	91	62	22	0	0
1951	100	88	12	0	0
1952	92	88	4	0	0

There is great variety in the treatment and care of Plainville infants, extending from the material paraphernalia used
to feeding and toilet training procedures. Differences are
most apparent between older and younger generations, and
within the younger generation between parents from better
educated, high-status families and those from low-status back-
grounds. Some young parents, for example, insist that infants sleep in their own cribs, not in bed with their parents
as they commonly did a few years ago (West, 1945:172).
Others, particularly, but not exclusively, lower prestige fam-

ilies, still follow the older practice. Older people especially, believe that "modern" parents who "sleep" infants in another room take unneccessary risks. "Why, what if the baby got strangled, or something like that? They might not even know it." [24]

More mothers bottle feed their infants nowadays than in 1939–40, when, as West (1945:171–72) indicates, not more than two or three followed the practice. However, as a young mother reveals, they may do so over criticism.

My mother raised heck when I gave my first baby a bottle. She thought it wasn't "natural" . . . acted like I was bound by duty to give him the breast. . . . I just let her rave . . . and anybody else that wanted to talk. It's a heck of a lot easier on me . . . and I can't see that it's hurt any of my kids.

Older women are particularly critical of the "modern" trend toward bottle feeding. They reason that mother's milk is best for the child and "young mothers just miss a lot of enjoyment when they use the bottle." One young mother, however, after trying to breast feed her baby, justifies bottle feeding on the grounds that "I didn't find it enjoyable at all . . . hurt like everything . . . and I couldn't see any point going through with it. Besides, I could never be sure the baby was getting enough milk." Many young mothers, however, still breast feed their infants, and some do this purely to allay criticism.

Plainville babies are fed when they demand it or, in the case of modern mothers, by flexible schedules—never by strict scheduling.[25] Most of the mothers we interviewed say that they wean their babies sometime between the first and second years. Supplementary food from the table, or commercially prepared baby food, is introduced into the diet within the first few months and is gradually increased from then on. As soon as the baby sits alone he assumes a position at the family table, at first on the lap of his mother who spoons food to him (see also West, 1945:173), and later on a high chair. Weaning is not severe and in most cases is not fully achieved until the child is around two or older.

Younger parents believe that children should not nurse much beyond two years of age, and in the few known cases of "stubborn weaners" the ultimate sanction applied is "shame." A large folklore still exists concerning late weaning and specific individuals who were late weaners. Some mothers, incidentally, still apply distasteful substances to the breast to discourage a stubborn child, but this practice is waning.

Our interviews reveal that Plainville mothers are little preoccupied with toilet training. A few young mothers start working with infants at around one year but are never severe in their methods. Methods commonly employed are placing the child on a "potty chair" or small receptacle at periods of anticipated elimination, or inducing the child to cooperate through imitation (see also West, 1945:175). Children are generally not trained until they can verbalize and properly understand the meanings and intentions communicated by parents. A young modern mother says:

I read Dr. Spock and the *Better Homes and Gardens Baby Book.* I tried too early . . . at about thirteen months. Looked like it was going to be a snap. . . . I had just trained myself. So, I just sat back and relaxed and decided not to rush things. I figure when she is older and can understand what's going on, we can try again.

If children are not trained by the time they are around two and a half, parents customarily resort to "shame" tactics, but again, as one older woman reports, "People around here just never get too excited about such as that . . . unless they're wettin' the bed when they get perty good size."

As each individual born into Plainville society begins to talk and to "understand," the language begins transmitting to him a series of kinship terms. Through observation, "correction," direct instruction, and innuendo, he learns to feel the sentiments and practice the behavior considered appropriate toward each relative (West, 1945:57).

Children learn, for example, that they are expected to obey and respect their parents. Parents on the other hand feel obligated to take care of their children until they are "educated," "grown," "married," or "able to make their own living." This "care" in-cludes affection, feeding, clothing, medical attention through home remedies and by doctors if necessary, and home discipline and teaching. Parents also owe their children an "education" the formal level of which may be determined by the child's own interest or ability, by a family's means, or by parental ideas about what amount of formal education is either useful or harmless to children (West, 1945:60–61).

Some parents, particularly younger ones with more money and educational values different from those of the older generation, are sending their children to college or contem-plate doing so. They belong to a growing number who value education and training as shortcuts to occupational and social advancement, whether one stays in the county or moves to the city. Some feel strong obligations to motivate their children in this direction, and to make the opportunity avail-able if this is at all possible. Others believe, however, that the problem of motivation is not too important, particu-larly for children with educated parents. It is assumed that they will "just naturally" want an education. In this respect Plainvillers realistically recognize that the life chances of children born to high-status families in their cultural system are more favorable than those of children whose parents occupy disadvantageous positions in the status rank system. However, in conformance with the American ideal that "any man can rise," children from low-status families are expected, particularly by high prestige people, to try to "better themselves" occupationally and morally. It is a real mark of distinction when one "from a family like that" con-tinues through high school and goes on to college.

As West (1945:61) says, "What children are particularly ex-pected to learn from their parents at home are morals, fi-nancial honesty, obedience, and work techniques." Few parents can state the formal training given children at home, though they are aware that they expect boys and girls to learn proper moral behavior through association with, ob-servation of, and a minimum of formal instruction from themselves and older siblings. The formal instruction that does occur during early years is mainly the responsibility of the mother, although the father may help, particularly with boys. Most parents expect that children shall grow up knowing right from wrong. Some parents instruct their children formally in sex matters, but find that "somebody has generally wised them up already."

The older generation is particularly critical of young parents who rear their children "with no ideas of responsibility." They contend that "youngsters" today do not know the meaning of money, that modern parents do not discipline their children, and that the present generation of Plainville parents as a whole is too indulgent. Younger parents are aware that their children have fewer work responsibilities than they themselves had as youngsters, and they know that modern technology minimizes the dependence on child labor which their parents felt. This, combined with the knowledge that most children "only go to the city when they grow up anyway," causes some parents to encourage children to take city jobs during school vacations. In fact, some fathers must hire temporary farm labor because their teenage sons work at summer jobs in Metropolis.

As for financial indulgence, today's parents firmly believe their children should have "all the things that we could not have." They readily admit that youngsters have more spending money than they had, but rationalize that children today have more things to spend money for, and "we have more to give them than our parents could give us." Most parents give their children pocket money at irregular intervals, depending on the child's needs or desires, and a few set up allowances for them. Some parents require their children to "earn" spending money by doing small chores, and some farmers' sons who work at home are paid wages similar to those paid hired workers. Farm children may also earn money from stock or poultry set aside for them and considered their "own" responsibility.

Generation differences regarding discipline are quite apparent. Older people sometimes sarcastically comment, in such words as the following: "We use to whip hell out of 'em. . . . Today they [younger parents] just talk to 'em." Though extreme, this generalization contains some truth. Younger and middle-aged parents remember being "whipped," "switched," or "licked" more often than they are willing to inflict these punishments on their own off-spring.[26] In fact, some parents say they have never given "a good licking" to their children, maybe "a good spanking," usually with a hand across the bottom, but "not a real licking." For that matter, anyone who whips his children severely is strongly criticized. There are some parents who do "really warm" their children, but they are exceptions rather than the rule.

Parents today emphasize deprivations, scoldings, and mild spankings as disciplinary procedures. While children are small the role of disciplinarian is assumed mostly, although not exclusively, by the mother. As children grow older their fathers become more involved, particularly in serious breaches of discipline. Fathers are, however, reluctant to discipline daughters physically, though some will do so if the occasion demands. Threat of deprivation, particularly of love, pocket money, or freedom of action, is the most common technique for securing obedience from children. Many parents, however, acknowledge that inconsistent application often renders the technique ineffective.

These inconsistencies, interpreted by older people as a symptom of weakness in the traditional authoritarian role structure of the nuclear family, are foci for criticism by Plainville's senior citizens. Their criticism is based on the assumption that the indulgence of young parents blinds them to the most obvious of their children's faults. The older critics, incidentally, are supported by some young parents, who cite as evidence, among other things, disciplinary problems in the schools. These problems, extensively discussed by Plainvillers, are considered more serious today than ever before. Old-timers and some young people attribute the break-down in teacher authority not only to passive discipline at home, but also to the actions of some parents who defend their children by supporting their denial of teacher accusations and, if necessary, applying pressures to insure that they not be punished. A former school superintendent, for example, is still severely criticized by older people because he yielded to these pressures and "favored" children from high status families—"wouldn't touch them." The present (1954–55) superintendent's popularity, on the other hand, derives largely from the respect accorded him for "not taking anything from them smart aleck kids," and for "treating them all alike." [27]

Defined relationships between siblings are few. The elder is expected to look after and protect the younger on the school bus and during play activities, but until they are grown and assume roles in nuclear families of their own, sibling loyalty is defined by the common loyalty which both owe to the family of their birth. As they grow older the patterned structure in this set of kinship connections, never pronounced, is less discernible, that is, highly individualistic. Married siblings should, if it is convenient, visit with one another, and to some extent expect to cooperate in economic matters. These are not, however, binding obligations. In fact, some siblings seldom seek each other's company.

The kinship connections between siblings after each of them marries largely determine the social relationships between certain other pairs of relatives. I refer specifically to the relationships connecting ego to his uncles, aunts, and cousins. Thus, if siblings maintain intimate social contact after marriage, affectionate bonds are usually created between them and their nieces and nephews. A child may, for example, like to visit, spend the night, and in other ways be around his aunts and uncles who, in turn, may "spoil" him with presents and other kinds of preferential treatment.

In the same way, if siblings maintain social contacts after they marry, intimate social relationships are likely to develop between ego and his cousins. Some adults, for example, compare favored childhood cousins with brothers or sisters. However, as West (1945:64) indicates, these close attachments usually disappear when the children grow up.

The terms "aunt" and "uncle" normally refer to consanguine relatives and their spouses, but are sometimes extended to include nonrelatives who stand in particularly intimate social relationships with one's parents. The terms are also used, to a much lesser extent, by some people to define their relationship with nonrelatives much older than themselves for whom they have a great personal liking and respect. This is the only consistent extension of consanguinal and affinal terms to people who stand in purely sociological relationships. On rare occasions one hears "grandpa" and "grandma" used as honorific terms for certain extremely old people.

Grandparent-grandchild relationships are still very much the same as West (1945:62) discovered in 1939: "Grandparents and grandchildren treat each other 'with the same affection' that exists between parents and children, but more familiarly. The same restrictions on obedience, respect, and mutual care theoretically obtain, but they are actually relaxed greatly."

Grandparents, then, are "expected" to be fond of their grandchildren and, inasmuch as this relationship is an affectionate and permissive one, it is believed "natural" that they should "spoil" them. That many grandparents conform to their role expectation is revealed in interviews with some of those who are most critical of the discipline techniques of younger parents. They, when asked if they discipline their grandchildren, structure their role so that it does not involve this responsibility, other than, perhaps, invoking mild corrective procedures, such as scolding, and then only if parents are not available. Paradoxically, their actions make some of them leniency figures in the eyes of grandchildren, and the latter expect them, if they are handy, to act as buffers against the disciplinary efforts of parents (see also West, 1945:63). The following rather extreme example illustrates this particular point:

Douglas Williams, learning that his son had not attended a boy scout meeting as the child had informed him he was going to do when he left the house, threatened him with deprivation of his weekly allowance. The boy had elected to spend the evening with his grandfather watching television. The grandfather objected to the action of the father, intimating that it was "cute" that his grandson had preferred to be with him rather than at the scout meeting, and implied that he would give the child spending money if the father did not. In this particular instance the boy knows that his grandfather is as good a potential source of pocket money as his father.

Grandparents are the logical foster parents of an orphan grandchild, providing, of course, they are not too old to care for him (see also West, 1945:63). They are particularly pleased to have children spend the night with them or stay for several days at a time, and it is a common practice in some families to send grandchildren from the city to spend part of their school vacation with Plainville grandparents. Many elderly Plainvillers, in fact, eagerly await visits from children, grandchildren, or other relatives who live in the city.

One set of kinship connections deserves special mention because of the impact a federal innovation has had upon it. This is the social relationship between adult children and aged parents, now influenced by old age assistance. By way of background we can quote West (1945:59), who in 1939 observed changes in this relationship.

Aged parents and grandparents are considered neither very entertaining, nor useful, nor wise nowadays, even in Plainville. They are considered to be "cares." They are less welcome in their children's homes than they used to be. They are made to feel that they are "tedious," and that there is not enough "room" for them. To avoid becoming "burdens," they are beginning not "to mind asking for the pension." The decline in respect toward the old works out neatly: father and mother formally "teach respect" for grandparents, but laugh at their weaknesses, foibles, and "old-fashioned ways" before the children. The children turn the tables by applying the lesson a generation later against their parents, thus intensifying the conflict and lack of mutual interest between the generations. When Old Age Assistance became available for needy old people, the old began to enjoy a new "value" in the eyes of children, who sometimes vie with each other to "keep" the parent whose maintenance may bring in from ten to twenty dollars a month.

This statement, with one major exception, is fairly accurate today. The major exception is that nowadays few children "vie" to keep parents who receive old age assistance. In fact, there are few known cases of aged parents who live in the household of a child. Most old people prefer to live by themselves, "maybe near the kids" if possible, but definitely not in the same house with them. This arrangement is approved by children, who express love for parents but "not under the same roof."

The most obvious factor liberating children from the obligation of caring for aged parents, and in turn liberating needy old people from the feeling that they are "cares" or "burdens" to their children, is old age assistance. The small stipend is barely enough to live on, but it does give some security to people who were unable to accumulate a surplus during their productive years of competition in the economic system.

Acceptance of old age assistance, which is steadily increasing, deserves special comment. Despite the obvious advantages which some old people can derive from the program, there are cultural factors which foster resistance to it. Many Plainvillers, for example, support the value that it is more "honorable" to earn one's own retirement than to be dependent on the government; therefore, some of the sharpest

critics of assistance to the aged are old people who have suc-
ceeded in the economic system. They criticize the past work,
management, and moral habits of recipients, and ridicule a
system which permits individuals with poor work reputations, "people who never knowed nothin' but sow-belly and
beans," to "retire" at the same rate of pay as an unfortunate
man who worked hard, suffered reverses, and really "needs"
and "deserves" the "pension." The values involved, however,
are deeper than this—some of these people by their actions
seem to say: "I am being robbed! I worked hard and earned
my right to retire. By what right does Orval Sparkman, who
never worked a day in his life, get a government subsidy in
his old age?" The sharp eyes and tongues of these critics are
constantly alert to real, or assumed, "foolish" spending habits
of recipients, and the pensioner who dares defend his position against certain of them becomes the target of a vicious
joking pattern. Community jokesters, critics of the system,
"confidentially" tell him that a neighbor is "drawin' more
than you are," and in other ways manage to keep him dis-
turbed, sometimes so much that he "hightails" it to the
county welfare office to lodge a complaint. Welfare personnel
by now, however, know the Plainville sources of such information and they handle the case accordingly. This kind of
treatment, combined with a constant flow of false rumors of
abuses in the system,[28] makes some recipients "ashamed"
that they receive "charity," and others so fearful of ridicule
that they go to great lengths, such as cashing checks outside
the community, to hide the fact that they are "on the rolls."

A further problem faced by Plainville's aged is that they
have no opportunity to achieve recognition in activities essential to the functioning of the community. Many spend
their time in gossip cliques with their peers, the only group
that takes them seriously, and some are socially isolated to a
very high degree. Still others attempt to create a position
for themselves in the moral structure of the community by
stressing such qualities as hard work, frugality, honesty, and

social acts of specific individuals as the only type of behavior to be expected from one who comes from "that" family.

The Plainville kin-group, however, is more than a framework of reference points for identifying other people. There are certain tenuous loyalties and obligations inherent in kinship bonds extending beyond the nuclear family. For example, the members of a kin-group should associate more among themselves than with nonmembers except where considerations of distance make this inconvenient.[32] They visit and eat together, particularly on Sundays, and sometimes exchange work. Furthermore, one normally expects to borrow money from a relative more easily than from someone else; certainly there is less urgency in repaying the obligation.[33] Relatives should rally round during sickness [34] or other misfortune, particularly if there is a death in the family. In fact, the internal solidarity of the kin-group is manifest at funerals more than on any other occasion that is likely to arise. The death and funeral of a relative attract kindred from distant points who, because they live so far away, do not participate in the normal kin-group relationships already mentioned. Individuals have returned to Plainville for a family funeral who had not been in the community, even for a visit, for years.

Many of the larger kin-groups formerly sponsored annual family reunions, a way of periodically reaffirming the solidarity of the kin-group. These, however, now seldom occur. Occasionally an extended family attempts a big reunion, hoping "to get everyone together just once more," but more often than not the affair is poorly attended. An elderly man, disgusted with his family's recent unsuccessful reunion, aptly observes, "You gotta die to git everbody together again."

An obvious factor weakening the solidarity of the extended family is the improvement of communications which facilitates migration out of Plainville. No longer are there neighborhoods, political units, or entire church congregations conforming to the limits of a kin-group, and the large, clan-like "hill" families mentioned by West (1945:58) are dispersed. As an example we can take the largest, oldest, and the most prominent of these, the "Ballou nation" (see West, 1945:58). Most of the Ballous are gone from the valley where their ancestors settled, so that today the "nation" is not so much reality as folklore. They, and the other well-known clan-like kin-groups, no longer maintain territorial solidarity, once characteristically a major trait in their identification. Instead, they now live throughout the county, and in various regions of the state and country. The Ballou surname is still common in Plainville, but the family is split into "branches" sufficiently differentiated through occupational and social achievement that no single trait, other than name, can be ascribed to the entire consanguinal group.

The dispersal of the large kin-groups is not a new process —to imply that it is would be to suggest a degree of isolation far greater than the facts warrant. It was, in fact, well under way even prior to West's study of Plainville, because, as he points out, once the area was settled land and occupational opportunities were so limited that at least half of each generation had to migrate (see West, 1945:18–24). The migration, however, has been accelerated since West's study, and the big catalyst was the Second World War, which speeded Plainvillers to city defense jobs and literally forced many "out" through the draft. The migration continued after the war because of a rapidly changing agricultural system— greater specialization, increased mechanization, and the concomitant trend toward larger farms. This, of course, threatens kin-group solidarity because, among other things, the overt forms of kin-group expression in Plainville all depend to a great extent on the physical proximity of the consanguine family.

Physical separation, however, is not the only factor involved. Mechanization of the farm, for example, minimizes the functional significance of social relationships developed by work-exchange partners. Since the most common source for these partnerships is traditionally the extended family, any condition which limits this type of interaction is sure to weaken the kin-group structure. Furthermore, it is apparent that the acceptance of new economic values, many of which stress the need for cash, causes considerable strain in some families. One manifestation is the frequent criticism of relatives as an economic risk ("I'd rather loan money to anyone but a relation"). In other known cases there is friction between close relatives over the repayment of obligations and refusals to lend money. West's observation in 1939 that "mutual helpfulness was greater when it cost only work, rather than money" is more true today than it was then.

In addition to the consanguine kin-group, ego acquires a special category of "in-laws" whenever he marries. He carefully distinguishes between kindred and in-laws,[35] even though the bond linking him and a spouse's relatives may be a warm and affectionate one. Women, especially, are likely to use terms of parental address when speaking to, or about, their parents-in-law. Men generally find it more difficult to extend these terms, and therefore usually refer to their parents-in-law as "my wife's folks," "Thelma's dad," or in some other way which specifies the wife as the connecting relative.

A marriage also defines a tenuous kinship connection between the two immediate nuclear families involved. This is most often expressed verbally and in patterns of social visiting, but sometimes appears in matters of mutual aid. Affinal ties, then, are the basis for some social relationships. In addition, they are, at the individual level, functionally important to some people as a means of extending their kin-group. As a consequence, parents are normally concerned about potential marriage partners for their children. Thus, children should not marry "down" in status but should "at least" marry "their own kind" or "better." [36] Most parents hope that their children will marry "good," and that their in-laws will be a "likable family," one with whom they feel that the neighborhood is the most important social group beyond the elementary family:

On occasions, a clique or friendship group may have the same membership as a neighborhood. In such cases, "the most elemental social group beyond the family in dispersed type of settlement is the neighborhood." However, throughout the world, in village and isolated farming areas alike, locality groupings are not as important in personality formation and individual orientation as the smaller friendship groups (1950:136).

One cannot help but be impressed by the seemingly endless number and variety of clique groups in Plainville. For purposes of discussion we can follow the definition of Warner and Lunt (1941:110–11), who say that the clique is a small, informal, non-kin group with a minimum of institutionalization. The following analysis of Plainville cliques approaches the problem of organization from the viewpoint of social visiting patterns. Visiting relationships were recorded as they became known and were observed in process. This information appeared in the visiting columns of the *Beacon* and was divulged through interviews with informants.[38] We discovered a great variety of these groups, acting in so many ways as almost to defy classification but, nevertheless, manifesting certain consistent characteristics. Locality, for example, is not an important identifying trait; rather, similarity of interests, age, style of life, and religious affiliation are the main basis for cliquing. Furthermore, Plainville cliques vary in size from two or three individuals to as many as fifteen or twenty, perhaps more, and they are both unisexual and bisexual. Size and composition vary with time and identification criteria. Some cliques are temporary, others quite stable; some are loosely structured around informal leaders who are not even aware of their position, and others focus on recognized leadership figures.

Plainvillers react negatively to certain kinds of well-established cliques, particularly if they think the clique is capable of manipulating some phase of the local power structure for the individual gain of its members. Board officials, for example, who wield authority in hiring, firing, and purchasing matters in the school, are, consequently, central figures in various cliques. These cliques are observed closely and with suspicion by those on the outside, and the actions and associations of board members invariably are topics for gossip and criticism, especially by those who feel their vested interests are threatened. As a further example, some businessmen feel they cannot restrict their friendship group merely to those with whom they wish to associate because, as a successful merchant puts it, "if I was to just buddy around with those people that I wanted to, right away everybody would start talkin' and figurin', tryin' to figure out what we was up to . . . like we was goin' to buy the whole town right out from under 'em." Another example, particularly significant, is that of the clique affiliations, assumed or real, of representatives of the government programs operating in the county. The actions and associations of these individuals, particularly the Extension agent, are observed closely. Thus, the agent is criticized because "he works with a little group on the east side [of the county]," because he operates within "his own little bunch . . . a little 'click'," or because "he works only with boys that's got the money," or "only with the outsiders." [39] Finally, we should remember that many Plainvillers associate well-established cliques, like classes, with superior or inferior positioning. These people resent exclusiveness in the social relationships of others; therefore, one commonly hears them derisively refer to certain people with such phrases as "they got their *own* little set" . . . "their *own* little bunch" . . . "they don't associate [with others] . . ." Still, no Plainviller denies his neighbors the right to "choose their friends."

The most obvious clique relationships, recognized by all the community, are those involving the aged. Older people who are leveled into common loafing and gossiping groups interact more frequently than do other age-grade cliques, hence their associations are more observable. One such clique consists of several old men who daily "hold court" in the square, or, during bad weather, in the pool hall. They relax on their benches, hold the community up for a sometimes critical, sometimes satirical, examination, spit, whittle, smoke, chew tobacco, and talk. They "kill time" by exchanging notes out of the past or disseminating (some say "garbling") current information, and some are even guilty of originating a fair share of community news. This group, more than any other, is a living link with Plainville's yesteryears, and their presence, plus the things they talk about, is a constant reminder of the past to younger men and boys who drop by the "court" for short visits during the day. The old men talk a great deal of the past but, contrary to the opinions of many younger people, spend equal time relating it to the present. Their talk constantly concerns change because they have observed and experienced so many first-hand changes in their culture. They evaluate local moral and technical changes as sometimes good, sometimes bad, and inevitably, to the consternation of some who are younger, permeate their conclusions, often apologetically, with some nostalgia for the "good old days." The old men are as fond of gossip as anyone in Plainville, and they enjoy nothing better than "a good scandal." I have many times sat through these loafing "bull sessions" and heard the comment, or complaint, "We ain't had a good scandal [or tragedy] aroun' here fer a long time." [40] The activities of these men are ridiculed by most young people, and by some of their peers, who "wouldn't sit with them old men for a hundred dollars," but when they "hold court" not a single person who sees them fails to wonder "what [or who] them old men are talking about now."

The concern which Plainvillers manifest in clique topics, such as that just mentioned, is related to the fact that gossip, regardless of its source, is an important mechanism for social control. Since it is generally believed that the various cliques of elderly people function only for loafing and gossiping, nonmembers are critical of the real, or imagined, activities of these friendship groups. In this respect, they are more critical of a few small cliques of elderly women than of those of old men. Most people believe that deliberate distortions are not as "vicious" in the male cliques as in the women's groups. This assumption derives partly from the awareness that the social relationships which structure women's cliques are not open to observation or partial participation by non-clique members, as are male loafing groups. In effect, then, the old women are subject to no controls whatsoever. As one elderly man says: "Them old women spin their tall tales behind closed doors . . . us men do it in the open. We might maybe stretch the truth . . . jus' fer fun, but they murder it." In addition, Plainvillers believe that women are inherently more "vicious" gossipers than are males. Thus, a few elderly women have reputations for deliberately "garbling" information in their gossip sessions and deliberately fabricating rumors injurious to character.

One category of male cliques, based on special interests, deserves some elaboration. These are friendship cliques which develop within given status levels [41] among those with similar interests in hunting and fishing.[42] In fact, some identification with these two activities is a minimum prerequisite for acceptance into certain male groups, and their significance for *full* acceptance into the male community cannot be too strongly stressed.[43] Many perceptive observers, for example, believe the present Extension agent would be much better accepted if he would devote more time to "hunting and fishing with the boys." Whether this is true is questionable but, nevertheless, the criticism emphasizes the need for this kind of identification. As a basis for friendship, the significance of these activities is further revealed in the comments of some men who indicate that they do not, and cannot, associate with given individuals because they are not adept enough, or do not participate, in the hunting and fishing sports. The following comment is typical of many received whenever the question was asked, "Do you ever visit or associate with [person on informant's approximate status level]?" "No. I don't hunt and fish, and that's all he wants to talk about or cares about doing . . . we just don't seem to have much in common."

Although the functions of friendship and clique groups in Plainville are many and varied, the primary function of most of them is visiting, which may in turn overlap with such obvious secondary functions as mutual aid and the pursuit of common interests. There are also less obvious functions which, for purposes of culture change, are of the utmost importance, including the function of friendship groups as communicative channels through which information is received, interpreted, and disseminated. Intimately related to this is the function of informal leaders in the decision-making processes of those who make up the clique. In the first case, Plainville clique groups so effectively disseminate rumor and fact that in a matter of hours news literally blankets the community.[44] In the second, holders of key positions in cliques are subtle but effective leaders. Even in groups where these informal leaders are not apparent, there may be individuals holding key positions in a specific network of relationships who, if appealed to in the correct way, can assume leadership roles. As Loomis and Beegle (1950:171) observe, "Those who will carry their programs to the people must relate such individuals both to the accepted formal leaders of organizations and to the informal 'grass roots' leaders." These are groups, then, which no innovative official or organization can afford to ignore.

NEIGHBORHOODS

In 1939 West (1945:69) observed that a farmer's close neighborhood included his house at the center, surrounded by adjoining farms containing the people "he and his family supposedly neighbor with most." He further indicated that this "close neighborhood" was not a tight unit, but rather, "differences in 'class' or 'morals' may make two separate, and what might be called 'geographically simultaneous,' neighborhoods out of the areas." In addition, a farmer also identified with his "big neighborhood" which, technically, refers to a locality center. "The big neighborhoods are named, after a church or school house, a natural feature, a leading or old-time family, or a combination of these" (West, 1945:71).

Plainvillers still recognize both of these neighborhood types, though functionally they vary considerably from what they were in 1939–40. In the first instance, a man formerly identified his close neighbors as those with whom he maintained various reciprocal cooperative relationships such as borrowing (including labor) and visiting. Today, however, borrowing is giving way to technological self-sufficiency, and visiting patterns extend far beyond the community. The breakdown in the type of neighborhood which the farmer defines in terms of social interaction is attributed mainly to mechanization.

The mechanization of farm and home is the most important factor contributing to the independence felt by neighbors. Farm tasks which formerly involved cooperative effort are now done more effectively with machinery, purchased or rented, or by hired specialists. In fact, many farmers definitely prefer hiring labor to obligating themselves, an attitude undoubtedly related to the fact that as they function more within a cash economy they become increasingly conscious of the economic value of time.

Besides the many mechanical changes which have fostered social independence for the farm operator, there are other innovations which have had similar effects on other social relationships. Improved roads and the increased use of cars, for example, obviate the necessity for farm wives to borrow household commodities ("Nowadays they just run to town when they get out of somethin'"), and these innovations facilitate intercommunity visiting so that few families now depend upon neighbors for this type of interaction. In fact, families commonly drive several miles, particularly on Sunday, to spend the day visiting or sightseeing. True, many object to these new patterns, especially the less mobile older people, but many of them admit that they themselves spend most of the time formerly spent visiting before a recent innovation, the television set.

In addition to such changes as these just mentioned, there have been changes in other types of interfamily contacts during recent years, specifically in more institutionalized contacts, such as those based on mutual interests in neighborhood churches or schools and, in some neighborhoods, commercial service units, such as a store or, perhaps, a post office. Changes of this nature are obviously related to functional changes in Plainville's "big neighborhoods."

The "big neighborhood" is the first area of residential identification, after community, which a Plainviller makes. Thus, a man acknowledges first that he is a Plainviller, and secondly that he lives in Pickett Bend, down near Pleasant Hill, over near Owl Roost, or in one of the other colorfully named neighborhoods.[45] The dimension of the big neighborhood has traditionally depended on the area of influence of one or more service institutions. In the past the most common of these were "country schools," "country churches," and general "country stores" and service stations combined.[46] Since 1939–40 most of these have ceased to function, consequently causing a change in the meaning of the neighborhood for those who live there.

Neighborhood grocery stores, for example, find it increasingly difficult to stay in business. In fact, the few that remain have reduced their stock inventory so drastically as to make shopping in them very unattractive to prospective customers. Major causes contributing to this type of business mortality are the steady decline in country population [47] and the increased mobility of farm people who have more money to spend and who value a style of life markedly different from that of their ancestors. These changes are accompanied by, and partially dependent on, shopping and buying habits increasingly adapted to city stores.[48] There is little functional need for the neighborhood store, and consequently people tend to identify their neighborhoods less in these terms. The patronage of such establishments was dealt a further blow by the consolidation of all rural post offices, most of which were located in country stores, into the central post office in the village. This eliminated the last major excuse which the farmer had for visiting and loafing at the crossroads store.

The decline in rural schools is even more dramatic than that of neighborhood commercial institutions. There were thirty-six rural schools in Woodland County in 1942, by 1950 the number had dropped to thirteen, and by 1954 there were no schools that had not been consolidated. Loss of a school reduces the solidarity of a neighborhood as much as any other cause, a fact clearly recognized by Plainvillers. They know that neighborhood school activities, "box suppers," holiday programs, and graduation exercises, integrated neighborhood residents into a common unit,[49] and the school house was the meeting place for community socials, political speeches, and a host of other activities, all fondly remembered by old-timers. The significance of the school as a symbol of neighborhood unity is apparent in the actions of people in some neighborhoods who insisted on retaining custody of the building even after consolidation was effected. The implications are obvious—many neighborhoods wanted desperately to keep their schools and gave them up only after bitter fights which sometimes split the group into hostile factions. Neighborhood loyalty, even identity, is difficult under such trying conditions.

The rural population decline has had its effects on many of the "country churches," because some neighborhoods are so thinly populated that there are not enough people to support one good church, even if all denominations were to band together. Other factors are church "squabbles" and the keen competition for members among village churches which causes them to encourage "country people" to consolidate with them, or come as families to town to worship. An accompanying, and possibly related, factor is the decline of interdenominational worship in both village and rural congregations. Parishioners and ministers agree that nowadays people do not worship across denominational lines to the extent they once did—"it's even hard to get people from other churches to turn out for a good revival." There are no obvious reasons to account for this, except possibly the declining interest in revivalism. Without this ingredient it is extremely difficult to arouse and sustain active interest in a small rural congregation.

The notion of neighborhood, then, for most Plainvillers, no longer involves functional types of interfamily activity patterns nor institutional identification. Now, for all practical purposes, identification with "neighborhood" is synonymous with geographic locality, a region within the community where one lives. There are two neighborhood groups, however, which because of their efforts to maintain solidarity through monthly "community" meetings deserve special mention. In each neighborhood meetings are held in an abandoned schoolhouse, retained as a "community building" by residents of the locality.

The most active group is the one made up of present and former residents of Happy Hollow, a small neighborhood in the timbered hill country about three miles from the village. The residents of this neighborhood, most of whom are older people, sustain a more highly developed complex of social visiting patterns than any other neighborhood group in the community. In fact, several elderly ex-residents of Happy Hollow return from other communities, where they now reside, for the monthly get-together.

The monthly Happy Hollow meeting was begun during the early forties by a former Agricultural Extension agent.

It was one of a few attempts to institute self-governing clubs of farmers, their wives, and their children [50] to function as a medium for recreation and a means of disseminating agricultural information. The organizing agent soon left Woodland County but, largely through the efforts of some elderly people in the neighborhood and the interest of the Plainville vocational agriculture teacher, the monthly meeting has persisted over the years.

The original agricultural orientation has been lost, although the vocational agriculture teacher and the county Extension agent are sometimes asked to discuss informally certain problems of interest, agricultural and otherwise. Social activities, on the other hand, are the order of the day. Wives bring great quantities of food, and during warm weather someone always brings a big freezer of ice cream. There is a brief program of children's specialty numbers, or perhaps musical numbers and readings by some of the adults. Most of the time, however, is spent visiting with neighbors, all of whom thoroughly enjoy the opportunity to "just sit and talk" on "meeting nights."

Some Plainvillers ridicule the Happy Hollow gathering as "folksy" or "hillbilly," but all agree that "them people down there have a real good time." The other monthly neighborhood gathering, which does not have the interest, participation, or historical tradition of the Happy Hollow group, is much less successful.

POLITICS AND LAW

The most significant political identification for Plainvillers is Woodland County, within which the people are essentially divided into a majority Republican party and a minority Democratic party.[51] The number of Republicans registered in the county exceeds the number of Democrats by slightly more than three to one, and in the Plainville precinct Democrats are outnumbered five to one. A check of local and county voting records in past county, state, and national elections reveal little quantitative variation in party strength. Anyone who votes across party lines is suspect, and his motives are seriously questioned.

Although the Republican party traditionally controls elective and appointive county offices,[52] this does not mean that the minority party is politically impotent. The Democrats, largely through superior organization, have been quite influential in local and county elections during most of the past twenty-five years. Their smoothly operating county organization attained maximum efficiency during the late 1930s and early 1940s. West (1945:87), for example, refers to the organization as a "machine," attributing its success in part, at least, to its leaders, who were drawn from politically active, wealthy farm families, linked together by kinship bonds. These individuals, through various manipulatory devices, controlled many votes, and made their influence apparent in the elections of Republican county officials. Their power and influence were enhanced by their party's national control and the many New Deal recovery programs at the local level. These drew administrative and other personnel from among local party members, and reinforced the control already accorded recognized party leaders.

The county Democratic machine, formerly described as "vicious," no longer effectively "controls" large blocks of votes. Three factors have contributed to the machine's loss of power. First, some of its important leaders have been forced by age to retire. Second, over-all economic improvement in the community, giving more people greater independence, has deprived other leaders of their former ability, because of wealth, to create obligations among constituents, Democratic and Republican alike. Finally, the national shift to the Republican party in 1952 was accompanied by a loss of patronage.

Most local political activity, whether Republican or Democratic, still operates along clique lines. "The heads of cliques are the 'politicians,' who for money, past favors, 'love of party,' and the gratification of controlling people and manipulating events attempt to accomplish the election of 'their candidates' " (West, 1945:87). Since the possibilities of patronage are limited, it is possible that most Plainville "politickers" are motivated chiefly by ego-satisfaction.[53] Whatever their motives, they are the ones who campaign, the ones who circulate "the word," usually very informally, among their friends and loafing groups, and along other clique lines which are available to them. They make effective use of gossip channels for disseminating and distorting information, and some of them are avid students of clique group interrelationships.[54]

Candidates for county offices, however, do not leave their political fortunes entirely in the hands of local politicians. Most candidates make as many personal contacts as possible, remind voters of their qualifications and of past favors which they may have done or secured for particular individuals or families, and make promises of things to come once they are elected. One successful candidate confided to me that since he did not have the money or time to contact everybody he developed a short-cut procedure by "figuring out who was most important in some of these big families." He concentrated his efforts on those in key family positions, hoping that they, in turn, would "pull" the votes of other family members. With most of the candidates and their key supporters emphasizing face to face contacts with potential voters, local and county elections are very personal for everyone concerned. This is particularly true of county primaries, "where the Republicans have to fight like dogs." Inasmuch as Democrats have little chance of being elected, they do not challenge in some races, throwing undue weight on the Republican primary, where a victory customarily insures election. Furthermore, since political issues are usually absent, candidates in "hot races" are, more often than not, elected because of personal memories and sentiments triggered in the electorate. There are some, in fact, who say that a hotly fought primary, or maybe a local school board election, so intermingles fact and fiction that "a person just doesn't know who to vote for."

Probably the most important idea which an office seeker must sell voters is that he "needs the job." True, such qualities as honesty and reliability are considered important, but need often takes precedence over these. This conclusion emerged from intensive interviews in which I attempted to evaluate the success of two or three candidates in a 1954 election, all of whom had poor credit reputations and were considered by many to be poorly qualified in other ways for the positions to which they were elected. This peculiar notion of political qualification is somewhat in line with the general opinion that "county government is rotten to the core," "all politics are tainted," and "an honest man elected can't possibly stay that way."

Contrasting sharply with their interest in local and county politics is the apathy of most Plainvillers for state and, except for agricultural matters, national politics.[55] They feel that most government affairs, agricultural legislation notwithstanding, are irrelevant to the immediate life of the community, and that "people like us" really have very little, if any, influence in state and federal policy. They believe this despite the fact that federal and state governments are more active at the local level than ever before. This sense of political futility, and some of the values which support it, is apparent in the reactions of many people to the government procedure for filling the two vacancies in the Plainville post office which were mentioned earlier. They are convinced that ultimately "them politicians in Washington will put in whoever they want to," that test scores and formal regulations are important only so long as they agree with the desires of professional politicians, and that politicians can always find loopholes in regulations.

The village of Plainville has a mayor and a town board of four members, all usually elected from among local businessmen. Aside from the duties of the secretary-treasurer of the board, whose task is to collect "a few cents on the hundred" (from five to ten cents per hundred dollars evaluation) property tax from village residents, the functions of this group are not clear in the minds of local citizens. The board meets periodically to discuss small expenditures from the tax funds, usually for minor street repairs, such as patching the paved main street or grading side streets, or for other small necessities, such as mowing the lawn in the village square. There is never much money to work with and, since the need for formal government is practically nil, there is never much for the town board and mayor to do. This frequently leads to conflict between the board and the local businessmen's organization, the Commercial Club. The latter, through assessments and dues, has more money to spend for community development and tries to keep some project in operation most of the time. Members of the town board, though, feel that they, as elected representatives of the public, should be consulted about the club's projects. Some of the club members do not agree; consequently, communication between the two groups is not always adequate to insure cooperation, even in projects where it might logically be expected. As matters stand there is some cooperation, but there is also much bickering, depending on the personalities who happen to be involved in specific projects.

Plainville has no village policeman and relies only sparingly upon the county sheriff for law enforcement needs. He is sometimes called to investigate drunkenness, fighting, accidents, and pranks, but for the most part Plainvillers object to outside interference in their internal affairs, legal or otherwise. I realized this when, shortly after my arrival in the community, an early morning gang fight occurred on the highway, immediately behind the local dance hall, near my house. The fight climaxed in a knifing, and someone fired two shots, whereupon the large crowd of witnesses rapidly dispersed. Due to the nature of this sensational fracas, the county sheriff launched an official investigation, and because the fight occurred on state property, the highway, rumors that state police officials would be involved quickly blanketed the community. Because of the threat of outside interference and the implicit possibility of becoming involved, witnesses to the incident suddenly became scarce, and people throughout the community were noticeably reluctant to discuss it. However, once official interest in the fight subsided, "authorities" gradually emerged with eyewitness accounts to "tell the straight of things." Even in a case as potentially serious as this one, many, but not all, people believe that outside authorities should not concern themselves, that the conflicting parties should arrive at a solution in their own way.

The most flagrant local rejection of outside authority is the resistance to state game laws, evidenced by expressions of overt hostility toward the resident conservation agent and his family. A former agent told me that when he came to Woodland County he had extreme difficulty renting a house, even though some were available. Several owners in Discovery, the county seat and his logical choice of residence, refused to do business with him. In fact, not until he found a house owned by an absentee landlord, for which he had to pay well above average rent, could he obtain living quarters for his family. Even under these conditions, friends in Discovery put pressure on the landlord not to rent him the property. This does not necessarily mean that he or any other agent is personally disliked—only that he stands as a constant reminder of outside interference which is resented, and which, according to some, should be resisted. Orval Sparkman, who has spent much of his life hunting and fishing, seriously observed: "We could git along with any of them conservation men if they'd jist come down here and fish and hunt like the rest of us!"

Many Plainvillers agree with the principle of game conservation, but most of them refuse to cooperate with the conservation agent because they believe that "people should regulate theirselves." This is particularly true of the people who still hunt and fish for part of their subsistence. They and many of their friends are convinced that state game laws are a violation of, as one man put it, the "God-given right to hunt and fish." [56] For other Plainvillers, though, the dictum that "people should regulate theirselves" presents a paradox when we consider that hunting and fishing now function primarily in the assignment of male prestige. For some men prestige depends on excellence in these activities, and the major criterion of excellence depends directly on the quantity of game secured. Sportsmen, then, are motivated to bag the maximum limit on those days when they can hunt or fish, even though they may have little or no interest in eating the game. Furthermore, others, for the sake of prestige, recreation, or subsistence, hunt and fish on days declared out-of-season by the state game commission. Some of them, however, see no violation of the law in their actions but rather, as already indicated, see the law as an outside imposition depriving them of a basic right.

The translation of this belief into action leads to the major complaint of conservation agents: that it is next to impossible to obtain convictions of known violators in the county courts. The defendant always requests a jury trial and, as one agent said, "Tell me where you could get twelve men in this county who would convict a man of illegal hunting or fishing." One state conservation leader told me that Woodland County is one of the most difficult enforcement areas in the entire state, but "if we could sell just one generation of kids our problems would be solved." However, lectures at schools and other appeals to children have little effect when the information is ridiculed by parents at home.

The reluctance of Plainvillers to submit to outside authority is apparent in areas of life other than those directly concerned with law enforcement. For instance, regulatory features of government agriculture programs are resented because of the implicit threat to the individual's independence; [57] the major criticism of the WPA and later assistance programs is that they originate outside the community and seldom take into consideration local values (the past work habits and morals of local recipients); some welfare programs, such as relief support for divorcees with families, are resented "if there is a family that can do its part"; and, finally, grade A dairymen constantly chafe under the rules and regulations imposed by milk companies and health inspectors.

Plainville resistance to outside legal and political authority does not, however, imply that its people are "lawless." On the contrary, there is a minimum of trouble disruptive to the normal everyday functioning of the community, because informal controls exist for handling most of the behavior defined as deviant or lawless. One of the most important of these is gossip. Most Plainvillers, as we have already indicated, are greatly concerned about what people think and are even more concerned over what others say about them. For example, some people support the churches, economically and by their attendance, because they do not want to be "gossiped about"; "moderns" leave Plainville for much of their recreation, particularly drinking and dancing; some women wear shorts or smoke only in their homes. The major exceptions are the very low prestige people who emphasize their lack of concern about what others say and who ridicule the fear of gossip so apparent in the actions of those in higher statuses.

Plainvillers believe that personal disputes should be resolved by the parties concerned. One or the other of the principals may seek advice or assistance from an informal clique group leader, but the disputants should resort to formal legal procedures only as a final measure. Occasionally personal disputes between men erupt into violence, a fist fight, but this is the exception rather than the rule. If it becomes necessary to take an issue into the courts, interest builds throughout the community and the pros and cons of the case are argued and contrasted with others in gossip sessions. Courtroom attendance in such cases is always good; in fact, some people enjoy attending court even when they do not know the principals involved.

ORGANIZED INTEREST GROUPS

There are many organized interest groups to which Plainvillers can belong and to which many of them do belong. One salient feature of these organizations is that their membership is drawn mainly from high-prestige families, who contribute most of the members and, more importantly, the necessary organizational leadership to keep the groups going. This leadership is particularly significant in some organizations because the rank and file of the membership is apathetic, and only by the concerted efforts of a small core of individuals can the groups survive.

There are several possible ways to classify the formal interest groups in Plainville. For our purposes, it is necessary to distinguish only between those that are agricultural and those that are nonagricultural in their interests. In the first classification, some of the more important groups to which Plainvillers can belong are the Farm Bureau, American Dairy Association, State Farmers Association, Extension Association, Extension Home Economics Club, 4-H Club, Dairy Herd Improvement Association, Angus Breeders' Association, and several other breed organizations, none of which have local or county chapters.[58] Groups organized around nonfarm interests are the Parent-Teacher Association, Commercial Club, Masonic Lodge, Eastern Star, Royal Neighbors, Boy Scouts, Bridge Club, Veterans' Organization, various church-affiliated groups, and the two neighborhood social clubs previously mentioned.

The number of formal interest groups increased slightly between 1940 and 1955, and the meaning and function of some of the old, well-established organizations have changed. Most of the newer groups reflect new agricultural interests and, though their membership is local, their organization was stimulated by forces from outside the community. These groups mark a shift in the interest of farmers away from lodges and insurance groups, and toward organizations that hold some promise of economic betterment. The following discussion is concerned only with some of the more important of these groups.

Chief among local farm interest groups is the Woodland County Farm Bureau. This organization, affiliated with the national body, is actively supported by many progressive Plainville farmers. Their participation and interest have accompanied a growing awareness that the federal government has been, since the 1930s, intimately involved in the local farm picture. The bureau offers a reasonable insurance program to its membership, and for some, admittedly, this is its main function. The more active farmers, however, support it rather because they know that this organization is more concerned with over-all national farm policy than is any other local interest group. These men see their economic destiny directly tied to Congress, and for them the National Farm Bureau is the best organization to pressure this body into favorable farm legislation.

Two formal groups represent the current (1954–55) interest in dairying and another actively supports the present interest in registered beef production. These are the American Dairy Association, the Dairy Herd Improvement Association, and the Angus Breeders' Association. The structure and function of these organizations have been analyzed in another context.

There is a complex of interest groups—the Home Economics Club, 4-H Club, and the Extension Association—organized under the outside stimulus of the agricultural extension services. These organizations, though governed by locally elected officers, have the advantage of services from professional leaders, the Extension agent and the county home agent (whenever one is available). They have in common a practical education orientation and strongly emphasize regularly scheduled meetings, project work, lectures, and practical assistance from paid specialists.

By far the most active and stable of the Extension-derived organizations in Plainville is still the Ladies' Home Economics Club (see West, 1945:84).[59] This club, like others of its kind in the county, still draws its members largely from high prestige families,[60] and includes several "town women" not directly concerned with farming. One farm woman, discussing the membership, commented: "We welcome town wives. In these small towns we are all country people. . . . We are all the same out here." The women meet regularly in the homes of members, where they undertake training projects in homemaking, usually directed by the home agent or an Extension specialist from the university, and sometimes they sponsor a social affair to which husbands and guests are invited. Those who are active in the club say it is practical and worthwhile and that they appreciate the chance to visit with neighbors and friends. Some of their husbands consider the group more a social club than one concerned with homemaking, but they are less likely to criticize the club's activities today than they were a few years ago. Although some men continue the traditional joking which implies that the major function of these, and other, female gatherings is gossip, they are aware that the Ladies' Home Economics Club has operated successfully for many years, and that most of its members are very serious about their roles in it.

Plainville 4-H clubs have never been as successful as the Ladies' Home Economics Club.[61] Participation over the years moves through cycles of popularity and unpopularity, both from the standpoint of youngsters and from that of their parents. Such fluctuations are traceable to inconsistent adult interest in the group, and resulting inconsistent adult sponsorship. The latter must be eliminated if the 4-H club is to succeed. Interested parents, for example, sometimes organize a 4-H club around specific projects, but their children lose interest or graduate, or the sponsor feels that other parents do not shoulder their share of the responsibility, and the club disbands. This has happened time after time. Furthermore, interviews with children reveal that many are little motivated to participate in 4-H club work, especially those whose parents or friends are likely to ridicule the "goings-on up there at school." The most interested children obviously are those whose parents are interested in the club. Many such parents, however, paradoxically rationalize a lack of active participation in or support for the organization. At present neither parents nor children show much overt interest in club work.

Since the structure and function of the Woodland County Agricultural Extension Association have been discussed elsewhere, it is necessary to repeat here only that the organization officially affects (according to the membership list) fewer than 200 families in the entire county, and that many of these are not directly connected with farming. Certainly businessmen and others should affiliate with and support the organization, but since it is the official sponsor of agricultural Extension work in the county, and has as its main function the formulation of Extension policy,[62] it seems logical that more farmers should belong. It is interesting, and in terms of the over-all acceptance of the organization important, that some prominent Extension cooperators are not members of the association. It is, however, more important that many outstanding farmers do not wish to be identified in any way with the organization. The factors underlying these problems are, of course, many and complex: politics, the awareness of some farmers that they need not depend on Extension authority for knowledge of new agricultural developments, and agent personality and methods. These factors are given more exhaustive treatment in other contexts.

The most important and active of the nonfarm interest groups in Plainville used to be the lodges. However, as West (1945:82) indicates, by 1939 the Woodmen and Odd Fellows had disbanded, and interest in the Masonic order was rapidly declining.[63] It looked for a time as if all the old-time lodges might disappear, to be replaced by formal groups focused on newly developed agricultural interests.[64] During and immediately following the Second World War, however, the Plainville Masonic Lodge was rejuvenated by new members so that by 1955 it boasted its largest, and probably its most inactive, membership of all time. In fact, sometimes there were not enough members present to hold the regularly scheduled monthly meeting. The increased membership brought in new funds, and some lodge leaders, in spite of the deteriorating participation, unrealistically set aside money and proposed a new building.

The rise in lodge membership is best explained by functional changes in the organization which give a different meaning to the group, not only for members, but for the rest of the community. This particular order has traditionally been "the lodge" in Plainville, a reputation derived in part from its exclusiveness and in part from patterns of mutual assistance, assumed or real, associated with it. Therefore, the prestige of membership and, in some cases, the possibility of securing economic advantages, motivated nonmembers to seek acceptance by the order. This, however, was not easy to secure until recent years. The lodge power structure was controlled by a small group of successful business and farm leaders, considered "the cream of the crop," who had relatively high social status in the community. Moreover, they jealously guarded Masonic prestige by freely "blackballing" those whom they considered unqualified. As conditions in the community began to change,[65] the "old-style" leaders were less effective; consequently their influence and participation in lodge matters declined.

Changes in interest and participation were already in motion when West studied Plainville. He suggested, but did not elaborate on, the following factors which he believed to underlie this condition:

Why the interest in Masonry is declining is less clear. I suggest the following main reasons: (1) a general secularization of life: interest has declined in formal "theology," and in all other rituals; (2) the decline in community solidarity; (3) the decline in small town "business" (the older business leaders were relatively "rich"; as lodge leaders they were worth being "brothers" with); (4) acceptance of new forms of entertainment: movies, radio, and all "enjoyments" made possible by the car (West, 1945:82).

All of these factors are undoubtedly significant. Two of them, however, the decline in community solidarity and the decline in small town business, are obviously related, and both are important in the waning influence of the "old-style" community leaders.[66] It is my hypothesis that the diminishing influence of these leaders, who were also pillars of the lodge, was accompanied by a functional shift in the criteria of exclusiveness and mutual assistance, both of which, in former years, were so important to Masonic prestige. Certainly, by the early 1940s most of the older leaders were no longer active, and younger men who did not, and still do not, think of the lodge as necessarily exclusive had assumed positions in the informal power structure of the organization. Furthermore, they were, and are, strongly influenced by changing economic values, and as they become more cash-oriented, lodge brothers are less apt to observe mutual aid obligations than they were when such matters did not involve actual money.

In short, as the older, more established functions change, the newer and younger members look upon the lodge as merely something else to join, and concomitantly use the blackball increasingly less. One indignant, older lodge member made the following succinct criticism:

While I'm on the subject, the Masonic lodge is something that has really changed here. It used to be that when a man wanted in, the lodge really looked him over, but nowadays, all a man needs is thirty-five dollars. Why, if you were to blackball someone up there, they'd run you clear out of the lodge. I've gotten so disgusted with it that I hardly ever go up there any more. . . . The Masons have gone to hell, and the reason is because they aren't selective any more. I've known some pretty important men in this community who tried for years to get into the lodge, and they used to be blackballed all the time. We don't have that any more. Everyone is a Mason!

There are known cases of serious personal differences between friends because one threatened to "blackball" the nominee of the other. Several older men, while going over the names of lodge initiates during the past several years, used the term "railroad" to describe the voting on particular individuals. They say that in the old days one member would not have applied pressure on another to vote "the right way."

The women's counterpart of the Masons, the Eastern Star, is more active than the men's organization. Its meetings, for example, are better attended, and through their sponsorship of public programs the women keep themselves in the public eye much more than the Masons. The only other women's lodge currently active is the Royal Neighbors, an organization with strong insurance overtones, but organized along the lines of a social group. It is interesting that both of these women's auxiliaries became stronger as the men's lodges declined.

Plainville's most exclusive interest group is the Ladies' Bridge Club. The club, which includes a few women from Discovery, has a long history and is, in the eyes of most of the community, made up of women from the "best" families. (Some say they "just think they're the best.") Despite the high-prestige roster, many women steadfastly deny that it is exclusive. They rationalize either that lower-status women never try to get in, or, more often, that "they don't go in for bridge." (It is true that lower-prestige families do not "go in for bridge.") One interesting myth to which some Plainvillers, and many people in nearby communities, give credence, is that the Bridge Club is an auxiliary of the Christian Church, and that bridge parties are held in the church basement. Card playing is, of course, criticized by Holiness and Baptist church members, many of whom think it particularly "sinful" that women meet regularly to play bridge.

Shortly after the close of the Second World War businessmen and some leading farmers joined together to form a commercial club, the purpose of which is to sponsor civic projects for the improvement of Plainville. During its early years the club conceived and carried through several ambitious and worthwhile projects: it paved the main street, constructed a highway park near the village, bought a mechanized street grader, and established a "city dump."

The club sponsors the annual "March of Dimes" drive and the children's Christmas program and, prior to 1955, sponsored a boy scout troop and the annual Fourth of July picnic in the square. The scout troop folded, mainly because of lack of interest among the boys and most of the parents— few people expressed much concern over its failure (see also West, 1945:85). Discontinuance of the Fourth of July picnic, oldest community tradition observed in Plainville, is considered a serious matter, particularly by older people. The Commercial Club stopped sponsoring the picnic because most of the members, many of them businessmen not native to Plainville, simply were not interested. Old-timers, who used to look forward to the annual reunion, are sorely disappointed, and various gossip cliques and outspoken individuals constantly complain about it. They say "That's goin' to hurt the businessmen in this town," but when asked "how?" they can give no good examples. On July fourth many ex-Plainvillers came home for the picnic, and their disappointment, relayed by Plainville friends and relatives, provides added fuel for critics of the Commercial Club.

The Commercial Club holds monthly meetings in the basement of the Christian Church. Ten to fifteen men attend and, for one dollar each, enjoy a tremendous dinner prepared by the Christian Church ladies. The dinner is followed by a short business meeting and then a program, customarily slides taken by some member, conservation films (despite antipathy to the game warden), or free films from national business firms. Visiting and eating together are now the main functions of the club, with business activities and development projects at an all-time low. The members say that poor economic conditions make merchants and others reluctant to finance community improvement, and that now is a poor time to try to initiate any program. However, a more accurate explanation of the club's inactivity is factionalism created by the mutual jealousies of some members and a feeling on the part of others that two or three men are trying to "run the show." This has led to virtual suspension of the club's interest in community development. In fact, only a strong interest in sociability, refreshment, and entertainment kept the organization alive during 1954–55.

If the Commercial Club cannot continue, Plainville will have lost the organization which has, since its beginning, filled the void caused by a lack of individual leaders. The club, with its original emphasis on cooperation from everyone interested in a better community, though inadequate thus far, can, if properly developed, more effectively cope with the changing economic conditions characteristic of Plainville today. This does not necessarily mean that it is the only kind of leadership possible, merely that it is the most effective that has emerged thus far. The problem of leadership is acute in small communities undergoing rapid social and cultural change such as this one.

EDUCATION

The most prominent symbol of community solidarity in Plainville is the consolidated elementary and secondary school. This institution commands the interest of a great number of people because it functions, along with the family, as a major socializing agency for Plainville youngsters. Interest in the school is not confined merely to learning, but depends partly on the awareness that for nine months of the year it is a major recreational source for both children and adults.

Practically all Plainville parents agree that education is the primary shortcut to occupational and social achievement— "it wasn't too important in the old days, but anymore you just got to have a little." There is, in fact, a sizable oral tradition about past Plainvillers who, through education, have distinguished themselves in the outside business and professional world. Such stories are an expression of the linked values of education and success, and support the related value that "anyone can make good if he just has the will and determination to do so." In line with these values is the belief of Plainville parents that education should be strongly utilitarian and pragmatic—learning for its own sake is a concept foreign to most of them.

Beyond this, however, areas of agreement are few. We find, for example, some people, particularly low-status families, convinced that the community is "crazy with schoolin' . . . they always gotta be doin' somethin' fer the schools . . . like more taxes fer this and that . . . buyin' them silly lookin' band uniforms that don't fit nobody. . . ." On the other hand, there is a small and often ineffective minority, holding the opposite view that Plainville's brand of education is "among the worst there is anywhere." These people complain of poor curriculum and low teaching standards, and ridicule fellow parents who assume that children are educated merely by spending a few years "inside the school-house."

On matters of education, as on so many other issues in Plainville, the most apparent differences of opinion are between generations. Most of the older people believe that the eighth grade (some say "maybe high school") is as far as children need go,[67] and that once this level is achieved parental responsibility ends. Younger parents, on the other hand, tend to hold more liberal views: children *should* get a high school education; and, as indicated previously, a few younger and middle-aged parents are convinced of the *need* of a college education for their youngsters. Paradoxically, they do little to motivate their children to prepare themselves adequately at the pre-college level. Expense, incidentally, is considered an impossible barrier by many who would like their children to attend college.

What, then, are the career objectives of Plainville's present generation of high school students? A series of English themes written by fifteen girls and fourteen boys, all juniors and seniors from varying social levels, and subsequent interviews with some of them reveal the following preferences for occupations after graduation. Six boys want to be mechanics: two of them automobile repairmen and four aircraft repairmen; three desire to be farmers; three hope to work as laborers in the city; one would like to be a veterinarian but does not want to attend college; and another wishes to study law. An interesting fact emerging from the themes is that eight of the fourteen boys expect to receive education in military service which will prepare them for future vocations as civilians. This expectation stems partly from the influence of military recruiting information available to them, and partly from their awareness that parents cannot give them more schooling. Three would-be mechanics hope to stay in the Air Force. Six want to live and work in Metropolis, one wishes to farm in an adjoining state, another is undecided on place of residence, and only three of the four-

teen hope to live in Plainville. Two of these want to be
farmers and the other hopes some day to own an automobile
garage. One of the boys who wants to be a farmer has never
lived on a farm. The reason for selecting farming as a voca-
tion is "independence"; in all other occupations the reasons
for choice are "would like that kind of work," and "good
pay." Only one boy wants to attend college.

Of the fifteen girls indicating occupational preferences,
four want to be business secretaries, four desire nurse's training so they can "work in a hospital," three prefer to be housewives, and the remaining four want to be, respectively, a
musician, a beauty operator, a kindergarten teacher, and an
orphanage or nursery attendant. Three girls hope to attain
their career objectives by entering military service. Five girls
justify occupational preferences by their desire "to be around
small children." The remainder prefer their professional
choice because of "good pay," "would like that kind of
work," or, in the case of the girls who want to be housewives,
because they like children and housewifely duties. Only one
girl wants to go to college.

In all cases, the students are aware that they will probably
leave Plainville. This is nothing new or strange to any of
them, but is merely the continuance of an emigration pattern
already well established (see also West, 1945:18). Between
1919, the year in which the community inaugurated a four-
year high school, and 1953, 562 individuals were graduated
from Plainville High, and eighty-two percent of this group
moved from Woodland County.[68] Like most of those who
did not go to high school, they migrated in all directions,
less because they wanted to than because they were forced
to.[69] When we consider that outside marriage there are few
local opportunities for girls and that the only occupation
open to boys (except for an insignificant number who ultimately enter local businesses) is farming, this is quite understandable. Furthermore, the lack of land, the reluctance of
fathers to retire, and the declining need for farm labor due

to mechanization restrict the number of boys who can stay on the farm.

Most graduating seniors, then, male or female, emigrate to the cities. They work as construction laborers or in defense plants, and become secretaries, or clerks with business firms; an occasional boy goes to another state to work as a farm laborer. Figures compiled for the period 1934 to 1953, involving 358 Plainville graduates, show that a small number, twenty-seven girls and twenty boys, entered college the year immediately following graduation. No figures are available to determine the number who received college degrees, but percentage estimates by informants are invariably quite low.

The fact that so many young Plainvillers leave the community raises the question of the functional adequacy of the high school curriculum. I refer specifically to a major area of specialization, vocational agriculture. The central position of this subject in the curriculum of male students can be shown by taking a number of years, say 1941 to 1950,[70] and determining the number of students who enrolled for agriculture courses. We find that eighty-four boys were graduated from Plainville High during this ten-year period, and that of this number seventy-seven took two to four years of vocational agriculture training. However, only fifteen of the seventy-seven ultimately entered farming, either in Plainville or elsewhere. The only other vocational courses offered are commerce and home economics. In addition to these subjects, students take academic courses in health, citizenship, history, speech, mathematics through algebra, biology, music, and English. However, due to the small number of credits approved by the state department of education, students have little selection during their four years of high school. With this background they compete in the city labor markets or, in the case of a few, enter colleges poorly prepared.

Interviews with students reveal that many are not particularly concerned about curriculum deficiencies but, rather, feel that their main objective is the high school diploma—

the acquisition of an "education" being somewhat incidental.[71] Their attitudes are shared by many parents who, unfortunately, are often more interested in the high school athletic program, the disciplinary ability of certain teachers, or school board politics than in academic matters. Such attitudes concern some teachers and parents, who, in their more sarcastic moments, criticize a system which sometimes graduates students who can hardly read. These conditions, of course, exist not only in Plainville but elsewhere in America, presenting an exceedingly complex problem which the present project does not propose to analyze. One important consideration does stand out, however, and this is a philosophy of education developed by many Plainville parents that their children are *due,* as opposed to earning, a high school diploma in the *public schools,* and woe unto the teacher who dares to stand in their way. The basic assumption seems to be that students learn by spending the required number of years in school; furthermore, that if they suffer academic or disciplinary [72] "injustice" at the hands of school officials, corrective action can be taken. The parent's position is understandable when we consider that the school is ultimately governed by an elected lay board,[73] the members of which are themselves a part of the community and subject to pressures from parents. The board is fairly close to the actual school program, and this makes Plainville teachers, many of whom, incidentally, are products of the community in which they work, potentially subject to parental controls channeled through board members. The amount of control varies, of course, with the independence of the individual members of the board.

Some Plainville parents are enough concerned about their school system to consider innovative alternatives which would be revolutionary. A small number of people, for example, advocate, though not too openly, the consolidation of Plainville High with other county high schools. A collaborative effort of this dimension could provide an expanded vocational program (which would better equip students to leave

They attribute many disciplinary problems to these student attitudes. They also complain, though again not too loudly, that most parents are little interested in education, pointing to the small number who normally participate in P.T.A.[75] and other school functions, and that so few rural parents are active in school affairs.

5 Religion in Plainville

A NEW RESIDENT quickly receives the impression that religion is a dominant interest among the people of Plainville. Among the first friendly overtures are those made by representatives bearing invitations to attend their respective churches. In fact, one of the first questions asked a newcomer is, "What church do you belong to?"[1] As he extends his contacts it becomes apparent that his Plainville friends consider religious affiliation a major trait when identifying their neighbors for him. Furthermore, it soon becomes apparent that there are a few militant agnostics, identified in religious contexts by one of the most powerful of all Plainville epithets, "atheists!"

The people of Plainville are divided for religious purposes into two broad categories, "believers" and "nonbelievers." In this connection, West, writing of the 1939–40 period, makes the following observation:

There are many nonbelievers in Plainville. Perhaps a fourth to a third of the people have been so permeated by rational ideas from the outside world that they no longer believe the received tenets of fundamentalistic Protestant theology, or they at least discredit any literal interpretation of the Bible (1945:142).

This condition probably still exists, though the number of individuals who overtly assume an agnostic role is not great. One extended family in particular has the reputation for never "darkening" a church door "because they don't believe in God," and a few individuals, who are accomplished students of the Bible, take great delight in arguing their position with fundamental religionists. Fear of social condemnation, however, prevents most "doubters" from public support of their views. Many agnostics, in fact, do not declare their belief, and at the same time advocate support of local churches, arguing that they stand for moral right as opposed to wrong.

The major religious identification for "believers," whether they participate or not, has traditionally been Protestant, further refined to mean Baptist, Methodist, Christian, or Holiness. Aside from these denominations there is little formal religious identification in the community. A few "Dunkards" still attend a small church about ten miles north of the village, but most of the sect have moved away. Catholic families are very few—three or four in the entire county, and only one in Plainville. Despite their small number, however, a little chapel has been built in Discovery, and it is occasionally served by priests from adjoining counties. Sometimes the fathers give information lectures in different communities, including Plainville ("Once in awhile one of 'em sets up in the square just as brave as anybody"), but most people are not responsive, because, as West (1945:145) wrote, "Of all the religions in the world, Catholicism is considered by most Plainvillers to be the most 'non-Christian.' " The only sect trying to missionize Plainvillers during our stay in the community was a Jehovah's Witness group which founded a "church" in a dwelling at a crossroads settlement about seven miles south of the village. They were having little success, mainly because Plainvillers condemn what they consider an "unpatriotic" stand: "Why they advocate our boys stayin' outa the army, and people not salutin' our flag, and sech as that!" Finally, a few Plainvillers attend church in other communities. Much to the consternation of the Holiness, for example, a few of their group sometimes go to the Assembly of God Church in Stanton. The Holiness believe that the "Assemblies" should not be encouraged because they speak in "unknown tongues."

Each of the four main denominations supports a house of worship in the village. The well-kept buildings and grounds are evidence of the improved (since 1939–40) economic conditions of the respective congregations. The Christian Church, a massive-appearing brick building much too big for its congregation, which was for many years the unrivaled religious showplace of the community, if not the entire county, remains the largest religious structure in Plainville. The local Baptist congregation, however, climaxed an energetic four-year building fund drive by erecting in 1955 a $15,000 brick edifice. This modern structure was made possible through subscription of local funds ("You'd never thought that much could be raised during a drought") and by labor donated by men from all village congregations. The Baptists are proud that their new building rivals the Christian Church in beauty, if not in size, and that in many respects it is more functional than the latter ("At least we can afford what we got"). Their pride assumes another dimension if we consider that church buildings in this area are traditional symbols of the relative economic position of the congregations.[2] Thus the oft-heard comment, "The Baptist Church is just as good as the Christian now," holds connotations of considerable importance for some. The Methodists hope to enlarge their building, but the Holiness are satisfied with theirs, which, though it is the smallest of the four, is, like the Methodist Church, a neatly painted, well-kept, white frame building.

The largest and most active Plainville congregation is the Baptist. This church in 1939 had an average weekly attendance of only thirty-seven, prompting West (1945:147) to make the following observation:

The Baptist church is the least active of the Plainville churches, chiefly because there are several very lively rural Baptist congregations in the trade area. The preacher who conducts services once a month in Plainville preaches to much larger country congregations on each of the other three weekends of the month. His Plainville revival meetings are also generally less successful than those in the rural neighborhoods, where he sometimes "saves" twenty or thirty people during a revival. He considers his Plainville church to be his "deadest" congregation.

The average weekly attendance during 1954–55, however, was seventy-eight, far larger than that of any of the other three congregations. The rise to prominence of this group since 1939 is based on several factors, some of the more important of which are the disappearance of "country" churches, the rising prestige of the minister, and the general enthusiasm behind the building drive.

The demise of rural Baptist churches and their subsequent absorption into the village congregation increased the size of the "town church" and improved its prestige by adding some of Plainville's more successful farm families to it. Paralleling the upgrading of Baptist prestige, in part contributing to it and in part the result of it, is the prestige rise of the Baptist minister. Besides preaching, he used to farm, but a few years ago gave it up and moved to town. He lives in one of Plainville's nicest homes, is county representative to the state legislature, and works as a carpenter in his infrequent spare time. He has been an effective leader of Plainville Baptists for some sixteen years, a ministerial tenure record not found in any of the other churches. Working closely with village and rural people, he has been responsible for orderly consolidation. He and his family evidence most of the qualities which Plainvillers most highly value.

The Baptists, with their attendance doubled over the past fifteen years, think of themselves as a "growing church." There are more active teenagers in their group than in all the other churches combined, and their adult congregation is almost equally balanced between male and female participation. Furthermore, several offspring of Holiness parents, and a few Methodists, have been converted to the Baptist faith.[3] As membership and participation grew, the church, under the skillful guidance of the minister, undertook its successful building drive. The interest generated by the campaign integrated the expanding group, and the building is, for the present, at least, symbolic of the congregation's unity. However, now that the structure is complete there are signs of emerging factions which may threaten the unity of the group.

Plainville Baptists are the only large congregation in Wood-

land County that has not broken away from a local organization to join one of the national Baptist groups. Much to the
consternation and perplexity of Baptist leaders in surrounding
communities, they continue to identify with a local group of
small congregations with "radical" and "emotional" revival-
istic tendencies. Sooner or later Plainville Baptists must face
the question of whether to continue their present provincial
orientation, which threatens to isolate them from other major
Baptist groups in the county, or to identify with the larger
Baptist mass movement and submit to a certain measure of
outside authority. When this occurs (and county Baptist leaders will eventually see that it does) informal factions, already
present, could serve as catalysts for disunity. One of the most
important bases for factionalism, the issue of "emotional" expression in religious services, will be discussed shortly.

West (1945:146) tells us that leadership in the Methodist
Church was formerly controlled by some of the town's "aristocracy," but with the failure of the Plainville bank in the late
1920s these families gradually moved away, and the Methodist
Church began to change. By 1939 its prestige position was
second to the Christian. It was still, however, the largest and
most active congregation in the community, with an average
Sunday-school attendance of seventy-four people per week
throughout the year. Since 1939 this number has steadily
dropped, so that the average attendance during our research
period was only forty-six per week.

Important factors in the Methodist decline are failure to
recruit new members to replace those who have emigrated or
died and, during recent years, ministerial problems that
threaten to split the group into two factions. One of the primary issues is "emotional" expression by some of the members
and their insistence upon a minister who conforms to their
expectations. This minority faction is referred to as an em-
barrassment by some more "modern" members. There are
several high-status families in the congregation, however, and
this undoubtedly contributes to the favorable prestige of the

church as a whole ("Methodists and Christians are about the same here . . . only two churches that can really get along"). The Methodists, primarily through the initiative, interest, and understanding of the retired postmaster, have the most active group of "junior-high-age" boys.

The Holiness group has dropped slightly, from an average weekly Sunday-school attendance of thirty-seven in 1939 to an average of twenty-nine in 1954–55. It is often called a "dying church" and, with considerably more justification, "an old people's church." For a number of years the Holiness has not replaced members lost through death and emigration because young potential members are obviously uninterested. Revivals produce few converts, and aside from occasional members already in the church few people attain, or even attempt to attain, the exalted status of "Holiness," or being "sanctified." Two or three prominent farm families in the community provide leadership, but most of the membership is drawn from families of lower socio-economic status, including an unusually large number of elderly female pensioners.

The Christian Church had an average weekly Sunday-school attendance of sixty-six during 1954–55, as against the forty-nine reported for 1939. This congregation, like others in the community, from time to time experiences minor attendance fluctuations traceable to ministerial personality and church "squabbles." It has, though, over the years maintained a fairly consistent attendance record. The congregation's major complaint is one shared with the Methodist and Holiness churches: too few young people attend, and even fewer are interested in joining. There are several high-status farm and business families in the congregation, some of whom have "run the church for years." The church as a whole, however, is fairly well united, and what factionalism does exist is confined mostly to the leadership group. The congregation is still mainly identified with the economic elite of the community, though it certainly is not exclusively so. One further characteristic of the group is a noticeable lack of adult male attendance.

The organization of all the churches is quite similar and, despite the beliefs of some Plainvillers to the contrary, the technical theological points separating them are slight. All denominations hold Sunday school every Sunday morning, but the frequency of church services varies. The Christian and Methodist churches hold morning and evening services one Sunday each month; the Baptist follows a similar schedule on two Sundays a month; while the Holiness insists upon services every Sunday morning and evening. The other churches imply that the Holiness can do this because it is not committed to a salary for its minister, but pays him *only* through the collection plate. However, some Methodist and Christian members say they could not maintain regular attendance even if they could afford full-time ministers: "One Sunday a month is about all we can get people out."

Some of the churches sponsor affiliated groups, but lack of interest generally limits multiple activities among all congregations. The Christian and Methodist ladies actively support auxiliaries, both of which meet regularly in the homes of members or, perhaps, in the churches. They raise money by selling food at public affairs such as athletic events, and sometimes at church dinners and farm sales, where for a small sum one can eat a large meal. The Methodist ladies hold "quilting bees" to raise money, and the Christian ladies have a monopoly on serving the Commercial Club dinners. Money made from these sources goes for missionary contributions, church maintenance, and a variety of other related activities. The Christian minister tried during 1954–55 to organize a men's group, but had little success: "Men just don't go much for things like that." The Baptist and Holiness churches sponsor young people's organizations, but since the Baptist is the only congregation with a sizable number of teenagers, theirs is the only successful one. Much to the consternation of the adults, youth groups in each of the churches tend to rise and decline. Their success depends on the number of teenagers who attend the church, the adult leadership available, and finally, a factor which many adults fail to recognize, the informal leadership provided in such groups by the young people themselves. The latter, for example, is an important ingredient in the Baptist youth organization. This became apparent when the 1955 high school seniors, many of them Baptists, organized their protest so effectively that the superintendent's selection of the Christian minister for baccalaureate exercises was overridden in favor of the Baptist minister.

As already indicated, the doctrinal issues separating Plainville churches are slight. There is, however, a prevailing belief that "churches here don't get along." Christians and Methodists, for example, say they work together in cooperative community functions, but that "the Holiness prefer to remain to themselves," and "the Baptists seem to like to go it alone." All the other congregations criticize the Holiness as "clannified," as a group that "sticks to themselves," and leaders in community-wide affairs, such as P.T.A., claim that invitations to Holiness are, except by one or two families, generally ignored. Actually, there is some justification for stereotyping the Holiness as "clannish." They, more than any other denomination, have developed a system of social relationships which permits them a substantial degree of social independence. (See also West, 1945: 129 and 147.) This is necessary because they emphasize "non-worldly" values and a belief system based on the highly emotional, outwardly manifest experience of "holy sanctification," features generally unpopular with the rest of the community. Furthermore, as Holiness members point out, most cooperative community affairs revolve around school children, and since their church has so few young people they feel no strong compulsion to participate in youth-oriented activities. Holiness members who are aware of their unpopularity in the religious community manifest their concern by criticizing "Holiness-fighters," that is, those who do not "understand our ways" and who make no attempt to understand them.

Baptists insist that they cooperate with other churches in

community affairs which "require" their participation. Several families are active in the P.T.A., and the church as a whole cooperates in the annual, interdenominational (except for the Holiness) Christmas program. The master of ceremonies for the occasion in 1954 was, in fact, the popular Baptist minister. The Baptists, however, refused to participate in a proposed interdenominational Vacation Bible School, telling the Christian minister, organizer of the school, that they prefer to hold their own. Many townspeople, including some Baptists, considered this "high-handed" and non-cooperative. A few Baptists, obviously dissatisfied with their church's decision, assisted the Christian minister's project.

There is, then, some evidence of non-cooperation among Plainville churches, but far less than many Plainvillers like to assume. The belief that "churches here don't get along" is kept alive by minor theological disagreements which, through argument and criticism, constantly force people to reexamine and affirm religious alignments, and which, to some extent, restrict certain social relationships. We found, for example, that, aside from family, people tend to engage in intimate types of social interaction (visiting in each other's homes) more often with fellow church members than with others.[4] As might be assumed, the intensity of this pattern is greater among the Holiness than in other congregations.

West (1945:146) indicated that emotional religious behavior was something of an issue in 1939. Referring specifically to the Methodist Church, he said:

According to many, including the retired preacher who served it in the old days, it has been overrun by people who prefer the more emotional kind of worshiping. Several local Methodist preachers are recent "converts" from the Holiness Church. The retired preacher says of them, "They like Holiness ways, but they like the Methodist pay. Of course, I still have to *go,* but it's a disgrace to listen to them." The county agent's wife, a Methodist, said, "I never did hear people anywhere else shout in a *Methodist* Church."

One of the most hotly debated religious issues in 1954–55 was that of public religious expression. Arrayed as polar extremes on this issue were the Holiness, sometimes called "holy rollers" because of their highly emotional and physically energetic religious behavior, and the Christian Church, traditionally known as "cold" and "reserved." Falling between these two extremes were the Baptist and Methodist, both with recognizable "emotional" [5] factions, sometimes called "Holiness-like Baptists" and "Holiness-like Methodists." The concern over this issue nowadays is all the more interesting when we consider that only a few years ago (West, 1945:148) [6] emotionalism was normal in Baptist and Holiness services, sometimes occurred in Methodist services, was typical of revivals in all three churches, and, within the memory of many people, was not uncommon in Christian-sponsored revivals. Today, however, most Plainvillers view such behavior as "outlandish" and "old-fashioned," a lag from an era when "people didn't know much better," and, for the most part, associate it with "radicals" and those who lack education. There are even some who, by inference, innuendo, or outright statement, attribute mental instability to the more rabid emotionals, arguing from the premise that a few "excessively" religious people have suffered "breakdowns," some requiring medical attention. Still others, actually a very small number, believe such behavior is innate, and argue that "you need churches to take care of that class of people. . . . Regular churches wouldn't have no appeal to that *kind*." Negative reaction is commonly registered by directing ridicule and criticism at those who follow the "old ways," and sometimes nonemotionals implicitly threaten coercion to silence their religiously "happy" neighbors.

Plainville's interest in religious emotionalism was focused sharply in a long tent revival held in the village square during the early weeks of research. The revival was sponsored by the regional Baptist group with which the Plainville church is affiliated, and was led by two revivalists, one a Plainville farmer-preacher. It was not, however, connected with the Plainville Baptist Church and was, in fact, boycotted by many of this congregation. The services were well attended by "Holiness-like Baptists," Methodists of the same category, and a small number of Holiness members. At times, large numbers of interested onlookers from Plainville and nearby towns sat in their cars or stood in the shadows "to watch the show." One regular onlooker jokingly said he came only for the "commercials," meaning testimonials but making an obvious analogy with television. He claimed he learned more about the financial dealings of one of the revivalist's relatives by listening to his testimonials than he ever could have done otherwise.

It was "one of the hottest," that is, most "emotional," revivals in years. Many, in fact, likened it to the "old-fashioned" prewar (1941) tent meetings and healing services. Nightly meetings until midnight or after were held for eight weeks. Each meeting followed a definite ritual form, beginning with hymns, followed by testimonials, often lengthy and very personal, and a sermon, with prayers and more testimonials interspersed at regular intervals. The climax, of course, came with the "invitation," the "call" for "sinners" to come forward to the mourners' bench at the front of the church and, with the assistance of the minister and the congregation, pray their way "through" to forgiveness.[7] On "good nights," when several potential converts came to the mourners' bench, services were unusually loud. The pattern of excessive noise, a manifestation of heightened interest, was exaggerated whenever individuals were "in trouble" at the bench and had to reappear night after night until they felt they had been "delivered from sin."

Most people said the revival was doomed from the start, that it could not long survive the "emotional" tone set by the two preachers. When it became apparent that this was not the case, and that participant enthusiasm was growing by the night, various negative sanctions were applied or threatened. Critics, including some liberal Baptists, effectively used established gossip cliques to stigmatize the meeting as "a disgrace to the community." They were not particularly effective, however, until the closing week of the revival when several young children were subjected to long hours of haranguing to "bring them through." The angry critics reasoned that since the children could not know when they were saved, the decision was controlled by adults, and therefore, that the preachers and some of the parents were exploiting the youngsters to prolong the meeting—and most of their listeners agreed that "them little kids don't know what it's all about," that "they don't even know when they're saved," while many agreed that such small children surely had not yet had a chance to sin. The anti-revival movement suddenly caught on, climaxed with threats of a petition to the town board to "cut off their [tent] lights," and rumors persisted that the county sheriff would be called in to stop the meeting on the grounds that it was becoming a public nuisance. The sheriff reportedly was seen circling the square on the last few meeting nights, and many construed this as a warning to "tone things down." However, no official action was taken by either the sheriff or the town board.

Excitement and controversy over the summer tent meeting had scarcely waned before the Plainville Baptist Church officially opened its annual fall revival. This one began calmly enough, but within a few nights "they got carried away" and "was actin' just like them people in the square last summer." They were "noisy," and the behavior of some who were "getting religion" supplied a topic for ridicule, criticism, and gossip. Many non-Baptists gleefully emphasized that some of those who were "cutting capers" had only recently condemned similar actions of their "Holiness-like" brothers. Leading Christians and Methodists, and a few liberal Baptists, openly criticized the lengthy testimonials, "bench jumping," and "moaning" of their Baptist friends. The revivalists were oblivious to their critics, or did not care, because they continued the meeting for four weeks. Plainville's correspondent to the

Discovery *Beacon*, a Baptist Church member, summarized the revival in glowing terms:

This is the greatest harvest of souls ever made in the history of the church within the memory of any of the body. There were 28 additions. A good spirit prevailed throughout the meeting. Many people shouted praises and witnessed the power of God working among His people. Visitors from other churches were revived and blessed during this meeting.

One particularly interesting development of this revival focuses on a condition which is taboo for discussion in Plainville—the competitiveness of the churches. Much to the consternation of non-Baptist parents and a few teachers, a number of Baptist youngsters who were emotionally involved in the meeting [8] permitted their enthusiasm to carry over into school activities. They were aroused by the "preparation for after-life" theme which permeated revival sermons, and which stressed immediate salvation as a prelude for death that might come at any time. Using "salvation before death" as their argument, Baptist youngsters sought to influence their peers to join the church without delay. A few non-Baptists became alarmed and there was some talk of complaining to school officials, but nothing came of it.[9]

Despite all the gossip, ridicule, and criticism of the emotional goings-on of the Baptist town church revival, no one suggested calling in the law to suppress their "noise." Since the implicit threat of legal action to curb noise had only recently been invoked against the tent meeting, several people were asked about the immunity from such action which applies to some Baptists and not to others. Most people recognize that there is a "Holiness-like" group of Baptists who would like to make every religious service a physically energized affair, but they distinguish this group from those who are "carried away" during revivals, but who, during the rest of the year, frown upon extreme religious expression. The minister and others who fall into the latter category command greater respect, have higher prestige, and generally occupy more desirable status positions than their "emotional" Baptist brethren.

Some people say that the implicit threat of legal action is the major cause for the decline of emotional behavior among the Holiness. They say that several years ago a man who lived near the church threatened to "call the law" if they continued their "late hours" and "loud yelling." Whether this is true could not be definitely established. Holiness people say that it is not. They deny that community criticism or threats of legal sanctions can force them to stop being "happy" in their religion; rather, "people has just changed. . . . They ain't as devout as they once was" or "they aren't as close to God as they were." That their revival behavior has changed was obvious in their fall meeting, begun during the final stages of the Baptist revival just discussed. The calm, rational approach of the young minister contrasted sharply with the "shoutin' and yellin' " Baptists, as townspeople were quick to detect because it was so contrary to expectations. Many people expressed the opinion that because community criticism of the Baptists was so great Holiness members purposefully refrained from any behavior which would reflect negatively on them. Again, Holiness people deny that this is true, and point out that there was, in fact, criticism from some older members because the revivalist "never really got the group warmed up."

Closely associated with emotionalism as an issue is the controversy over revelation of grace or conversion. The Christian Church believes that a person should offer himself to God in a rational manner, and that this is a choice made by the individual only after considerable thought, even during revivals. Most Holiness members and Baptists, on the other hand, and many Methodists, believe that an emotional experience is preliminary to the revelation of grace or conversion. A person from one of these three churches will, during a revival, sometimes pray for hours at the mourners' bench to induce "an experience." However, if one joins the Methodist or Baptist church during regular services he is spared this ordeal. Not so in the Holiness church, where every person who seeks salvation, during revivals or otherwise, must outwardly manifest an expression of "sanctification," an ecstatic feeling which comes only after God bestows upon him His "second blessing" as evidence of His forgiveness of past sins.

Many people believe that salvation or the deliverance from an evil habit, such as drinking, "cussing," or smoking, does not necessarily have to occur in church. Several Holiness, Baptist, and Methodist converts can recall the exact date, time, location, and what they were doing when they "got religion," or were delivered from an "evil" habit. One man, for example, tells of being "saved" while driving his tractor; another was "saved" while sitting in his living room where he was suddenly seized with a tremendous and uncontrollable urge to sing and dance; an elderly woman "got religion" while sewing; and a high school boy is disappointed because he was saved in church rather than in a favorite location he had previously chosen for the event.

Another point of difference currently separating Plainville's congregations involves educational values, particularly training for ministers. This issue sometimes appears as a sermon topic and in arguments by interested parties. The Christian Church, for example, stresses that its pastor must have a college degree from an institution accredited by the national organization, and most Methodists prefer that their minister be college trained, though a small minority do not support this view.

Baptists believe that ministers are "called to preach the gospel," that formal education is not a prerequisite to pastorship. When an adult Sunday-school class discussed this issue, except for two or three dissenters who said that "times are changing" and that ministers should be educated to change with them, majority opinion was that preachers should not attend college. Arguments against ministerial education focused on three points: (1) a minister goes away to college, and thus is exposed to the "sins of colleges"; (2) educated ministers get their sermons from "books" (other than the Bible) or compose them before delivery, and "preachers should give their sermons as God tells them what to say"; (3) educated ministers "use words too big for us common people to understand." During this particular discussion several people opposed college for their children because "kids go away to college and are exposed to worldly evils." However, as one of the more vehement critics explained, "practically all kids orta have a chance fer a high school education."

Holiness members firmly believe that ministers are "called" to preach, and under no circumstances should they write out or otherwise prepare their sermons ahead of time. The local church sometimes appeals to a nearby Holiness college for revivalists or temporary pastoral replacements, but these young men are never popular because their delivery is not emotional enough and they do not in other ways meet expectations. This further convinces Holiness members that "the best preacher is one that never got to college." They believe that a minister has, above all else, a responsibility to "preach the Bible," and that neither college-educated Holiness ministers nor preachers of other religions do this. The favorite story of one Holiness man concerns some "high-toned Campbellites [Christians]" he once knew who "spit in a Holiness preacher's face for preachin' only the Bible at 'em." His friend Silas Wolf describes the ideal minister as one who "talks real fast," and Chris Upton, a Holiness leader, says, "You can't give people time to think . . . they get restless if the preacher don't keep comin' at 'em with somethin' all the time."

Other minor disagreements separate Plainville denominations. The method of baptism, for example, is still occasionally argued, though few people nowadays hold extremist views of right or wrong regarding it. During the tent revival there were disputes over "infant damnation," and one sometimes hears arguments about whether a person can "fall from grace." In the main, though, the similarities among the churches and their problems are far greater than the differences.

Some of the obvious trends in the changing religious behavior of Plainvillers are (1) withdrawal from intense involvement in religious matters, particularly evident in declining revivalism and decreasing "emotionalism," already discussed; (2) the appearance of new values which redefine church participation and attendance; and (3) a greater reliance upon science and modern technology in coping with various problem areas.

West had the following to say regarding Plainville revivals:

The climax of the religious year is the revival. The Baptist Church holds two revivals nearly every year. The Holiness Church often holds several. The Christian and Methodist churches ordinarily hold one each. Each revival is scheduled to last a fortnight, with nightly services, and occasionally (except at the Christian Church) with morning sermons too. If the revivalist fails to arouse interest, the meetings sometimes close within the fortnight. More frequently, however, they last longer, if conversions are coming in fast toward the end, or if it is felt that a few more sessions might "bring through" any mourners who are having a particularly "hard time" at the mourner's bench (1945:151–52).

During the year of my research the Baptist, Holiness, and Christian churches each had a revival; the Methodist had none. Only the Baptists believe theirs was a success. Many people in the Christian Church complain that the results of their meeting did not justify the expense: "We didn't get a person that wouldn't have come in anyway." Actually, a few people in each congregation, unpopular as their stand may be, question both the need for and the function of modern revivals. Most members feel that they are needed to "fan up interest," and assume that this will result in better attendance and participation in regular church and Sunday-school services. However, when measured against Plainville values which define church attendance and participation, revivals seem no longer adequately to serve this function.

Most of those in the Christian and Methodist congregations confine their religious activities to a few hours on Sunday, and during the rest of the week show little interest in church-sponsored affairs unless they offer some recreational value. In fact, some people identify with these churches more as a matter of civic responsibility than anything else. For them it is easy to rationalize that civic and religious obligations are satisfied so long as they are represented at scheduled religious functions. The representative is usually the wife in the family.

Holiness and Baptist families are more likely to view attendance and participation in church and Sunday school purely as religious actions. They, particularly the Holiness members, are less concerned about criticism if they do not attend church than about how they themselves will feel. But even in these congregations, there is no longer the strong compulsion to become involved in religious matters that there once was. The Holiness, for example, who still, more than any other congregation, approximate "living" their religion seven days a week (see West, 1945:147), now accept new values which affect attendance and participation. The Dovers, a prominent Holiness family, confide, "It wasn't too many years ago when we thought it was a terrible sin to miss a day of church," but now they "often" stay home to rest or receive visits from children or friends, or maybe "drive to see the kids." A prominent Holiness man lamented in a Sunday evening prayer service that "people anymore are so busy just making a living" that they have too little time to "think about religion like they use to." Mr. Dover, his friend and neighbor, who was not present, when informed of the remarks said: "Some people are crazy with religion . . . just as crazy as they come. If people just think about nothin' but religion they'll go just as crazy as bats . . . people need things to do and other things to think about. Look at Mrs. Carson—she just set around all day with her Bible in her hands . . . she wouldn't talk nothin' but Bible." A prominent Holiness woman agreed with Mr. Dover and then added that she no longer enjoys the "big camp meeting" (West, 1945:148) as she did a few years ago:

The other day me and my husband went to a big tent meetin'
over by Hill City. It was an all-day meetin', and towards the
middle of the afternoon I was so sleepy [attributes her condition
to physical fatigue resulting from hard work] we just packed up
and come home. I just couldn't git aroused. . . . Wouldn't a
been thataway a few years ago . . . I woulda been there from
early mornin' till two in the mornin'.

The plain and simple fact is that nowadays people in all
congregations not only "have too many things to do," but they
have a great number of activities which they prefer to church.
This cuts into the time formerly given to religious matters,
and minimizes the functional importance of the revival as a
vehicle for "stirring people up" and "getting them in the
mood" to participate in regularly scheduled religious activities. Complementing this is another obvious sectarian trend
—the tendency to go only to one's own church. People used
commonly to go to the church that was holding services or a
revival, regardless of denomination, but nowadays there is
less courtesy visiting across denominational lines.

The increased dependence of Plainvillers on modern technology and science as the best way rationally and empirically
to control their environment has been stressed in the preceding pages, and need not be given full discussion here, though
one particular feature deserves special mention. There is very
little overt religious healing today. Only a few years ago many
Holiness members and some Baptists and Methodists preferred "prayer healing" to the services of a physician, and
there is a considerable oral tradition about those who died
"because they refused a doctor . . . had people prayin' over
'em instead." Now any person who knowingly refuses the services of a physician in favor of healing by prayer is ridiculed
by most of the community.

There are, nevertheless, some people who say that certain
ministers are supernaturally endowed with healing powers,
and still others who believe that "gifted" individuals are
"healers" even though they are not "servants of the Lord."

Two Holiness men, for example, spoke in an interview of the "blood-stopping" powers of two "un-Christian" individuals as "witchcraft." These men believe in the healing power of prayer, and they believe that supernaturally endowed preachers can heal because "they live closter to God and know his ways better'n us common people." They also believe that the two "blood-stoppers" are effective, but condemn their ability as coming from the devil rather than from God. Neither of these men has any qualms about going to a doctor: "God said he'd send gifts down from above . . . and, son, them doctors and preachers and medicine, them are gifts from God." A few people believe in the healing power of a regionally well-known radio evangelist, citing as proof testimonials offered by him. Some of these "religious radicals," as they are called, recently drove to Largetown to see for themselves the powers of the "healer," and upon their return became very angry at some Plainville men who ridiculed what they reported.

No statement of Plainville religion is complete without mention of the importance assigned to the last rites for every citizen. News of a death spreads quickly to friends and relatives, and sets in motion a complex of activities which most people consider absolutely necessary: kinship bonds are tightened and relatives rally from far and wide; friends hasten to express condolence, provide food, and in other ways pay their respects. Relatives and close friends sometimes visit the "undertakin' parlor" to view the corpse, particularly if the deceased is an ex-Plainviller "brought home" for burial. The dead person is the center of community attention—for some, it is the only time that so much interest is directed their way. In fact, it can be said that a Plainviller's prestige invariably improves after death because most of the talk about him stresses positive rather than negative qualities. "If people here don't know nothin' good about a feller when he dies, they'll make somethin' up."

Families expect to give their deceased a "nice burial," which means nowadays that the body is embalmed [10] and, after appropriate religious ritual, interred in a "good coffin." Most Plainville families spend from four hundred to six hundred dollars for these "necessities," a debt that some must take years to pay.

The focal point of the activity set in motion by death is the funeral, normally held in the church attended by the deceased or his family. Friends and relatives are expected to attend, and the family, and perhaps a few close friends, are expected to demonstrate their affection for the deceased by a proper display of emotion. Relatives who do not do this may be criticized, but at the same time, "they shouldn't overdo it like folks use to." In this respect, funerals are less emotional occasions nowadays than they formerly were, when, as many people remember, they sometimes lasted for three or four hours. "Then . . . people carried on a lot more than they do now." In fact, some ministers were known to "practically turn funerals into revivals . . . even use the casket for a mourner's bench." An elderly Holiness woman in an interview voiced approval of this practice and said that she has given her minister permission to use her casket for this purpose "if he thinks it would save my kids [by getting them into the church]." Without identifying the lady, I asked several people about this custom, and all of them reacted similarly: "She's crazy!" "That ain't been done fer years." "Some of the Holiness and Baptists use to do things like that . . . but even they don't do it no more." "It would be highly irregular and downright embarrassin'."

Several factors determine the success of a funeral. The minister, for example, should not "break up" (cry) while delivering the sermon. Furthermore, his words are always balanced against personal knowledge of the deceased "to see if he done a good job." The major criterion of success, however, is the size of the audience, and no funeral rates higher than one which people remember thus: "Why, there was so many people there they couldn't all get in the church." It is, in fact, "respectful" to attend death rites, "even when you consider it a 'duty'," and this is the only religious service which some people ever attend. Others, however, admit they go "more outa curiosity than anything else" or "maybe to see how the family carries on." One factor more apparent in recent years, certainly a reflection of better times, is the prominent display of flowers sent by relatives and friends. A funeral with a large number of floral arrangements is invariably considered a big success.

The climax of the ritual comes when the entire congregation files by the casket to view the deceased for the last time. The strong feeling of Plainvillers about this privilege undoubtedly explains their opposition to closed-casket services and may be one of several related factors in their opposition to cremation. It probably also helps to explain the strong desire of most families to bring "home" their "kin" for burial.

Once the body has been viewed by the congregation and the members of the family have paid their last "respects" in private, the casket is taken to the cemetery. Only relatives and very close friends make this trip. The family's final "duty" comes later, when a tombstone is erected to mark the Plainviller's final resting place. As West observes (1945:205), tombstones vary in size and quality as one proceeds up the social scale. The family that does not mark a grave with some kind of monument is severely criticized.

Most obituaries appear right away in the *Beacon*. In addition, many families place small "remembrance" ads in the paper on each succeeding anniversary of the death. These are sometimes poetry, traditional or written by some relative. The content invariably reaffirms the family's love for the deceased. Occasionally circumstances surrounding the death of the person are included, particularly if these were considered "tragic." Plainvillers are not likely to forget too quickly those who die under tragic, unusual, or violent circumstances.[11]

6 Status Rank in Plainville

JAMES WEST chose Plainville as a community for research with the assumption that it had "no recognized 'aristocracy' or other well-defined 'social classes' " (West, 1945:viii). The first residents he met told him: "We're all just one plain old class of common average working people here. You don't find no very rich people here, and no very poor people, like you find lots of places" (West, 1945:viii). It took only a short while, however, for West to realize he was "dealing with a discrimination system of enormous complexity" (West, 1945:xii). He was advised that he should talk, visit, and be seen with certain people in order to gain the most respect from the community. "Judgments of neighbor on neighbor, and all evaluations of individuals, appeared to be repeating patterns of great uniformity, despite the wariness with which they were phrased" (1945:xii). West accordingly set out to determine if "this system of discrimination took a form which should be described under the label of rigid social classes" (1945:xii).

He found that Plainvillers' persistence in denying the existence of "class" complicated his gathering of data: "Due to the society's muting of the concept of class, and also to the peculiar styles followed in local humor and gossip, comments suggesting class ranking are more frequently made by inference and innuendo than by outright statement" (West, 1945:118). However, he identified a class system in Plainville which he described as

a "superorganization," because it provides for every person living there a master pattern for arranging according to relative rank every other individual, and every family, clique, lodge, club, church, and other organization or association in Plainville society. It provides also a set of patterns for expected behavior according to class, and a way of judging all norms and deviations from these norms in individual behavior (West, 1945:115).

West describes two main classes, upper and lower, each comprising approximately half of the community. Most of the "upper class" were referred to locally as "good, honest, self-respecting, average, everyday working people"; a few were called the "upper crust." The "lower class" was subdivided into three groups: the "good, lower class people," "lower element," and "still lower is a small group of people who are considered almost sub-human; their behavior is not judged by the conventional standards of 'responsible people.' They are often called 'people who live like animals' " (West, 1945:119). West (1945:116) wrote that these labels "are the most frequently repeated terms, among a wealth of synonyms, by which upper-class people classify both themselves and others. The . . . labels were selected and appended, after listening during fifteen months to hundreds of Plainville people discuss, criticize, ridicule, condemn, and approve their neighbors."

He says (1945:118) that no two people control exactly the same facts about any individual in the community, nor do they weigh the facts equally. Furthermore, Plainvillers do not fully agree on the importance of different criteria in evaluating the social status of their friends and neighbors. In his delineation of the Plainville social stratification system, West's most significant contribution is his analysis of the differential perception of the system depending upon the individual's position in it.[1]

I, too, was told by initial informants that I should talk and be seen with "the right people" in order to gain ready acceptance by the community. And I found, just as West had found, that most people steadfastly denied the existence of social classes in Plainville. I also found, however, general agreement that status differences exist, and that these differences are traceable to the assignment of social prestige according to a set of criteria previously defined by West. These criteria are discussed in the following pages, but for the moment let us consider the problem of social class in Plainville.

Three principal techniques are used in this study to determine whether classes exist in the community today (1954–55). These are: (1) analysis of informant statements, particularly to determine if labels are used to identify strata stereotypes; (2) determination of distinctive subcultures, particularly as these might be manifest in differing "styles of life" valued by different status groupings; and (3) analysis of observed social behavior, particularly as this applies to organizational membership and more intimate types of social interaction.

1. Plainvillers do not use labels with sufficient consistency, applied to a specific group of people, to warrant their use for descriptive or classificatory purposes. It is true that the terms "good" or "bad," "better," "honest," "average," and on occasion "lower element" or "high-" or "low-class," are used by some people when speaking of certain families or individuals. However, consistency is not such that particular terms denoting inferior or superior are associated with a specific group.

Particular attention was paid to the term "people who live like animals." I found this term voluntarily used by only one elderly man, who, when pressed to identify specific families in the category, either could not or would not do so. Many people were confronted with the term, and a few did express the opinion that "maybe we use to have people like that." When pressed for identification of criteria for such a group, they normally described an extremely low level of living as evidenced by "filth," "low morals," or being "backwards" in the sense that the people seldom came to town, but preferred to live in isolation. No such families could be identified in 1954–55. It is significant, however, that no Plainvillers objected to the class terminology used by West. When questioned about the terms, most people seem to consider them very general, and do not object to them until there is an attempt to correlate terms with specific families—to draw class lines. Then, informants are very inconsistent.

2. An attempt was made to determine whether different status groupings, correlated with particular "styles of life," might indicate class realities, an approach implicit in much of the data reported by West. Except for some of the Holiness group, most Plainvillers agree upon the components of a desirable "style of life." Their general acceptance of a particular mode of life, though one not obtainable by all, contrasts sharply to the situation reported by West when there were two distinctive ways of life.[2] At that time, there were some who valued a subsistence-type livelihood and who identified mostly with hill residence, and there were others who valued a more "modern" style of life identified mainly with prairie residence. In view of this, subcultures probably existed in 1939, and if these can be termed "classes" then classes also existed. Since then, however, largely through diminishing isolation and changing economic conditions, "style of life" values have been leveled. We found that social status is derived not from the acceptance of one value system as opposed to another, but rather from the possession of commonly desired symbols indicative of economic achievement. This is, in fact, the greatest change in the Plainville prestige system since the original study, a point which will be developed more fully in the pages to follow.

3. West (1945:133) reported that nearly every friendship clique, lodge, club, church, and other organization could be ranked according to its position within the social stratification system. We found that this is still partly true. Intimate social relationships, for example, are mostly, but not entirely, restricted to those between individuals or families of similar prestige, and the Bridge Club is definitely restricted to higher-status women. Farm organizations, on the other hand, draw their membership mostly from higher-status families, but not exclusively so. The same applies to P.T.A., the Commercial Club, Masonic Order, Eastern Star, and Royal Neighbors. The two major political parties include people from all status positions, and the two "rural" community gatherings include

people from a wide status range. Churches are ranked according to the general status composition of their members,[3] but identification with a church does not automatically relegate one to a specific prestige level. There are other variables, such as "emotionalism" and level of living, which intervene. The basic problem involved in determining class on the basis of associations in Plainville is whether separation along the lines of interaction is relatively permanent, and whether persons interacting in the various organizations, cliques, and the like, are really behaving as social classes. Plainvillers say that they visit and associate with those whom they like, those with whom they have "the most in common." The facts do not entirely support their claim.

In view of the preceding facts, I believe that a hierarchy of social classes with appropriate divisions and labels did not exist in the minds of the people of Plainville in 1954–55. Rather, they ranked people along a status continuum of imperceptible gradation between two extremes. The two extremes are identifiable as small groups of people on either end of the continuum: those families and individuals assigned high status according to the criteria to be discussed shortly, and those families and individuals assigned low status according to these criteria. In between the two extremes lies the bulk of Plainville's families, any one of which is assigned to a prestige position on the basis of high or low status in the criteria considered important for ranking. It is possible to subdivide the community in many ways on the basis of a single criterion of status, and the validity of doing so for heuristic purposes is recognized. I believe, however, that such divisions are a frame of reference imposed on the community, constructs, and do not indicate real categories.[4] This brings us to the concept of status rank.

THE CONCEPT OF STATUS RANK

All societies classify their component members according to the roles they play and according to certain ascribed qualities and personal achievements. Ascribed qualities are those over which the individual has no immediate control, whereas personal achievements depend on individual initiative and capability.[5] The differentiation of a society's members according to these criteria results in a ranking of individuals for a variety of purposes, and according to the interests of the group. For example, different societies may rank individuals according to their social prestige, ceremonial position, physical strength, or in a number of other ways.

The ranking system that is analyzed in the following pages is the one based on social prestige. Prestige is that quality "which a person is accorded by others when he *does*, or *is* or *owns* or '*stands for*' or is *associated with* something which is valued" (Cuber and Kenkel, 1954:5).[6] The individual derives social prestige through the mechanism of criteria, ascribed or achieved, which are culturally defined as having social value. The sum of all pertinent personal qualities and attributes and the roles he has played produces his status rank in the social prestige system of the community. This generalized sort of status is also referred to as "social status" (Hoebel, 1949:287).

Once an individual is assigned to a status rank he is expected and permitted to play roles which may in themselves serve as criteria for future ranking. For example, in a specified situation an individual, through the accumulation and proper manipulation of wealth, reaches a high-status putting him in a position to play certain political roles, thereby achieving legitimate power and the prestige associated with this criterion. Thus, the status rank system exhibits a self-influencing quality in that the position which the individual occupies influences his future status rank. This is one of the major differences between "status rank" and "class rank." The latter is characterized by a degree of rigidity not found in the former —"class" refers to a group, "status rank" to individuals. "Class" connotes definite strata, ranked by the society as superior or inferior, the members of which conform to a particular way of life and, most importantly, are aware that their group is distinctive. "Status rank," for our purposes, refers to the individual's *relative* position in the Plainville prestige system.

The concept of status rank is used in this study to analyze the processes of change that have occurred in the culturally determined criteria for the establishment of differential social ranking in Plainville. The status rank system of this community, as described by West (1945:116–28),[7] was characterized by six criteria: residence, lineage, technology, wealth, morals, and "manners" (style of life). With modifications, to be discussed later, some of these criteria are still important in the assignment of social status by most Plainvillers. The latter derive social prestige on the basis of roles they perform, behavior in accordance with certain values, and personal qualities, according to each of the ranking criteria. The social prestige derived from various combinations of the criteria causes individuals and families to be assigned to a positional rank, or social status, relative to other individuals in the community. People occupying different social statuses conform to certain expected behavior patterns depending upon their relative positions in the system of status rank, and these in turn have a prestige value.

For example, higher-status Plainville families are identified by farming and business achievement as indicated by the accumulation of property. These families and individuals have reputations for being ambitious and industrious. Their farms are larger and more mechanized, their homes are more modern, and most often they are beef or dairy specialists. They comprise most of the membership, and contribute all of the leaders, in agricultural and social organizations, and are expected to take the lead in community affairs and religious duties, as, in fact, they do. They attach the highest value to education and take the greatest interest in the local school. Most of them belong to the Christian, Methodist, and Baptist churches, and they ridicule the "emotional" goings-on of the Holiness and certain factions of the Methodist and Baptist. Their church attendance is not necessarily regular, but they are seldom criticized for this. High-status families devote more time to expensive leisure pursuits, such as annual vacations, they buy more expensive sporting equipment, and they make more trips to the city. The most obvious of all status differences, however, are the possessions of farm and home which connote superior economic position: impressive houses, cars, clothing, and farm machinery.

The least respected families, those occupying the lower-status positions in the community, are those who are least energetic and least successful. It is obvious that they are the ones who have failed to achieve economic success, who have smaller property holdings, who do not have the means for obtaining the symbols associated with the higher-status "style of life." They take little active interest in community, particularly school, affairs and their participation in local organizations is very erratic. Higher-status families make little effort to induce them to participate in such activities. Their visiting tends to be more along familial lines. Moral criteria are more important in assigning prestige to them than to higher-status families. The latter make an effort to conform to certain moral standards, whereas some lower-status people frequently flout moral traditions and criticize higher-status families for being too conscious of "what people think." Higher-status Plainvillers believe that their lower-status neighbors "should" attend church, "should" be industrious, "should" be trying to "better themselves." Lack of industriousness is a particularly frequent criticism of lower-status families, though they may not have the land resources or other means to demonstrate their industriousness.

As we have already indicated, the gradations in Plainville society are most discernible in cliques, membership and leadership in some organizations, and possession of obvious status symbols correlated with economic achievement. Furthermore, from what has been said, one factor, economic achievement, is the most important underlying factor in the assignment of social status in Plainville today. To a lesser extent this was true at the time of the first study.

For example, West's discussion of the criteria considered

important for ranking purposes in 1939 shows an obvious economic thread running through technology, wealth, and "manners" criteria. He does not imply that this is the sole determinant of rank in Plainville, but indicates that moral behavior, lineage, and residence also contribute to social status. Lineage and residence, however, are closely tied to the other criteria in the ascription of status. For example, prairie residence was identified mainly, though not entirely, with modern technology which returned greater farm income spent for a style of life which set prairie families apart from their hill neighbors. Most of the people identified as "prairie" valued highly their use of technology and their over-all style of life. The "hill" people, on the other hand, lived on the "worst" land, attached little importance to "prairie" technology (not suited to their small farms), and supported different values regarding wealth, style of life, and certain moral criteria. Most of them valued highly pioneer virtues that not too many years before were accepted by most of the community: subsistence-level living based on patchwork farms and strong dependence on hunting, fishing, and timbering. Technology, wealth, and style of life, then, contributed to the distinction between "hill" and "prairie" lineages. The salient feature of the Plainville social stratification system, as West describes it, was that economic symbols underlay some of the status determining criteria, and that major importance derived from the values assigned to the status symbols in each respective group, as evidenced mainly by style of life, rather than from the achievement of one set of symbols valued by all the community.

The interrelation of the economic system and the status rank system is not unique to Plainville. Talcott Parsons (1949: 178–80), Robin Williams (1952:92), Bennett and Tumin (1949:472), and Warner (1949:294), among others, agree that in American society wealth and its manipulation contribute importantly to the ascription and achievement of status. Furthermore, many studies emphasize the prestige-determining significance of occupational roles. Concerned specifically with rural America, Paul Landis (1948:269, 275), Arthur Raper (1949:309–32), Carl Taylor (1942:850–52), T. Lynn Smith (1940:332–33), and Useem, Tangent, and Useem (1942: 331–32), to mention only a few, stress the importance of economic factors underlying status rank in farm communities.

In view of the significance accorded economics as a major factor underlying status position in Plainville and elsewhere in rural America, the following guiding hypothesis was formulated: changes in economic methods, organization, and values in Plainville are accompanied by structural changes in the status rank system of the community. My interest in Plainville status ranking, then, is mainly in those changes in the status rank system which have accompanied economic changes in the community, and more importantly in the processes by which these changes have occurred through changes in ranking criteria. I should like to reiterate that the concept of status rank, as employed in this analysis, is not synonymous with "class," and does not connote definite community strata such as class implies.

PLAINVILLE STATUS RANK CRITERIA

Commenting on the criteria for higher or lower status in Plainville, West (1945:118) wrote that "to an observer who patiently listens to Plainville gossip, the criteria of discrimination by which Plainvillers judge and rank each other seem at first to be nearly infinite, because every item of human possession and behavior seems to be involved." He did, however, as already indicated, discover that six basic criteria were most often used, alone or in combination, to differentiate social status in Plainville.

We found that some criteria of social status today (1955) are the same as those reported by West, but that since his analysis some of their meanings have changed. The following discussion examines the structural changes in these status-determining criteria, attempts to verify identification of the criteria as crucial, and illustrates how they function to establish an individual's position in the status rank system.

RESIDENCE

West defined two social classes for Plainville which, at the broadest level, were correlated with geographic residence patterns—most hill people were "lower class" and most prairie people were "upper class." The exceptions were hill families with a "prairie" style of life and people physically located on the prairie who lived like "hillbillies." Village residents were often categorized as being of "hill" or "prairie" ancestry. West says that

many of the "good prairie families" are connected by various links of kinship with many hill families, and since people have no hesitation in "stating their kin," the present arrangement of families in the class structure must have arisen since 1870–90, when the prairie was brought under cultivation (West, 1945:121).

His analysis emphasizes, and my later contact with him substantiates, that "hill" and "prairie" identification was extremely important in 1939. I found few people, however, who refer to this residence dichotomy today. A very small number of elderly, life-long inhabitants of Plainville make the distinction, most often in a historical context, but younger people say that place of residence as such has little bearing on status prestige. Moreover, most people who have recently moved to Plainville are not aware that a residence dichotomy ever existed.

Several factors possibly contribute to the declining importance of residence location as a status determinant. Most people say, for example, that this criterion *was* (during West's time) closely related to subsistence techniques. By 1954–55, however, few individuals, and even fewer families, approximated the subsistence level of the large group of families classified as "hill people" in the first study. Furthermore, since 1939–40 many of the small, subsistence-type farms have been consolidated into larger units—there has been a fifty percent decrease during this period in the number of Woodland

County farms of 100 acres or less. Most of the consolidation of small units came after 1945, that is, during a period of rapid growth in the technology that is now such an integral part of Plainville minimum living standards. The implications are obvious—farming and farm life have changed.

Plainvillers are explicit about the standard of living they now desire, and know that it demands greater cash income. To earn more money the farmer specializes and expands, both activities requiring large cash outlays, a particularly critical problem for the subsistence-level farmer. Two state farm experts told me that Woodland County is now (1955) in its last generation of "marginal" farmers, and by "marginal" they mean those who live at near-subsistence levels. Certainly there is little incentive for hill, or prairie, children to stay on small farms. They are aware of their new wants, and they realize the cash potential of a small unit—they are not content to embark on a life of subsistence living. They, and some of their parents, resolve their dilemma the easiest way they know, by going to the cities or other states to get salaried jobs. Some of the old people sell their small acreages to an expanding neighbor and retire to the village.

Another factor which influenced the economics of "hill life," as it was known in 1939, is the decline of the wood market. Many families who formerly depended on the sale of posts, ties, and fuel for their small cash needs, cannot do so today because there is little demand for these products. As one lower-status bachelor says, "I could cut all the wood this whole town needs iffen I jus' wanta work that hard."

It is significant that those who were called "hill families" in 1939 have since raised their level of living, and even more significant that they value the style of life enjoyed by their more fortunate neighbors, though they do not have the income potential to realize it. The following is from an interview with a very low-status former hill farmer.

Me and my wife done all right lately . . . got us a ice box [a used refrigerator] from one of the kids. Our home been wired and that done a lot. . . . Hell, son, I can 'member when 'lectricity first come in here. I didn't have no use fer it . . . I was young and didn't know no better. Why, I tole my wife them town people was goin' to git sore eyes from them bright lights. Funny how people change, ain't it? We got a 'lectric washin' machine . . . and I can 'member when my wife laughed at 'em. . . . Hell yes, I'd like to have my place fixed up like Bill Schwartz's. A man'd be crazy not to want a setup like his'n.

One important economic condition that forces many elderly Plainvillers into a dependence on cash, thereby eliminating a large segment of would-be subsistence dwellers, many of whom lived in the "hills," is old age assistance. Many "pensioners" have more cash to spend each month than they formerly earned in several months on their small farms. A substantial number of them now live in town where facilities are handier, and the phrase so many Plainvillers use, "they never had it so good," is, in some cases, true.

Just look at old Ezra Duke and his old lady. Why they never had it so good in their whole lives. . . . Use to nothin' but sow belly and beans. . . . Both of 'em on the pension and jus' rollin' in money. . . . I mean for them. . . . They never had nothin' . . . and look how they spend their money . . . foolish as can be. They jus' can't handle that much money. . . . Broke by the fifteenth of ever month.

Another factor which contributes to the declining significance of "hill" and "prairie" identification is that many business owners and a few farm families have moved to Plainville since 1939. These people are not aware of, or more often do not attach significance to, the intimate details of family history available to native Plainvillers, which the latter consider important in evaluating their neighbors. "Hill" and "prairie" are geographic terms to the newcomers and do not have consistent social implications.

People agree that one of the characteristics of the "hill" families reported by West was "clannishness," and that this was correlated with lack of mobility ("Some of them people use to hardly come to town . . . never went to Liberty or Largetown. Just stayed out in the timber"). However, as we have indicated elsewhere, accelerated emigration threatens this kind of family solidarity, and certainly with improved communications there are no longer "rubes" who have never been out of the county.

It is interesting that some Plainvillers use the term "hillbilly" to refer to someone considered "backward" in much the same way as it might be used in the city. Sometimes families are referred to as "living on the prairie" or "back in the hills," but these are more often descriptive phrases signifying geographic location than terms of derision or compliment. Residence cannot be considered a major social status criterion as in 1939, because value differences attached to the two styles of life described by West have been largely erased.

LINEAGE

West (1945:121) had the following to say about lineage as a status-determining criterion:

"Good families" . . . are contrasted with "poor families," . . . or "lower-element," or "no-account," or "trashy" families. So rigid are the restrictions governing courtship, visiting, worship, and so forth, and so firmly set are the patterns of behavior expected from each member of the society according to "what kind of a family he comes from," that lineage can almost be described at present as an absolute criterion.

Our data shows that lineage per se does not always ascribe a person to high or low status. It definitely is not an absolute criterion. This is especially evident in some of the very big, and old, extended families which include within them individuals or nuclear units ranging from very low to very high prestige. Thus, Elzie Ballou's family has high prestige, but his cousin Horace and his family have low status. Plainvillers today, in fact, very often evaluate a person less by his lineage than in terms of achieved criteria. In this community everybody knows everybody else and most contacts are face to face, consequently a particular economic position, set of moral criteria, and style of life come to be identified with a specific family, and as a result higher or lower status is assigned to them. The longer the family lives in Plainville the more their neighbors learn about them, and the more traits are associated with their lineage position. Relative newcomers to the community are judged first by their economic position and style of life, secondly by their moral behavior, and finally by their acceptance of local standards. Education and manners which denote superior social position held outside the community are not easily evaluated by Plainvillers except as these attributes are associated with status symbols, such as automobiles, with which they are familiar.

A *few* higher-status people sometimes attribute inferior mental capabilities to certain long-standing lower-status families, but this is not common for the community as a whole. In fact, children from one or two such families who distinguished themselves in high school are constant reminders of innate mental capability regardless of social background. However, when children from lower-status families get into trouble at school, others are likely to infer that it is a reflection of their "background": "That family has always meant trouble to the schools." The implication, though, is that style of life, not heredity, is to blame. In this respect, some higher-status parents caution their children "not to run with" low-status kids "because they might be a bad influence." These parents are particularly concerned that dating patterns do not involve marked status differentials, but, as noted earlier, "kids around here just grow up knowing who to run with."

Lower-status people have little difficulty accurately assessing the limited life chances available to them in Plainville. They know that changing economic conditions, particularly in agriculture, limit their opportunities for local achievement even more than in the past. They realize that their children, like those from high-status families, must leave Plainville, and they are aware that when they leave they take with them a competitive disadvantage. They do not have, for example, the benefit of parental financial assistance which an upper-status child is likely to have. As one lower-status father bitterly says, "Shore, I turn my kids loose in the city. . . . I ain't got no choice. . . . They git there and they got to scrub jus' like they done here. I cain't help 'em none." This may be one of the explanations for the fact that lower-status emigrants often completely sever connections with Plainville: "Just go away and we never hear from 'em again."

An important factor which contributes to lineage as a status criterion is morals. Since morals are discussed more fully later, they are mentioned here only to further emphasize that lineage as a status criterion is largely defined by achievement and ascription in the other status criteria. Thus, "The Stankey family is a real thievin' bunch," "The Quincys are a fightin' outfit," and "The Wolfs have always been a real religious family." In most cases such characteristics are not actually attributed to heredity, but this is "just the way they always been," because "they don't care" or "they're just not interested in being like most of us."

TECHNOLOGY AND AGRICULTURAL ECONOMICS

Technology, as the term is used here, refers to the varied techniques for making a living, particularly as they apply to agriculture. Within the Plainville agricultural system, as previously discussed, there are alternative patterns for making a living, each characterized by a definite organization of roles and role behavior.

Scientific farming was innovated in Plainville about 1870 when techniques and tools became available for breaking the prairie.

Other sons (and their wives) joined with a second wave of settlement from outside the county and helped to homestead the prairie. These "second settlers" were prairie-seekers, who brought with them the steel-beamed plow (the "plow that broke the plains"), a need for sawn lumber, and the knowledge that men and livestock could live on the prairie, apart from springs, if wells twenty to forty feet deep were dug. The bull-tongued plow, with its affiliated traits of frame houses, wells, and prairie farming, can be taken as a symbol of the first social revolution in the county. In its wake came corn planters, steel cultivators, mowing machines, binders, threshers, and (more recently) tractors and combines—in short the whole evolution of prairie technology and "manners," by which hill life and frontier traits have been devaluated to the point of being considered "comic," and the present class system has been established (West, 1945:208).

West shows that the differential acceptance of modern technology, closely correlated with residence, constituted one of the criteria for status in 1940. "The 'way a man makes a living' is an important item of social discrimination" (West, 1945: 120). He further noted that technical innovations, largely through the impetus of federal farm programs, were being introduced to the community in 1940 at a rate faster than at any prior period in its history.

We discovered that technology is still an important criterion for status assignment, but that it functions in a way considerably different from the way it did when West studied Plainville. He found that many prairie farmers used "modern" practices, whereas others, particularly hill farmers, rejected scientific methods and machinery, rejected "book farming." The acceptance or rejection of methods and equipment then considered modern established the basis for technology as a status determinant. Farmers today say, however, that the "way a man farms" contributes little to his prestige position in the community, that status derives, rather, from the ownership of symbols indicative of his achievement as a farmer. The facts do not fully support their claim, however, because the few men who still use "old-fashioned" technology are ridiculed as "backward" and their status is, accordingly, negative. Our interviews show that Plainvillers have forgotten, or do not take into consideration, that the philosophy of scientific agriculture, mechanization and methods, has been generally accepted by Plainville farmers since 1939–40. In fact, they have become so accustomed to change in agricultural technology that they anticipate it, and innovative agencies caught short with nothing new to offer are criticized.

The acceptance of modern methods and machinery by Plainville farmers has resulted in a new status differentiation, based not so much on acceptance or rejection of modern technology as a pattern of behavior as on a broader criterion of agricultural economics, consumption patterns. For example, the major difference in the mechanization of Plainville farms is in the quantity, size, and expense of equipment, all traits used in judgments of neighbors on neighbors because they represent known economic referents. Thus, a farm family derives greater or lesser prestige through ownership of technological equipment which now becomes an end in itself, a symbol of economic achievement. Those who invest heavily in machinery gain, among other things, considerable prestige satisfaction, whereas those who do not are judged as "backward," "behind the times," and "tight."

The other aspect of technology, modern methods, is also generally accepted by Plainvillers. This does not mean that all farmers follow Extension recommendations down the line, because there are deterrents, already mentioned, such as unpredictability of weather, and always the question of whether the expense justifies the risk or the increased return. Today it is not so important to a farmer's prestige that he accept modern technology, as most of them do, as that he manipulate it to achieve greater cash income to be turned into status symbols such as better homes, appliances, and machinery. Obviously, methods are not the sole determinant of agricultural success, because such variables as size and quality of farm, specialization, the industriousness of the farmer, management, and "luck" are also important.

This brings us to another aspect of technology, and the major basis for status differentiation on technical grounds: the prestige advantage of "big operator" specialists over small-scale farmers. The trend to beef and dairy specialization firmly established these two facets of technology as the best way to earn the most money in agriculture. This advantage, and others, causes high value to be attached to them.

Economic outlay and income potential are the two factors which contribute most to the general prestige of these two specialties. It costs more to set up and operate a beef or dairy farm, but the outlay is balanced by an income potential that far surpasses that of the small, general-type farm. Admittedly, a small number of older general farmers are accorded high status because of their economic achievement (in former years some of them turned this advantage to political power which further raised their status) but they are exceptional cases. Most people agree that those who make the most money, the "ones who are getting bigger" (and "bigness" symbolizes achievement), are beef raisers and dairymen. They are the ones who talk of fifty to sixty thousand dollar layouts, and they and their families have the most money to spend, are the most "progressive" on farm and in home, have better cars, and dress their children the best. Everyone is aware that "general-type" farming, adequate for subsistence-type living, does not satisfy needs for "steady" cash. Thus, the trends are to specialize, mechanize, and get larger farms, and as they are set in motion the agricultural life chances of children born to small farm owners become even poorer than in the past. The very exclusiveness of farm specialization, then, intensified by the selective factors involved in getting a start and becoming a big operator, contribute to greater prestige for these specialties.

Again I should note briefly that there is more prestige derived from being a "beef man" than a "dairyman." Several factors are involved, one of the most important of which focuses on the work requirements in each of the specialties. Many dairymen and general farmers hope someday to "get enough laid by to go into the beef business." They are motivated by a stereotype of beef farming which defines more leisure time for the owner, and more money for less work. Considering the work hours demanded of a dairyman, and the tediousness of general farm chores and pursuits, their attitude has some justification. In short, the successful, full-time beef farmer stands at the pinnacle of economic achievement in Plainville farming, a fact forcibly demonstrated to many by the large number of "small beef men" who were forced out of business during 1953–55 because of the drought. The ones who stayed are stereotyped as the most financially successful men in the community.

WEALTH

West (1945:121) wrote that his question to Plainvillers, "What gives a man his rank among his fellows?" usually received the reply: "The only thing that counts in other people's eyes is, how much money has he got." He found that the average wealth of the prairie family exceeded that of the hill dweller, creating two materially different styles of life—prairie farmers had better homes, more expensive automobiles, more "modern" farm equipment, and better livestock.

Wealth identified with a family is still an important consideration for assignment of status, but of greater importance is the manner in which it is accumulated and manipulated. The significance of wealth as a criterion of social status, then, is that ultimately it is an index of achievement, and it serves as the base for acquiring symbols which contribute to a desirable style of life.

Highest prestige comes from wealth that is earned in Woodland County. The strong value of industriousness, combined with the knowledge that at best it is difficult to distinguish oneself economically in Plainville, leads to strong criticism of "outside" money spent locally, or of local individuals who "inherit" their start in life. There is nothing wrong with parents helping their children—they "should" assist them with a minimum start—but then a child should achieve his economic success through hard work, honesty, and clever management. In former years frugality was also considered an important criterion. Criticism of parental assistance develops only if the assistance is initially too large and continues for too long a period. Similarly, "outsiders" who have moved into the county, and who have bought and developed large acreages of relatively cheap land, are criticized severely because their improvements were made possible by funds derived from "outside." Concomitantly, the Extension agent is criticized for "spending more time" with them than with the "homefolks."

Industriousness, honesty, and frugality were originally the traits considered most important in the accumulation of wealth. We found that industriousness and honesty are still important, but that management definitely supersedes frugality in Plainville economic values. Involved is a split between generations over how best to manipulate wealth. Older people were conservative about debt and their spending habits were frugal. They invested surplus money in land for leasing, loaned to neighbors "at eight percent," or if the quantity was sufficient lived it up in retirement. The younger generation accepts a standard of living which requires greater cash income, and their emphasis is on enjoying life as one lives it, with minimal concern for old age independence, so important to their parents. They readily accept installment buying, because management to them often implies the manipulation of funds which they do not have but, rather, have the potential for obtaining. The older people, most of whom have weathered oppressive droughts and economic depressions, criticize their children's careless spending habits and say that they have never known "true hardships."

Several economically secure older people in the community are remembered as having had high status in the county. Today, however, they are criticized for their frugal ways—ways which formerly were highly valued—because they do not spend their money for the things which young people, especially, agree are desirable. Many older farmers, in fact, spend large sums to improve their farms and to mechanize, and they espouse the values of labor-saving, comfort-giving items "when we can afford them." Interviews with some of these conserva-

tive families show they feel they cannot afford to live in the
style of their neighbors because they still believe that nothing
but land should be bought until it can be paid for. This leads
many of their children to criticize them openly because they
"spend everything they get on land . . . they're land crazy,"
and because they do not "fix up" their homes and "make life
easier and more enjoyable for themselves." Older people are
likely to agree with the style of life which their children wish
for them, and which their children hope to achieve, but they
criticize the way young people manipulate wealth, particularly
installment and credit buying. They have much greater respect for wealth measured in cash and freedom from debt—
younger families measure wealth more as income potential.

One significant change, hitherto mentioned only briefly, is
the motivation underlying the achievement of wealth. We
have indicated that until a few years ago money was accumulated and invested in a frugal way to insure old age "independence"; status largely resulted from the success with which
this was managed. Today, wealth is achieved so that one can
buy status symbols that contribute to a more enjoyable style
of life.

My old man made money all his life . . . and he really socked
it away. Me . . . I can't save money . . . guess I don't really
figger it's to be saved. I can't see savin' everthing till a feller gits
so old he can't enjoy life. . . . I'm goin' to git me a TV soon's
I feel I can afford it . . . then I'll git an indoor toilet.

To reiterate, we found less emphasis on frugality, less reluctance to buy on installment, and less fear of debt. Frugal habits
are ridiculed in favor of spending, and one should enjoy the
present rather than work toward independence in old age.

Finally, the achievement of wealth should be through ethi-
cal means compatible with local values of honesty and fair
play. The attitude prevails, for example, that merchants'
profits should not be too large, that these should, in a sense,
be shared with customers by giving them "good deals." Merchants are aware of this, and some take great precautions not

to risk gossiping criticism by seeming ostentatious. As an example, one family told me they want to buy a new car but they are afraid of criticism should they buy one; another merchant wants to air-condition his home, but is afraid of the criticism he "knows" would result. This points up a value inconsistency which has arisen with the improved economic conditions since 1939–40. There is on the one hand definite prestige in conspicuous consumption manifest by the proliferation of traits considered normal to the style of life in 1954–55, and more especially by new values concerning the disposal of wealth. At the same time, people generally criticize ostentatious behavior, particularly if displayed by merchants. Similar behavior by farmers is more mildly criticized as "poor management," "they dress too fancy," or "they give too much to their kids." Implicit in this differential criticism is the value of economic achievement through farming, also acknowledged by businessmen, as more desirable than by other means, and the belief of most people that farm labor is more difficult than other kinds of work, and thus farmers can legitimately elaborate their consumption patterns.

MORALS

West (1945:122) comments: "As a fifth criterion, 'morals' is given much local lip service. The common moral traits which most people agree in stressing are 'honesty' . . . willingness to do hard work, 'temperance' (regarding alcohol), and performance of all domestic duties." Other "severer" points stressed were "church membership, or 'salvation,' . . . taboos against drinking beer or spirits, dancing, cardplaying, smoking (especially cigarette smoking, and particularly cigarette smoking by women), other uses of tobacco, swearing, obscene talk, ostentation in dress, and so forth" (1945:122). He further says (1945:122) that "within the upper class, morals are a critical criterion only for approval and 'respect,' therefore only for relative rank within the class," but "morals count for more in judging lower-class people. Except for its lowest and smallest group, the lower class is subdivided mainly by the criterion of morality." He found that this criterion was not sufficient to assign one to upper or lower class, and that one's perception of moral criteria depended mainly on his reference group. Some of "the lower class," for example, were allegedly moral because most of them had been "saved," but people from this class had to possess the additional moral trait of willingness to work, and to conform to the accepted moral standards mentioned above, in order to maintain the "respect" of the community.

With two significant exceptions, we found roughly the same "morals" situation as West found. These two changes have to do with the moral criteria "willingness to work" and church membership and participation. In the first instance there is a value shift regarding what constitutes hard work, and in the latter case there is new significance attached to church membership and, more especially, to behavior in church.

During and prior to the initial study, before the advent of diversified labor-saving machinery, a successful farmer worked long and hard, but a definite value was attached to his physical capabilities and his, or his family's, willingness to work. The widespread use of machinery, however, has altered this situation so that now industriousness is defined in other terms (see page 56).

The farmer who achieves economic success with the latest equipment is accorded highest status, whereas the one who refuses to buy labor-saving machinery, particularly if it is thought he can afford it, is ridiculed by his mechanized neighbors. Some older farmers who do not invest heavily in machinery say they have gotten along without it thus far, and besides, as one of them reminded me, "I got more time than anything else . . . and hard work never hurt anybody." Their younger neighbors, however, stress the time- and energy-saving qualities of mechanization, and constantly contrast these with "old-fashioned" methods and equipment, and the long hours required to "just get by," that characterized the preceding generation. The few men in Plainville who are still known for their physical strength are generally stereotyped as "slaves to hard work," and though some say they enjoy working as they do, many more characterize them as foolish. One unusual example highlights this generation conflict. Mr. Carmen, one of the most progressive farmers in the community, owns all the latest equipment, enjoys an enviable style of life, and is considered the most industrious man in Plainville. His younger neighbors, though, criticize him because he will not take it easier—he replies that "this fancy life keeps me busier than ever." In this case, Mr. Carmen follows the "old-fashioned" economic rule of paying cash, but accepts, and conforms to, the style of life values of the younger generation. To pay cash and live as he does requires continued hard work.

Most Plainvillers definitely believe that work hours should be shortened, that people should have more time to enjoy life. Thus, one who buys machinery and still works as hard and long as ever, such as Mr. Carmen, goes beyond the status requirements of industriousness, and is considered "foolish." In short, leisure time is more important than ever to Plainvillers, as evidenced by the large number of television enthusiasts, those who take vacations, and, among men, especially, money spent for sporting equipment, as well as the time and money spent on hunting and fishing expeditions within and without the state.

West (1945:130) says that the churches in Plainville form a social hierarchy, with the Christian highest, followed in order by Methodist, Baptist, and Church of God (Holiness). He further observes that this rank order is reversed by Holiness informants. Prestige based on religious affiliation in Plainville involves a strong correlation between economics and church membership, and at the time of the first study the Holiness group mostly comprised families and individuals from the lower economic categories. We found very much the same situation in 1954–55 except that a few families occupied economic positions in the community that were average and above. However, since their social status was not commensurate an effort was made to determine why. We found that the consumption behavior of the more economically secure of these families was a negative factor in their prestige potential. Their church establishes a value framework which permeates many everyday activities considered secular by other churches. The Holiness members, for example, negatively value most worldly goods; therefore, those who do have the money do not conform to the ideal "style of life" norms because of religious taboos against the use of wealth for such purposes. The following comment from a leading Holiness farmer is quite revealing in this respect:

I farmed most all my life with mules and horses. . . . I didn't buy me a tractor until 1948 . . . and then my boys kept after me till I done it. They kept sayin', "Dad, why don't you make things a little easier for yourself?" I never minded hard work . . . and the Lord don't mind it neither. . . . I've gone most of my life without "soft things." Yep, I bought me a tractor in 1948 and I'm still ashamed some that I done it. . . . Lotsa times I still work my team and leave the tractor be. I'm not shore the Lord meant us to have it so easy . . . them things [list of traits commonly found in homes and on farms] should never come before the Lord.

Of equal or perhaps greater importance is the fact that the Holiness group, like certain Baptist and Methodist families, ranks low in prestige because of its "emotional" type of worship. To some upper status people this has connotations of mental instability—the devout Holiness members interpret it as nearness to God—and they say that "you have to have a church for people like that . . . that kind don't fit in regular churches."

The significance of religion, then, as a criterion for social status, lies mainly in the behavior of the individual in his worshiping and, in the case of the Holiness member, rejection of "worldly values" considered important by the rest of the community. Actual identification and participation with a congregation is more important for lower-status than higher-status families. Most of the latter see to it that some member attends church, and this is generally considered sufficient, whereas nonparticipation and nonmembership among low-status families are often interpreted as "irreligious," and generally condemned.

Plainvillers still criticize drinking, women's smoking, the use of obscenity, and other minor moral matters. That these "vices" are present seems fairly obvious, but fear of gossip drives them, particularly among higher-status people, behind closed doors. This is especially true of drinking. Several women in the community smoke, but those of higher status generally confine their smoking to the home. A few people "buck the churches" on minor moral issues, such as those mentioned here, but for the most part the negative connotations of such behavior are continually strengthened and reinforced in church services and gossip sessions.

"MANNERS" (STYLE OF LIFE)

The criterion of "manners" is the same as that referred to in the social stratification literature as "style of life." West (1945:124) had the following to say about it:

The sixth criterion of class is of enormous complexity, because it involves all the other criteria, renders them meaningful, and in a sense supersedes them. At the same time it governs interclass relationships and is critical in matters of class mobility. This criterion is "manners." The number of traits associated with manners is so nearly infinite that no effort can be made to describe them all. All relate in some way to the fundamental division of the society into two main "ways of life": the older, more isolated, and more self-subsistent hill life, and the newer, more up-to-date life on the prairie. . . . People on the prairie have better and more modern cars, improvements, farming implements, livestock, furniture, clothing, etc., than the hill people have, but such things represent not only the greater productivity, or wealth, of the prairie; they represent also the habits and tastes of prairie people, and their "feelings" of what it is appropriate for their class to possess, use, and display, in their increasing efforts to do things as they are done in better farming regions outside.

The significance of this criterion in 1939 lay more in the values which people assigned to a style of life, than in the style of life itself. West says that the hill people's way of life, for example, was attributed, according to local thinking, to ignorance on their part, and to the fact that they "like to live" the way they live.

We found that style of life is just as important, maybe even more so, as a status criterion than it was in 1939. Its importance, however, derives not from two separate and distinct ways of life, each valued by a group of people, but more from a leveling of values regarding desirable and adequate living standards. This leveling has accompanied, and is at the same time the result of, general acceptance of a great proliferation of labor-saving and comfort-giving traits (see Chapters II and III). The acceptance of these is so general that the differential values attached to the two ways of life in 1939 have dissolved. Instead, prestige derives from the quality, quantity, kind, and expense of traits that are identified as the level of living of each Plainville family. The obvious exception to this predominantly material style of life, as already indicated, is the Holiness group.

The all-inclusiveness of style of life is manifest in a set of moral attributes assigned to most families, and invariably mentioned when a Plainviller "adds up everything" he "knows" about someone. These moral criteria include those previously discussed, and also the amount of, and value accorded, education in a particular family. The latter trait is, in fact, becoming more significant as many younger parents become concerned that their children should have an opportunity to attend college, or at least an advanced trade school. "They got to anymore to make something of themselves."

One interesting style of life feature, identified mainly with higher-status families, which points up the new interest in leisure, is vacations. Taking a trip just for the sake of going somewhere, perhaps to hunt, fish, or sightsee, and not offering as the major reason a visit to relatives, is a privilege which only high-status families enjoy. Many lower-status people consider such trips conspicuous consumption.

MOBILITY

This feature of Plainville status rank deserves brief mention. West (1945:135) observed the following regarding social mobility:

Practically, the two main classes are rigidly exclusive systems into which people are born. Movement across the line separating the upper class from the lower class is virtually impossible, without leaving the community. It is not easy even by way of migration, because local manners, training, viewpoints, and the initial contacts of migrating Plainvillers with the outside world are pretty apt to place them in a first job or social setting from which no very great "rise" is likely.

However, "one of the proudest points in the Plainville credo is the point that 'Anybody can rise. Any feller can git just about where he wants to be if he's got the grit and determination' " (West, 1945:134). When West made his study, "among people still living, or recently living, in and near Plainville, only three real shifts in class status [had] occurred" (1945:137). Two of these were upward, from extremely low to high positions, and the other represented a descent from very high to very low status. No such outstanding examples of social mobility are known to have occurred since 1939–40.[8]

Despite the lack of extreme status shifts, social mobility is a common process in the Plainville status rank system. The minimum-maximum limits possible without emigration, however, and the conditions under which these occur, are problems for further investigation. The three cases described by West show that it is possible to rise or descend through the complete status continuum, but such radical shifts are obvious exceptions. This does not mean, though, that Plainvillers are not concerned with mobility, because most of them are. One factor constantly appears in our interviews to support this hypothesis—people invariably rank a person by first contrasting his present position against that of his family: "what he comes from." And, when viewed in this manner, there are many who have risen in status, and a lesser number who have descended. Furthermore, Plainvillers exemplify mobility in their society by commonly contrasting different time segments within the lives of specific individuals.

Plainvillers evaluate social mobility more in terms of economic achievement than through acceptance by, or association with, a particular group of people, set of associations, or cliques. This emphasis on achievement, of course, contrasts sharply with the former emphasis on ascribed criteria, and results mainly from the leveling of value differences previously mentioned.

Opportunities for improving one's status through economic achievement are locally limited to farming and shopkeeping. Thus, the life chances of children from lower-status families, already traditionally circumscribed, particularly in agriculture, are more limited than ever. This condition accompanies the shift from subsistence to cash farming, and trends toward specialization, mechanization, and larger farm units. Farmers, for example, now estimate about $50,000 as the amount necessary to buy and outfit a farm "the way a feller would want it." This is a vastly different situation from that which existed in 1939–40, when, as West (1945:23) observed, a man could " 'start up good' on $1,000," and is a deterrent to one with no alternative but to start at the bottom and work his way up the agricultural ladder. Furthermore, a person without money, particularly if he does not come from a business background, who goes into business in Plainville has a difficult time. To take only one example, everyone knows that Bill Kendall, a low-status business owner, constantly verges on "going broke." He is referred to as a "pitiful" example of someone with no financial backing and no business acumen. People attribute what meager business he has to those who feel sorry for him—still, few high-status families buy from him.

It is possible to alter one's financial position locally within limits, but opportunities to rise high via the achievement ladder are extremely limited unless a person has adequate "money behind him." In addition, the economic changes already discussed, particularly larger, more specialized farms and changed shopping patterns, further restrict local opportunity. The logical result is emigration in all status levels, draining off a potentially large unemployed laboring group which might otherwise result in a clearly defined class grouping.

7 Summary and Conclusions

OSCAR LEWIS (1953:466–72) distinguishes four types of restudies:

(1) Those restudies in which a second or third investigator goes to a community with the express design of reevaluating the work of his predecessor; (2) those in which the same or an independent investigator goes to a community studied earlier, to study culture change, utilizing the first report as a base line against which to measure and evaluate change; (3) those in which one returns to study some aspect of the culture not studied earlier; and (4) those in which one studies more intensively and perhaps from a new point of view some aspect of the culture studied earlier.

Plainville Fifteen Years Later falls into the second category. It does not supplant the original study. Rather, it is built upon the earlier work, and brings up to date the record of culture change in Plainville between 1939–40 and 1954–55.

A restudy in the category of *Plainville Fifteen Years Later,* other considerations held constant, is only as good as the original work. For this reason, a follow-up project must assess the reliability of the base line. This means weighing the findings of the first researcher against the second, taking into consideration such factors as diverse research interests, methodology, theoretical orientation, and, perhaps, personality differences of the researchers as these are known or become known in the field.

COMPARISONS WITH WEST'S FINDINGS

On the whole, the year which I spent in Plainville gave me a new and greater appreciation of West's study. I found his analysis of the community an adequate base line from which to measure and evaluate changes, and further found, on the basis of my own research and checks against his materials, that I can agree with most of the data which he reported. This is, I think, obvious in most of the preceding pages, as are our points of difference.

The over-all view of Plainville presented by West differs considerably from mine. This does not mean that one is right, the other wrong, but rather that the community has changed extensively during the fifteen years separating our visits. West describes a community relatively isolated, resistant to outside influences, and peasant-like in the sense that agriculture was more a way of life and much less a business for profit (Redfield, 1956:27). I found a community not so peasant-like, a community of "farmers," as Eric Wolf (1955:452–71) uses the term, who see land as capital and commodity. They are relatively less isolated, now anticipate change in many facets of culture where it was formerly resisted, and have urban value commitments greater than at any prior period in Plainville's history. The present volume is, in fact, concerned precisely with the forces and processes responsible for such changes.

The major difference between West's report and mine, explained partly by culture changes in the community and partly by differences in theoretical orientation, is our treatment of Plainville's social stratification system. West describes the system by using the concept social class whereas I describe it by using the concept status rank.

West determined the criteria considered important by Plainvillers for prestige differentiation, and our data firmly support these as crucial for 1939 and, in fact, show that with structural and functional changes some of them defined the Plainville prestige system in 1954–55. This has just been discussed in the preceding chapter. The crucial point, of course, is: were the classes which West describes social realities, meaningful social entities for the people involved, or were they heuristic devices for conceptualizing differential rank in the community?

West seems to accept the division of Plainville into two social classes made by his upper-status informants. Furthermore, he saw the classes as clearly crystallized and tightly structured, with boundaries almost *caste-like*. He determined only three examples of mobility (1945:134–39), all representing *extreme* status shifts, a difficult achievement whether the stratification system is conceptually viewed as class or status rank.

I can see that possibly there was a system of dual social classes in 1939, that these may have split unevenly along the hill-prairie residence dichotomy, and in terms of the values involved could have been meaningful subcultural units for Plainvillers. I cannot, however, definitely conclude that there were classes, because I found the hill-prairie residence criterion no longer a basis for prestige, and the value differences formerly attached to these two ways of life largely leveled into a common system. Not only that, but with the current emphasis more on achievement of status and less on ascription, many people have great difficulty retrospectively according these prestige variables the importance they must have had in 1939.

My data does support West regarding extreme status shifts —in fact, I found none occurring between 1940 and 1955 so striking as those he described. I do not, however, believe the status system was so rigidly crystallized as his seemingly narrow conception of mobility indicates. Based on the situation as we found it in 1954–55, and taking into consideration the present-day emphasis on achievement, I believe that in 1939 and before there was movement within limits, not extreme, up and down the prestige continuum by some of the large mass of Plainvillers depicted by West (1945:117, Fig. 3) as falling in the middle range of the status hierarchy. Certainly our data shows considerable mobility of this nature, facilitated mainly through marriage and economic achievement, and in some cases through education.

As I have previously indicated, I am convinced that West's most outstanding contribution to the social stratification literature is his analysis of differential perception of the Plainville prestige system. This analysis (1945:130, Figs. 4–7), in effect, argues against a definitive social class system recognized by *most* Plainvillers, though they do recognize status differences, and points up the significance of reference groups in the differential evaluation of prestige criteria. From my own experience in the community, I consider this by far the most insightful material about the prestige system developed by West. In this respect, I cannot help but wonder if his analysis of Plainville social stratification, particularly mobility, might have been more meaningful if viewed in a status rank conceptual framework rather than that of social class. I am also struck by the possibility that the dual class system reported by West's upper-status informants and what it seems to me his view of mobility may have caused him to accept, was not really a well-defined system but, perhaps, an incipient class structure which, because of the many changes analyzed in this volume, never fully crystallized. Certainly I found no clearly established system of social classes, though Plainvillers are quite aware of status differences, and the hill-prairie dichotomy, the "most visible and obvious criterion of class status" (West, 1945:120) in 1939, is no longer important.

I should like to make one further observation about West's treatment of Plainville social stratification. I cannot agree with his choice of the label "people who live like animals" for those on the absolute bottom of the prestige system. My data does not reveal consistent application of the label; therefore, considering the extreme semantic implications possible from such a descriptive phrase, I believe it a poor choice.

West's analysis of historical change in Plainville is excellent, as is his understanding of the changes in motion in 1939, and the forces underlying them. In view of my particular interest in Plainville, I can easily appreciate his material on all counts; it enabled me generally to make careful comparisons. We do, however, differ on one significant point. He says (1945:221) that the agricultural movement in Plainville in 1939–40 was, among other things, toward "shifting land from soil-depleting

crops to leguminous pasture or hay, and simultaneously shifting cash incomes from crop sales to sales of livestock and poultry and their products." Our data, corroborated by the farm
census reports, show this not to have been the case; rather,
Plainvillers at the time of the original study already depended
on livestock for most of their earned income (see Chapter III,
pp. 46–47).

Some readers will be conscious of differences in dialect between the quotations recorded by West and those recorded by
me. This can, I think, be attributed to two main factors. First,
I use far more local talk of *all* levels than did West. There
are a number of dialects spoken in the Plainville region,
ranging from standard to substandard English, and in my
quotations I deliberately stress the notion of dialect levels.
West obviously was aware of these because they appear in his
quotations (see also West, 1945:xv). He did not, however,
emphasize them as much as I have done. Second, I am convinced that with the decline in isolation there have been
subtle changes in Plainville diction, so that today far fewer
people speak the substandard English dialect that appears
frequently in *Plainville, U.S.A.* On this score, many of those
who spoke standard English in 1939 complain that West
stereotyped the community dialect so that "everyone who
reads that book must believe that we all talk that way." This
criticism, interesting because it reveals their reaction to the
first study, is not completely accurate because it fails to recognize the subtle dialect distinctions which West does make.

CULTURE CHANGE IN PLAINVILLE

The major specific culture changes in Plainville between
1939–40 and 1954–55 have been analyzed in the preceding
chapters. We should now conceptualize, as nearly as possible,
the actual processes by which changes have occurred and, at
the same time, look at some of their broader implications. We
can start by saying that culture change in the community dur-

ing this period is best generalized as the result of the following interrelated conditions: the steady disappearance of geographical and cultural isolation; pressure for change from the larger culture surrounding Plainville, involving at some points actual interference; [1] and the acceptance of new living standards focused on material comfort and increased efficiency. We can generalize further and say that the major culture change process is urbanization,[2] that is, that Plainvillers are entering into relationships drawing them into ever-widening circles of awareness of, participation in, and dependency upon the surrounding urban world. Central in this process are the extension of technology from the greater mass culture [3] to Plainville and the subsequent adjustment of Plainville systems of values to altered conditions. This process is actuated mainly by forces outside the community.

CONJUNCTION OF DIFFERENCES [4]

West (1945:214) says that the 1939–40 generation of Plainville youth had their minds

saturated, as were no previous minds in the community, with the material and social values of the outside world, which reached them daily through talk, trips, movies, radio, newspapers, weekly picture magazines, "comic books," and so forth. . . . Due more to the car and the radio than to all other influences combined, the fifth generation had many new wants and needs, and a growing discontent with the community's poverty in money, resources, opportunity, and entertainment.

It is obvious that this pattern of diminishing geographic and cultural isolation not only continued, but expanded and accelerated to the point that opportunities of young and old for frequent and close contact with the mass culture have been greater since 1939–40 than ever before. In the broadest sense this can be tied to three major influences, all of which have facilitated the conjunction of differences between Plainvillers and the rest of their society.[5] These influences are the reform programs growing out of the "New Deal" era, improvement in local communications systems, and developments associated with the Second World War.

The New Deal programs were innovated during the natural and social catastrophes of the 1930s—a decade inaugurated by economic depression, complicated at midpoint by scorching drought, and climaxed by rumblings of global war—and brought home to Plainvillers, with emphasis, that theirs was a world suddenly grown small and complicated. They, and other "Plainvilles" in America, were caught up in a mass society which was rapidly centralizing administrative authority. Locally, this meant innovative interference by centralized agencies in areas of Plainville life formerly considered autonomous. A great era of social planning was under way as the larger mass society assumed the major share of responsibility for alleviating the crisis. This responsibility, manifest in a national reform program, ultimately filtered down to Plainville through AAA, FHA, Agricultural Extension, Old Age Assistance, ADC, CCC, NYA, Vocational Agriculture, and Social Security—all common household phrases when West left there in 1940. Agencies representing these programs acted as professional advocates, that is, sponsored specific innovations, and for the first time the community felt the full impact of directed culture change.

At about the time the reform program appeared, a cross-country highway was built through the community (1940), and shortly afterwards (1941) the country was plunged into the Second World War. Because of the war some Plainvillers went into military service and others went to the cities to work in defense plants. In the meantime, the new highway funneled a steady stream of outsiders through Plainville, had an immediate effect on the business structure, facilitated the development of new shopping and marketing patterns, and removed the last significant vestige of geographic isolation. The conjunction of these three influences in such a short time made their effects mutually reenforcing and accelerated the tempo of change during the early 1940s.

The government programs, of course, continued in one form or another up to the time I visited the community, and since the close of the Second World War communications between Plainvillers and the surrounding mass society are much improved. This is possible through television, better roads attributable to the state's assumption of construction and maintenance responsibility, and greater use of cars and pickups. Not to be forgotten is the flood of mass media which daily pours into the community from the outside, and which parades before Plainvillers the same ideal living standard, and the same complex of modern technology believed minimal to achieve it, that is paraded before their urban cousins. Most of the mass media originate in the cities and with the central agencies of authority and, because of this, traditionally represent sophisticated, urban points of view.

MEETING NEW NEEDS

A major result of the Plainviller's increased contact with American mass culture is new expectations of what constitutes the desirable in various areas of his life.[6] Among other things, he has developed new standards of adequacy based on models drawn from urban America, that is, cities and more urbanized farm communities. These are mirrored in the dominant pattern of change—a newly defined standard of living involving expectations of material and nonmaterial comfort and efficiency. This pattern, axial in a complex of economic changes, permeates and, in large measure, integrates most of the changes which have occurred in Plainville since 1939–40.

Since the depression of the 1930s many of the specific changes introduced into the Plainville subculture have been designed to raise the level of living a notch closer to what is considered a desirable standard. This has been, for example, a major objective of most of the farm programs. At the practical level the agencies concerned have met the problem with innovations designed ultimately to bring more cash into the community. More specifically, the innovations involve modern technology and specialization as ways to accelerate the long-term shift in emphasis from self-sufficiency to a cash economy.[7] Because of this, quality dairy and beef farms are more important in the total economy, and land use patterns have undergone considerable change—about one third of the available cropland is now in pasture. Acreage planted in traditional crops like corn, wheat, and oats is down about one third, but through extensive acceptance and use of commercial fertilizers, conservation methods, and improved grains, particularly hybrid corn, yields are up. Concomitantly, greater attention is paid to improved pasture programs and more extensive use of soil-building legumes.

Of the two major farm specialties, dairying is the one that currently (1954–55) receives the greatest attention by Plainville farmers, and the one which holds prospects for a great number of related changes. Interest in dairying stems from the knowledge that it can provide a relatively regular and predictable monthly income, an important consideration for those who support their present level of living with newly accepted patterns of installment buying and who, because of this, have bills that are regularly due each month. In this sense the increased scale and economic importance of dairying, and the decreased importance of diversified farming, are the main factors underlying the change to basically male labor in the care and handling of milk. A further explanation of the male role in dairying derives from the underlying cultural assumption as to the normal or desirable, and therefore "just," economic contribution of the male compared to his spouse in the over-all farm enterprise. Men should make most of the family's money. This does not mean, however, that women have completely withdrawn from dairying. Rather, modern mechanized milking is done with optimum efficiency if the family operates as a tightly knit, cooperative unit. Speed is more important in this specialty than in any other phase of Plainville farming, past or present, mostly because large-scale dairying makes monotonous demands of the farm family. There are two milkings at specified times every day of the year, and equipment maintenance following each of these involves a rigid routine. This inflexible schedule, previously unknown in Plainville farming, does, in fact, lead to the rejection of full-time dairying by some farmers. At the same time, the desire of dairymen for relief from such monotony [8] predisposes them to accept technological innovations which cut the time spent handling milk.

Interest groups focused on dairying and beef production, like most other interest groups in the community, have arisen largely through outside stimulus. These newer groups are more impersonal than older organizations, that is, stripped of social implications. They are, however, instrumental in linking Plainvillers to regional and national interest groups, some with such specific goals as influencing prices or farm legislation, others concerned more generally with technical education. Concomitantly, these alliances impose submission to outside authority (see p. 242) for technical innovations and, more specifically, for breed, production, and marketing standards, or, in the case of dairymen, innovations in linked traits involving such intimate matters as personal cleanliness. Acceptance of such authorities as Extension, American Dairy Association, Farm Bureau, Angus Breeders' Association, Farmers Home Administration, or The Red Rose Milk Company is not without its elements of personal conflict, particularly for those who desire to preserve an autonomous way of life. These conflicts are, however, secondary to the greater consideration, and awareness, by Plainvillers that their economic destiny is now tied more closely than ever to the larger mass society.

Many people find, some rather painfully, that the consequences of a shift in emphasis from relative self-sufficiency to a cash economy are indeed great. Some, for example, must leave small farms, generally for the city, and others must abandon diversified farming, because small or diversified farms cannot satisfy a standard of living based on consumption patterns which require a cash economy. This is, in fact, the major explanation for the twelve percent population decline in Plainville between 1940 and 1950 (seventeen percent for the county as a whole during the same period), the thirty-seven percent drop in the number of farms in the county between 1945 and 1954, and the trend toward larger individual land holdings, from an average farm size of 151 acres in 1945 to the 217 acre average in 1954 (see p. 43). The modern Plainville farm family seeks, and needs, additional land to expand beef and dairy farms in order to earn more money, and thus to realize greater advantage from the constantly expanding complex of modern technology which it continually incorporates into its ideal standard of living. Those who cannot make it are increasingly motivated to leave Plainville, further ramifying kin and friendship bonds, each a potential and intimate avenue of communications with the outside. To cite only one corollary social change at this point: weakened solidarity of the Plainville extended kin groups is related, among other causes, to dispersal of kin through outward migration.

Specialization, then, is Plainville's major answer to the need for more money to sustain a more desirable level of living. Certainly through specialization Plainville farmers shared in the economic prosperity of the war and postwar years to a greater extent than could otherwise have been expected. Between 1939 and 1949, for example, the total Woodland County farm income from products sold increased from roughly $665,000 to $2,400,000, and during the same period farmers, who make up seventy-one percent of the county labor force, realized income shifts as shown in the following table.

TABLE XIII. FARMER INCOME LEVELS, WOODLAND COUNTY, *1940–1950* [9]

Income Level	Percent Reporting with Specified Income	
	1940	*1950*
Under $250	22.6	12.3
$ 250 to $ 399	17.4	10.4
400 to 599	19.9	10.0
600 to 999	22.6	10.0
1,000 to 1,499	9.7	16.8
1,500 to 2,499	4.7	18.9
2,500 to 3,999	1.8	9.0
4,000 to 5,999	.5	7.3
6,000 to 9,999	.5	2.6
10,000 and over	.0	2.6

The improved status of Woodland County agriculture contributed to an upturn in the retail business volume of county merchants—from average gross sales of $5,300 per business in 1939 to $27,600 per business in 1949. Another major factor boosting the buying power of Plainvillers during this period was the influx of money into the community through government-sponsored programs. Income from old age assistance, welfare, conservation and other farm programs, and salaries of administrative personnel in local government agencies still accounts for as much as twenty percent of the effective buying power in the community and the county.

Improved economic conditions from all sources during the 1940s resulted in a median income in 1949 of $852 for all farm and nonfarm families in Woodland County. This is more than double the most reasonable estimate possible for ten years earlier, but still less than one third of the $2,619 reported for the nation as a whole in 1949.[10] This disparity, however, did not keep Plainvillers from identifying with the consumption patterns of their more affluent neighbors in the mass society.

Partly because of the new wealth derived from farm specialization and government programs and partly because of greater contact with the mass society, Plainvillers developed expectations of a constantly expanding standard of living. They were so thoroughly aroused that their prewar traditionalism which assumed a fixed standard of living for some, particularly "hill" residents, disappeared. Plainvillers began to look on technology as the way to enlarge economic opportunity and as the way to realize greater material comfort. They did not, however, create their favorable image of technology unassisted. Reform agencies hammered away at it, their own contacts with urban and more successful farm communities contributed to it, and the mass media had always glorified the productive process. In fact, as Plainvillers are increasingly drawn into the mainstream of American mass culture they find no escape from it.

Suddenly, then, the community was caught up in a postwar "revolution of expectations" from which it has never recovered. The people of Plainville, and the rest of America, daily feel the impact of accelerated postwar American advertising, which turns novelties into necessities, and they, and the rest of America, daily sense the productive might of a war-fattened industry, hungry for peacetime consumer markets, which makes yesterday's purchases obsolete today. Little wonder that technology is a dominant concern and that Plainvillers' interest now focuses sharply in technological change.

We find, for example, that living conditions thought ideal in 1939–40 are now considered archaic. We have, in fact, already traced the specific patterns of change which have made this possible. Modern farms and homes are now important to Plainvillers, and they accept, at least in theory, a vast complex of labor-saving and comfort-contributing appliances. They have, in short, developed a highly expansible set of material wants, the greater part of which, significantly, cannot be satisfied locally. This has the effect of linking them with urban communities where their consumption needs, particularly those involving price and quality alternatives, can be met. To illustrate with only one example: the mechanization pattern of Plainville farms alone requires such a great variety of equipment, qualitatively and quantitatively, that it is not economically feasible for any local firm to try to satisfy the farmers' demands for equipment and services. Farmers logically turn to urban communities where they have a choice. In greater or lesser measure the same is true of the appliances found in modern homes, the cars Plainvillers drive, the recreation patterns they find desirable, the clothes they wear, and the foods they eat.

The people of Plainville, then, of necessity have shifted their consumption patterns toward the vast urban market places, with the immediate consequence, of course, of greater local interest in money and finance arrangements, because urban economic relationships are defined and mediated almost solely in these terms. The cost to Plainvillers, however, is more than an economic one. These changes in traditional shopping patterns have created emotional tensions between consumers and businessmen. Such statements as "Plainville is the highest damned place in the state" or "The store owners here are gittin' rich" are common among consumers, and just as common are statements by merchants that "These farmers don't want to pay the goin' price fer anything" or "The people here won't buy what little we do have to sell 'em." Not to be forgotten in this context is a further complicating, and crucial, factor which contributes to these tensions. I refer specifically to the new role of village businessmen as farmers specialize. The farmers, particularly dairymen, sell directly to urban markets, and they and the cattlemen no longer define any symbiotic relationship between themselves, as buyers and sellers, and the village businessmen as intermediaries with outside markets.

TECHNOLOGY AND QUANTITATIVE VARIATION

The widespread acceptance of modern technology by Plainvillers, and its focal position in their culture, demands that we examine more specifically the function of technology in the cultural change process in this community. This immediately poses the question of the incentives which motivate people in this area of their economic behavior (technology). A major consideration in this respect is what Barnett refers to as the desire for change involving quantitative variation. In Barnett's words (1953:167), "Many changes are welcomed because existing mechanisms do not provide enough of something that is valued." Thus people innovate, and also accept changes, because of their desire for something new which "involves more or less people, things, money, space, time, behaviors, ideas, efforts or the qualities of these things" (Barnett, 1953:167). It is our hypothesis that Plainvillers envision technological change as necessary to satisfy certain desires for quantitative variation. We now turn our attention to some of these desires and the influence of technology upon them.

As we have already indicated, a major desire of Plainvillers is more money. The propaganda of government reformers, and their own contacts with the mass society, caused the people of Plainville to enter the 1940s convinced of the need to raise their level of living. This ultimately led to the acceptance of new living standards which stress, among other things, new definitions of personal comfort and consumption patterns mediated only by cash. The desire for more money, then, is an important factor in several changes in the economic behavior of Plainvillers which are ultimately valued for their increment or decrement qualities, and which involve to some extent technological change. To mention only a few such changes: dairymen produce *more* milk through mechanization, the acceptance of modern bookkeeping methods, and scientific breeding and feeding practices; land improved by chemical fertilizers *increases* crop yields; feed costs are *reduced* with improved strains of grains and grasses which resist drought and pestilence; and *better* beef is produced by scientific breeding, feeding, and disease controls.

These are only a few of many changes which involve quantitative variation in the social experience, economic or otherwise, of the people, and which depend to some degree on technology. There are, in fact, many other changes not involving

technology which Plainvillers accept mainly, but not necessarily entirely, because of their desire for more money. Again,
to mention only two of the more important: they accept installment buying to *extend* financial deadlines necessary to
buy equipment and in other ways avail themselves of modern
technology; old age assistance, praised for the economic *security* it affords older people, is criticized less, and more willingly accepted, now than it was in 1939–40. A complete listing
of all such changes would be tedious and is unnecessary. It
is important at the moment only for us to realize that the
desire for added income is strong in Plainville, that this is conditioned by the acceptance of new living standards which, in
themselves, largely depend on technology, and that Plainvillers view the solution to the problem of more money as
lying mainly in technological change.

At this point we can better understand the role of technology in the culture change process by exploring some additional changes, the relationship of these to the Plainvillers'
desire for quantitative variation, and the influence of technology upon these desires. This requires a brief examination
of some of the linkages which concomitantly give meaning to,
and are the product of, a desire for this kind of change. Two
conditions which immediately come to mind are the new
values regarding work and the new significance accorded time.

I have already called attention to the fact that in some technical areas Plainville farmers are "over-mechanized" (see p.
55). One, but not the only, explanation for this is contained
in the present Plainville definition of the farmers' ideal role
—defined less as physical labor and more as owner and manipulator of machines (see p. 56). A major concern of most farmers is, in fact, efficiency, which they define mainly as the speed
and ease of meeting work requirements. Thus, farmers accept
"combine maize" because it is harvested with machines and
not by hand, or a piece of equipment because it is more efficient than another, and so on. Consequently, they are attracted
to technology which conserves time and effort, which in turn

are put to more enjoyable use, such as hunting and fishing, trips to the city for visiting or shopping, watching television, vacationing, or any one of several other patterns of leisure to which they are becoming accustomed. This is true of other Plainvillers. Housewives, for example, desire a great variety of appliances because many of these make the role of mother and wife an easier one. However, whether by housewife, farmer, or businessman, the acceptance of technology designed to reduce time and effort usually increases expense.

Thus, though Plainvillers accept technology to make more money, other values intervene to cause them to accept other innovations, in this case labor- and time-saving machines and appliances, which increase their living costs, for some to dangerously high levels. Part of the explanation, as already stated, lies in the emergence of hedonistic values, but this does not tell the whole story. The extra expense is sometimes so great —for example, when measured against labor and time reductions, as in the case of heavy-duty tractors and other large equipment—that we must look further to explain what seem to be apparent contradictions in the ordering of Plainvillers' desires.

This leads us, then, to the important consideration of the influence of modern technology on the prestige system and the organization of status rank therein. We find that the acceptance of modern technology in the home and on the farm is so general that the differential values attached to the two ways of life, "prairie" versus "hill," in 1939 are no longer present. Thus, prestige does not derive from accepting or rejecting modern technology, as during West's study, but now derives from the quality, quantity, kind, and expense of the technical traits assumed integral to the present standard of living. The make and model of car one drives, the tractor or other equipment one uses, the house and appliances one owns are important criteria when neighbors make prestige judgments about neighbors. These, and other objects, are symbols of one's ability to earn and spend—tangible, quantitative evidence for invidious comparison in evaluating persons with respect to worth. In other words, a major facet of prestige acquisition is a comparatively unsystematized process which we can call conspicuous consumption. Among other things, ownership of technological equipment, which is only one pattern of conspicuous consumption, becomes an end in itself for some, a symbol of achievement to many. This being the case, then, it is our hypothesis that the incentive for many Plainvillers to gratify their desire for quantitative variation is the possibility of raising themselves in the status rank system. Thus, one accepts technology to quantitatively vary comfort, efficiency, conservation (of time, labor, or natural resources), or income, and the quality and quantity of the technology assume symbolic importance for prestige purposes.

SOCIAL CONCOMITANTS OF TECHNOLOGICAL CHANGE

The social concomitants of the rapid acceptance of modern technology are many. In fact, the full adoption of technological changes involves sweeping readjustments in just about every phase of rural life. Our immediate concern is with some of the more important changes which have accompanied the extension of technology into Plainville.

One of the most likely areas of change is, of course, the prestige system. Since we have already discussed in some detail structural changes in specific ranking criteria, there is little need to do so again. It is worthwhile, however, to reiterate that the most obvious over-all effect of technology and related economic changes on the prestige system is to shift the emphasis from ascription to achievement in the assignment of social status, and to point out that this results mainly from the disappearance of value differences applying to technology, style of life, and wealth, three criteria strongly linked by an economic thread. Today there is overwhelming importance assigned to achievement of social status measured mostly in money terms or concomitant symbols, especially the manipulation of money in consumption patterns which support a desirable style of life.

Other considerations, stemming from technology and related economic changes, which bear on the status rank system in Plainville can plausibly enter our discussion at this point. I refer specifically to certain conditions which indicate the possibility of future crystallization of status differences and, perhaps, definite class units. For example, one outgrowth of agricultural specialization and mechanization is bigger farms, with the possibility that the trend will continue. Conceivably, then, land-holdings, in so far as they are an index of achievement and income potential, can become even more important in reckoning prestige than they are now. Furthermore, the importance of conspicuous consumption, which results in constantly accepting new traits as part of the desirable style of life, can lead to a greater awareness of status differences. In other words, the gap in general well-being between those who have sufficient land and technology and those who do not may well widen. One of the major indices of this is the availability of technology symbols. We might better phrase this as an hypothesis: given the social prestige criteria which exists in Plainville, increased wealth, unequally distributed, will result in a proliferation of status symbols; the status symbols, unequally distributed, cause a greater awareness of social differentiation.

Other concomitants of Plainville's rapid acceptance of modern technology are specific changes in economic attitudes. One of the most significant of these is the redefinition of economic relationships between the individual and his fellows, in this case his neighbors and his kin group. This change involves the qualitative, not the quantitative, dimension of individualism.[11] The latter distinguishes the degree of individualism, and can only be measured against its polar opposite, cooperative behavior, which exists whenever a number of individuals work together for a mutual goal, as when a kinship unit secures a food supply shared by all. This kind of cooperative behavior is distinguished from collective effort, which means helping individuals with their own, respective, private work. Collective effort, then, can and often does exist where there is a high degree of individualism. This, in effect, has been true in varying degrees in Plainville throughout much of its history. The fact that it was true in 1939–40 is indicated by West (1945:72–75), who reports economic exchanges between neighbors, that is, "mutual help in harvesting and threshing, in butchering, and sometimes in sawing wood." Furthermore, "men lend ordinary work freely . . . or 'lend a boy' to work for a neighbor. They often 'give' work lasting less than a day." Our own data show that such patterns were present then and that they were more binding between members of the kin group, such as father and son or brothers, than between neighbors.

It is our hypothesis that economic individualism has qualitatively changed, that more work is accomplished individually and less work jointly at present than was formerly the case, and that the major contributing factor is the acceptance of modern technology. The collective activities just mentioned, for example, have all disappeared. The entire harvest complex of threshing crews, preparation of large amounts of food (see West, 1945:73), and other activities disappeared with the introduction of the combine, hay baler, and assorted mechanized traits which permit two or three men to do in a short time what formerly took many men a longer period to accomplish; butchering is now mostly done by two specialists who, with specially constructed facilities, streamline the entire process; sawing wood, as an individual or collective effort, is not important today because of modern heating and cooking appliances and fuels. These changes are obvious, and are the result of accepting technological alternatives in the interests of comfort or time and labor efficiency—kinds of quantitative variation already discussed. It is important at the moment, however, to note that they are accompanied by significant attitude shifts by Plainville farmers. Thus, ideally one should no longer have to depend on kinsmen or neighbors for assistance, nor ideally should one be obligated to extend assistance to them. These new attitudes, then, among other things, make it imperative to Plainville farmers to mechanize, because only through mechanization can they achieve this kind of social independence. Such attitudes, in fact, focus sharply in current beliefs regarding owership of machinery: Plainville farmers believe so strongly that "it's best for every man to own his own equipment" that frequently close relatives who live on adjoining farms duplicate major and expensive machinery (see pp. 57–58) .

These attitudes also appear in a corollary social change, in the broadest sense related to technology, particularly mechanization, which also involves some elements of the Plainvillers' changing conception of economic individualism. For example, "big neighborhoods" are no longer institutionally defined (see pp. 141–44) in terms of country school, store, or church, as they once were. Now, because of technological changes which permit larger farms, new living standards which demand more money and city shopping, improved roads and greater use of automobiles, these service institutions are mostly consolidated at the village level. Thus, people nowadays define their "big neighborhood" mainly in geographic terms.

Of greater significance for our present argument, though, are changes in what West calls, following Plainville usage, "close neighborhoods." These were formerly defined in terms of specific social relationships such as visiting and reciprocal cooperation in minor economic matters, that is, borrowing household items and tools, and exchanging work. However, as stated in Chapter III, improved communications obviate the dependence on neighbors for social relationships like visiting and borrowing. Furthermore, "work swapping," more important for our present consideration, is also waning. Al-

though this is partly explained by the emphasis on individualism, which stresses that one should not be obligated to another,
this explanation is insufficient. We must, therefore, broaden
it by introducing at this point the second major change in
economic attitudes, a greater tendency toward commercialism.
"Commercialism," according to Watson (1952:89), "can be
stated as economic rationalism, a tendency to appraise factors
of economic importance more in terms of conscious, measur-
able, tangible economic goods or appreciable economic advantage, and to appraise them less in terms of non-economic
values." In short, Plainvillers now value work, and time particularly, more in money terms than as the performance of
kinship or friendship obligations. Thus, if a farmer has a great
deal of work to do the ideal solution is to hire someone. "That
way there ain't none of this addin' up to see if everbody is
gittin' his fair share."

Exchange labor, of course, is not the only area of economic
behavior affected by "commercialism." In the broadest sense
such attitudes support the present interest in cash income
farming, and are prominent in emerging values which define
farming more as a business and less as a way of life.

DEPENDENCE UPON EXTERNAL AUTHORITY
AND THE EXPECTATION OF CHANGE

Conjunction of differences and the desire for quantitative
variation do not adequately explain the culture change process
or the nature of changes in the Plainville subculture, nor are
they intended to do so. We must, therefore, turn our attention to two other conditions which have had their impact.
These are (1) a growing dependence upon external authority,
in this case external authority sometimes committed to securing change and providing needed assistance, and (2) growing
expectations of change by the people in certain areas of their
culture. In Plainville these two conditions are intimately
linked.

Under the impact of rapid culture change and accelerated

contact with the mass society, Plainvillers are confronted with many problems too complex to be resolved by customary internal adjustments. This causes them to surrender, sometimes happily, sometimes not, local authority and responsibility in many decision-making processes to sources outside the community. This, in itself, is a major culture change for Plainvillers, perhaps *the* major culture change, and is a logical consequence of their greater involvement with and dependency upon the wider urban world about them. Significantly, however, urbanization as Plainvillers are experiencing it is not the extremely impersonal process which sometimes characterizes contacts between non-western, underdeveloped, rural areas and our own complex western society. Rather, Plainvillers are increasingly drawn into the mainstream of modern urban America, and have been since 1939–40, as much through the efforts of the mass society as through their own initiative. For example, as previously indicated, most scientific farm traits in the community are innovated by federal agencies which act as intermediaries between centers of development and the ultimate application of changes on Plainville farms. The complexity of many of these innovations is obviously such that we could not expect them to be invented locally. The people of Plainville, and similar communities, are fortunate that authority has been established specifically to transmit such complex changes to them.

Local units which represent the centralized authority of the mass society, and are charged with innovative responsibility, such as ASC, Extension, welfare, FHA, conservation, and others, influence to some extent, then, the direction of culture change. Furthermore, educational programs of many of the agencies contribute to the development of certain change expectations by the people. It would be erroneous, however, for us to assume that these expectations are solely the product of such educational effort, because some are partly due to the influence of mass media. To take one example already mentioned, Plainvillers expect a constantly expanding standard of

living which, more than anything else, they define in technological terms. This is partly the result of government programs, which have directed technological changes in their
culture, and partly that of increased contact and involvement,
through mass media and, among other things, new shopping
and marketing patterns, with a mass society which has firmly
established technological materialism as the very heart of its
economic system. Some innovative agencies have, in fact, so
convinced Plainvillers that technology is the solution to their
problems, and so convinced them of the agencies' function in
transmitting new technology to them, that the people particularly expect changes in this area of their behavior. This
whole approach, of course, is indirectly buttressed by mass
media which constantly emphasize the unlimited potential
for technological efficiency and comfort, so crucial in materially dominated modern life, made possible by seemingly endless frontiers of American industrial enterprise.

Unquestionably, Plainvillers associate many technical
changes, particularly in production and conservation, with
one or more branches of the federal farm program. In fact,
some depend on external authority so strongly, and define the
role of certain agencies so rigidly in terms of change, that
representatives of the more energetic programs, such as Extension and conservation, are criticized if they are not constantly advocating something new. This does not mean, of
course, that the people are necessarily receptive to all the innovations, merely that they have come to expect certain kinds
of alternatives from specific sources. This condition is correlated, obviously, with the development of specialized knowledge, particularly in the field of agriculture. However, we
must pursue the problem a little further and refer to a condition mentioned earlier, the trend toward centralization of
authority in the mass society, and the subsequent greater interest and control of the federal government in the institutionalized areas of society. This factor, as much as any other,
helps to explain the Plainvillers' developing dependence upon

external authority as sources of change, as well as the nature of some of the changes which have occurred.

The involvement of government agencies in Plainville life goes much beyond the obvious attempt to improve farm production and soils. To take a few related cases: the Farmers Home Administration not only provides for the economic assistance of needy farmers but also aims directly at educational guidance (see pp. 41–42); parity insures price supports but also introduces production controls; Extension and its affiliated interest groups aim at improving all facets of rural life. If we look beyond the realm of farming we can see other examples of interest and control expressed by the federal (and state) government through several innovative programs combined into one administrative unit, the county welfare office. This can be demonstrated by briefly examining only one program, the most significant one under welfare jurisdiction as to the number of people affected and the social and cultural changes wrought: old age assistance. Through old age assistance society not only assumes the economic burden of indigent people at a given age, freeing younger members of the family from these obligations, a condition which in itself creates changes in the family structure (see pp. 127–30), but in various ways interferes with the behavior of the older people. Thus, those who receive assistance are not free to travel beyond certain limits nor to be gone from home longer than established periods, and they feel compelled to limit gardening activity, and in other ways to refrain from materially contributing to their subsistence, through fear that "pensions" will be reduced or stopped. In these and other ways the arbitrary limits on earned income set by old age assistance and social security programs restrict initiative.

The federal government is not the only source of external authority which influences the process and nature of change in the Plainville subculture. The state government, usually in conjunction with federal agencies, is more active at the county level now than ever before. This authority, for example, is involved in some of the programs already mentioned, particularly Extension and welfare, and in addition assumes most of the cost of maintaining and improving local roads, a burden which the community and county cannot sustain.

Aside from government agencies, there are other external authorities which the people rely on, and which, in various ways, affect the course of culture change. One particular area of social organization, interest groups, is heavily influenced by extra-community forces. Admittedly, many such groups were stimulated into being by government agencies, especially Extension (Extension Association, 4-H clubs, womens' home demonstration clubs, balanced farm groups, etc.), but there are others which are nonpolitical in origin. For example, as already noted, specialization in agriculture was accompanied by interest groups, almost all of which were organized under outside impetus, which in most cases function specifically to control breeding and marketing procedures. Some of these organizations are the Dairy Herd Improvement Association, Angus Breeders' Association, the American Dairy Association, and the State Farmers Association. At a broader level, more and more Plainvillers are taking new interest in such specific goal-oriented groups as the national Farm Bureau.

There are many other examples, some formal and others informal, but all function to shift specific decision-making autonomy out of the hands of Plainvillers, and in so doing integrate them more effectively with larger units of the mass society. The grade A dairyman, for example, conforms to the regulations of the company to whom he sells his milk; local Baptists are split in their own congregation, and with others in the county, as to whether they should affiliate with the national Baptist movement; the state is more insistent than ever that Plainvillers and others in Woodland County obey the game laws: veterans look to county, regional, state, and national organizations to further their cause; modern Plainville mothers depend less on tradition and more on Dr. Spock, the

Better Homes and Gardens Baby Book, and others as guides for rearing their infants; and in 1954 the federal Congress authorized the extension of social security benefits to farmers.

And so it goes—the community of Plainville has opened up more to the socio-economic impact and cultural influences of urban American society since 1939–40 than in all of its previous history. As urban values steadily penetrate the Plainville subculture it is little wonder that the people increasingly depend upon external sources of authority for innovations and assistance. They, and similar rural communities, are caught in a complex web of the mass society which now impinges in some form or another upon most institutionalized areas of their behavior.

West, writing of 1939–40, aptly said: "One fact . . . is very clear: though many Plainville citizens would gladly 'go back to the old days,' there is no way to go back, because Plainville is no longer isolated" (1945:221). It is symptomatic of the rapid social and cultural change in Plainville since then that only a questionable few today would really want to "go back." True, there is considerable nostalgia expressed by certain old-timers, some of whom I am sure expressed the same sentiments possibly more strongly to West than to me, but their number is rapidly declining. They sometimes talk, actually reminisce, of values and a pace of life which by now is strange to their grandchildren, but when West was in Plainville these advocates of a tradition-oriented social, religious, and technological system could command a sizable following. Today their potential listeners are intimately involved in a mass society which deprecates such values, and which does, in fact, encourage, pressure, and cajole them to accelerate the urbanization process. Again, as West graphically wrote of Plainville in 1939–40, "The roots of her tradition are still in the frontier, but the leaves and branches of that tradition have already begun to touch and chafe against the boughs of all other American 'traditions,' rural and urban" (1945:221). Today we can modify his statement to say that the historical roots of Plainville *were* in the frontier culture, but the leaves and boughs of that tradition are being lost (for the present generation at least) in the entanglement of other American traditions, especially those of more modern rural and urban communities.

CONDITIONS AFFECTING ACCEPTANCE OF CHANGE

Plainvillers have not been involved to any great extent with the actual process of innovation. Rather, considerations of change from the viewpoints of the persons involved have to do mainly with acceptance or rejection. We turn our attention now to this particular, but by no means simple, problem, and find that basically there are two conditions which influence Plainvillers to accept or reject innovations. One of these concerns the advocator of the change, when this is known, and the other has to do with qualities of the innovation as perceived by the people when they project it against an already existing background of social experience.

In the first instance it is significant that many of the changes presented to Plainvillers have professional advocates. These range from advertising firms, which design promotional schemes for dissemination in the mass media, to the personal protagonists who represent innovative agencies of the government in face to face contacts with the people. In addition, there are nonprofessional advocates, such as the personal protagonist who emerges in a local organization or, perhaps, the central figure in an informal clique. It is with these personal advocates of change that we are concerned.

It is convenient to distinguish two kinds of changes presented to Plainvillers: optional and nonoptional. These are conditions which, considered alone, can be expected to affect the change process. However, our immediate concern is how the characteristics of advocates influence others to accept or reject these two kinds of innovations. We find, for example, that the acceptance of optional changes is certainly affected by the personality features of the protagonist involved. This is especially manifest in the response to recommended practices innovated by Extension, where success or failure often rests heavily on agent personality. The conditions underlying this have been analyzed earlier (see pp. 39–41). This, however, is not an isolated case. To take a few other examples: some dairy farmers reject the scientific testing program of the Dairy Herd Improvement Association because of the person making the tests; community development projects have rough sledding in the Commercial Club if sponsored by certain men not particularly "liked," perhaps because they are stereotyped as too "aggressive"; or, more personally, Jason Jackson fights realignment of the school district simply because his neighbor favors it.

Another and more important feature which influences the acceptance of optional changes is the nature of the personal relationships which link a potential accepter to an innovator. Again, this is especially manifest in the major optional-change-inducing agency, Extension, where the successful agent, as Plainvillers define him, is one who establishes personal rapport with individual farmers. This may be done by social visiting, by giving certain families individual professional attention, or, perhaps, by engaging in various kinds of activity socially acceptable, if not necessary, for males. The latter may be loafing with gossip groups, "hunting and fishing with the boys," or using any one of a number of other ways to identify with the ingroup. In other words, an advocate's success in securing acceptance of optional changes depends strongly on personal relationships, and these can be defined in many ways. This is true of professional advocates, such as the one mentioned, and applies equally to nonprofessional sponsors. For example, those who make such proposals as community development projects to the Commercial Club, policy changes to the school board, a program to the Extension Association, or, perhaps, a change in the informal rules of the bridge club, first secure acceptance by personal appeal to kinsmen and friends. This kind of "politikin'," in fact, permeates most decision-making in Plainville, whether or not involved with culture change, and is a kind of behavior which most people seem thoroughly to enjoy.

It is important to note that advocates of conservatism, that is, opponents of change, particularly when faced with specific alternatives to the status quo, find appeal through personal relationships, especially those mediated by kinship, friendship, or religious bonds, the most effective way to register opposition. In this regard, the importance of personal relationships in the culture change process derives partly from the fact that the most effective communicative channels in the community are intimately linked to informal friendship cliques. The bases for these, and their significance for change, are mentioned elsewhere (see pp. 135–39).

This brings us automatically to another important characteristic of advocates, particularly nonprofessionals, and that is prestige. As West said in 1939, "for the average farmer a new habit or trait must 'get into the tradition' through acceptance by neighbors before he ceases resenting it enough to try it" (1945:223). With qualification this statement is still true. We should have to say, however, that the number of initial accepters is far greater today than in 1939, and consequently the rate of acceptance is generally faster. Other than this, conditions surrounding acceptance are pretty much the same as then: initial accepters are among the more prominent farmers, those who have emerged superior in the competitive agricultural system and who, because of this, command favorable prestige in the community. They are soon imitated, frequently sought after for advice, and as advocates of change are listened to by those less successful. For example, people went to "old Mahlon" for years because he was the most successful farmer in Plainville. "He could tell you the best there was to know about any kind of farmin' you was interested in . . . he done a little of all." He was, in fact, one of the early "total converts" to scientific farming and New Deal farm programs, and through his prestige led the way for many others. West said of him: "His farm, with its outbuildings, crops, pastures, and livestock, is a model. . . . His corn ordinarily grows a foot taller than corn separated from it by only a line fence; and people can count his wife's egg crates as he delivers them to the produce house" (1945:223). But Mahlon has long since retired, and in many ways is now the major symbol of a passing era—the prominent general farmer. Today, as already indicated, farming is tending to specialization. Thus, "If a feller wants to learn about dairyin', he'd look up Frank Stanton or Carl Lindsey," or if one needs information about cattle raising he would turn to Mack Staples for Herefords or Norvel Ballou for Angus.

Favorable prestige of advocates or, to be technically correct in the present context, initial accepters, speeds acceptance in areas of Plainville life other than farming. For example, those who first acquired television, home freezers, modern bathrooms, and a host of other items now part of the ideal living standard stand high in the status rank system and are the acknowledged "style-setters" of Plainville. These people, often with more and better contact with the mass society, and certainly with more money for buying the items mentioned, are models for imitation; theirs are the homes admired the most; theirs are the consumption patterns eliciting the greatest envy.

The knowledge, however, that they are paradigms, and that their position rests mainly on prestige, makes some of them, under certain conditions, advocates of conservatism. They may willingly assume the role of advocate, or even strive for the distinction of initial accepter in an area of behavior where most of the community appreciates change, such as the technological materialism underlying the standard of living,[12] but be noticeably reluctant to identify overtly with change in other areas. The Blaxton family, for example, is one of those that sets the pace in desirable life style for other Plainvillers, but Mr. and Mrs. Blaxton say it is unthinkable that they might use their prestige to advocate teenage dances for the town youngsters. They are not opposed to dancing—in fact, they sometimes dance when they are away from Plainville —but are convinced that to advocate locally such recreation, defined by some as "sinful," would "ruin us."

In some ways all of the variables just discussed—personality, nature of personal relationships, and prestige of advocates— also apply to the resistance, or lack of it, with which Plainvillers greet nonoptional changes. Most of the latter, of course, are regulatory features of government programs, many of which have professional or nonprofessional sponsors at the local level. Some nonoptional changes are supported by most of the people, but a great number of these, because they do involve regulations and restrictions upon one's behavior, are resented. In this respect it is worth noting that resentment is greatest against those advocates and those changes specifically identified with the minority political party. This region is strongly Republican, and since the New Deal era, at least, Democrats are stigmatized by many as regulatory. Our data, in fact, show that some farmers resent proposed changes, nonoptional and optional, and in the latter case refuse to cooperate, on political grounds. This was particularly true of the early history of full-time Extension in the county. Whether people would have the same reaction to similar programs proposed by the majority party cannot, for the moment, be determined. The Republican party had been in control only two and one-half years at the time of my study and had made few changes in farm policy which were meaningful to the people of Plainville.

We turn our attention now to those qualities and values which people associate with innovations, and which, because of this, affect their receptivity to them. Several considerations immediately come to mind, some already alluded to in other contexts. The more important of these are values related to efficiency, cost, pleasure, and advantage which Plainvillers associate with innovations, and compatibility and meaning of the innovations as perceived by the people against their background of social experience.

Since three of the values mentioned—efficiency, comfort, and advantage—were referred to in our discussion of the desire for quantitative variation, there is little need to elaborate them further. I should like, therefore, to focus attention briefly on cost, especially since money and money values have become so important to Plainvillers since 1939–40. "Cost," as Barnett (1953:316) says, "is a relative judgment . . . a function of an individual's economy of preferences." Thus, a small number of people in Plainville, though they have the money, figure that a full inventory of work-saving, comfort- and prestige-contributing technology is not worth the cost. They, however, are few compared to the great number who psychologically accept a vast array of changes, but cannot translate many of them into action because they cannot afford them. Or, to look at the cost factor in a different light, one individual, when he measures expense against return, may reject an Extension program such as "permanent pasture" or a complete application of fertilizer to bring soil up to maximum potential, but does not consider a heavy mortgage on his farm too much to pay for new equipment, some of which is dysfunctional when measured against cost, upkeep, and needs. In these cases, cost, or "an individual's economy of preferences," is obviously meaningful only when understood in its relationship to other values, such as efficiency, comfort, or some specific kind of advantage, such as prestige. These are the real factors which ultimately influence acceptance or rejection whenever cost is an issue in the assessment of an innovation.

Turning our attention now to compatibility and meaning, we can say that their influence on the acceptance process is obvious. Stated another way, one of the major generalizations which anthropologists make about culture change is that the selection or choice of innovations by a host culture is governed largely by the principle of compatibility (Linton, 1940), and another is that the *sine qua non* for acceptance is the meaning which an innovation has for an accepter. There are, however, important qualifications which, in each instance, should be made. In the case of compatibility, for example, Spicer (1958: 433) cautions that this, and other generalizations, may be questioned when referred to the social structure of contact situations. Though he refers specifically to the "culture change which goes on when two societies with differing cultures come into contact," Spicer's thesis is equally applicable when one is concerned with the socio-cultural integration of a subgroup into the larger mass society. Thus, though Plainvillers tend to resist changes which are not congruent with their basic value system, they do, nevertheless, accept some such changes, and the acceptance of these is understandable when viewed against certain unique features of contact with the larger surrounding society.

To pursue this a bit further, a major thesis of this study is that culture change in this community is, to a great extent, influenced by the deliberate interference of professional advocates who represent innovative agencies sponsored by centralized authority in the mass society. In light of our present concern, then, the social structure of contact involves on the one hand Plainvillers and on the other innovative agencies, some of which manipulate legitimate power to secure acceptance of specific changes. It is this legitimate power differential which, for the purposes immediately at hand, defines the social relationship. This power may be in the form of legal sanctions accompanying nonoptional changes or the distribution of economic rewards to ameliorate resistance to those which are optional. In either case our concern is only with those changes which at first appear incompatible with existing value systems. I say "at first," because such changes, once introduced, tend to have a socializing effect upon the people, perhaps generating a new zone of value. This, in fact, seems to have been the case in Plainville.

We can, perhaps, see this a little better by looking back in Plainville history to the point when people began to experience at first hand the efforts of centralized authority to direct change—for our purposes, the New Deal farm and social reforms of the 1930s. In writing of this period, and of some of the changes that were occurring and the forces behind them, West (1945:216) says that Plainvillers resented, among other things, federal programs which presumed to reward farmers for not farming, distributions of money (especially for relief and old age assistance) which "disregarded local opinions of the morals and past performances of the recipients," and WPA "because 'worthless men' (in native eyes) were hired, and because much of the work was 'made work.' " These and other programs conflicted with Plainville values and were resisted because of this, but innovative agencies, nevertheless, used their legitimate power to introduce them to the people. Such innovations were, in fact, only part of a broad reform program which became the foundation for a vast complex of regulatory and assistance measures that followed, and which, inevitably, linked the people more closely to the mass society. Analysis of some of the more important of these to appear during the period covered in my research, and their impact on Plainville life, has already been made in the preceding pages. For present purposes, therefore, we need only emphasize one important feature which all of them hold in common: they substitute external for internal authority in areas of Plainville life where decision-making responsibility has heretofore been considered autonomous. And this, as we have indicated, represents probably the most significant change in the Plainville subculture —the people not only accept but are dependent on external authority, particularly the federal government, as a directive source of change.

So far as meaning is concerned, we need only mention that it is the identification of an innovation by Plainvillers, not that intended by an innovator, which is important in its acceptance or rejection. To cite only a few specific and obvious examples:

some oppose old age assistance because they identify it as "charity," but there is less initial opposition to social security because of the widespread belief that it represents "earned" retirement; many farmers originally refused, and some decline even today, to cooperate with Extension because of an assumed identification with the Democrats; the permanent pasture program received initial impetus, and subsequent rejection by some, because of an erroneous assumption that grasses were developed which could produce throughout the entire year; and artificial insemination was initially accepted, and later rejected, by some dairy farmers who fallaciously assumed that it would continually improve production.

IMPLICATIONS FOR THE FAMILY FARM TRADITION

The story of Plainville as just presented is not just the story of a small cultural island lost in the vast society we call the United States. There are, in fact, thousands of Plainvilles because millions of Americans still live on small farms and are subject to the same forces of social and cultural change as those we have been discussing.

Plainville, in microcosm, exemplifies many of the changes which have affected rural America since 1939–40, and shows some of the effects of the concern for the family farm tradition in our society translated into action. In broad outline the more important changes in Plainville and the rest of rural America can be stated as follows:[13] social-cultural linkage between rural and urban communities has proceeded at an unprecedented rate; the welfare of the farmer now depends more on state and national farm policy than on the individual efforts of the farm family itself; and there have been revolutionary changes in technology with concomitant social changes.

During the past two decades (1935–55) rural communities have been increasingly drawn into the urban sphere of influence. This results largely from improved communications, better transportation, and, more than anything else, clear-cut urban technological and economic dominance. As MacIver and Page (1949:330) so aptly put it,

The city has the prestige of power and wealth, and specialized knowledge. It holds the key of finance. It is the market to which the ruralite must turn in order to buy and sell and borrow. Its people, habituated to many contacts, have the advantage, when city and country meet, of being more articulate, more expansive, and, superficially at least, more alert.

More than anything else the increased interaction between farm and city has the effect of greatly reducing rural-urban differences. Stated another way, farm families in most sections of America now accept values characteristically urban, and these values, in fact, integrate changes in many facets of rural life.

Concomitant with the urbanization trend in rural America, and with all the newly felt needs, desires, and frustrations which it produces, is the rapid extension of centralized authority, in this case the federal government, as a supportive prop for the family farm tradition. The assumption is that price supports, acreage restrictions, conservation, credit, farm purchase programs, and educational activities can make life on the family farm equitable with that of nonfarmers. The failure of these programs to achieve their goal is a matter of recent history. The consequence of this failure is a matter of current statistics, namely, stepped-up migration of farmers, poorly equipped for urban labor markets, to the cities.

Those who stay on family-size farms are caught up in a technological revolution which, if accepted in its entirety, threatens their very existence. The full adoption of technological changes for modern farms and homes, for example, poses several imperatives: more land, more livestock, increased mechanization, more capital, and greater management skill. Obviously those who find it most difficult to achieve these imperatives are the approximate one and one half million farm families who now live on substandard farms—most Plainvillers are included in this number. For them, it is questionable whether mechanical power can be efficiently adapted to their farms or whether income from their produce can even offset the expense of recommended soil-building chemicals, let alone permit them a standard of living which psychologically they already accept. And there still remains the most important question of all: can they ever compete with more fortunate family farmers and the growing number of industrialized farmers short of outright, full subsidy?

Ours is an economy with an embarrassing agricultural surplus. The latter is tied to a rapidly expanding technology. This technology, though adaptable to the family farm if used successfully and efficiently, demands the imperatives previously mentioned. This in turn renders an archaic farmer, or one limited by land resources, ineffective in his efforts to sustain a desirable level of living on a family-size unit. Viewed in this way it is doubtful that the latter tradition can, or should, survive in American society, regardless of the sentiment attached to it.

We must face the problem squarely: do we intend to sustain, or even increase, the present number of *substandard* family farms through a public subsidy program or should we strive for maximum efficiency through industrialization and concentrated management? [14] The first solution—government controls to preserve some semblance of an autonomous way of life—is completely contrary to the rural values of independence and self-sufficiency. The second course, if successful, involves several major factors: abandoning a fallacious stereotype, deeply rooted in American tradition but inconsistent with social, political, and economic reality; reorientation of farm policy in line with technological advances and national and international needs; and, most important, *extensive and realistic social planning to protect the welfare of the one and one half million families directly involved.* As West (1945: 226) says: "Since there are millions of 'Plainvillers' in America, the problem of Plainville is the problem of America." The challenge seems obvious: planned, orderly change to create the conditions which permit the maximum realization of human potential consistent with the democratic value system.

Notes

1. All place names and personal names have been altered. I have used most place name pseudonyms as they appear in *Plainville, U.S.A.* The only significant exception, the community which West called "Y," I refer to as Liberty. "Today," or "the present," of this book unless otherwise indicated is August, 1954, to August, 1955, when the field work was done.

2. A family farm can be described "as one sufficiently large enough to provide steady employment for family members but not large enough to require a great deal of supplementary labor. In addition, the family provides its own capital and management. Actual physical size would, of course, vary with such characteristics as type of enterprise and degree of mechanization" (Bertrand, 1958:201).

3. *Plainville, U.S.A.* (1945).

4. Oscar Lewis (1953) classifies restudies, and indicates that this is not a particularly popular approach to the analysis of culture change. He lists examples of restudies which have, however, used this approach.

5. See U.S. Department of Agriculture, *Development of Agriculture's Human Resources: A Report on Problems of Low-Income Farmers* (1955:1–2).

6. Walter Goldschmidt (1947:241) says of this image:

This picture is "as American as apple pie." It is hallowed in our poetry, our art, our novels, and our soap opera. It grew out of homesteading and free land, and has in the past been a real and living tradition for a segment of our farm population. To be sure, it was not applicable to much of our rural society, and the area of applicability has long been dwindling. Yet it has its basis in an historic reality; reality which appeals most particularly to that segment of the urban population which . . . remembers an earlier farm life somewhat, if not exactly, like that tradition.

7. See particularly Ackermann and Harris, eds., *Family Farm Policy.*

8. It is interesting that non-Plainvillers frequently express the opposite view: that West presents the community in a sympathetic light.

9. Many Plainvillers believe that books are written only to make money, and that if one writes a book he is bound to make a lot of money.

2: THE SETTING

1. Adapted from the Woodland County Extension Agent's Annual Report for 1954.

2. A factor in the decision of some to drill deep wells is the possibility that existing wells will not supply modern plumbing facilities. One "water witch" reports that so many "town" houses are now "modern" that septic tank lines foul his calculations.

3. Adapted from United States Bureau of the Census, Population, for years indicated.

4. Adapted from United States Bureau of the Census, Vital Statistics, for years indicated.

5. Adapted from United States Bureau of the Census, Population, for years indicated.

6. Adapted from United States Bureau of the Census, Population, for years indicated.

7. An expression which colloquially means a person who has not been out of the county or the immediate region.

8. There is one well-thumbed copy of *Plainville, U.S.A.* in the Plainville Library. The real names of people and places are penciled in the margins opposite pseudonyms used by West. Many conflicting stories, some obviously fictional, explain how the book first got back to the community.

3: THE ECONOMY OF PLAINVILLE

1. West (1945:vii) refers to the community as a "relatively isolated and still 'backward' American farming community."

2. "The average farmer is deceived into feeling that he operates more in the 'money system' than he actually does. Most town people, too—even the most prosperous—are oriented to the patterns of local farm life, and spend no money for much of their subsistence. . . . The majority of farmers raise most of what they eat. Some raise practically everything except flour, sugar, and coffee. Others, more prosperous or less 'saving,' buy many luxuries" (West, 1945:40–41).

3. U.S. Census of Population, Missouri, General Characteris-

tics, 139. The figure is adjusted to $898 for the rural and urban nonfarm families in the county.

4. See West (1945:40–53). *Sales Management,* Vol. 48, No. 8, 1941 Missouri County Data, estimates the "effective buying income" for Woodland County in 1940 at $820,000. This same report indicates that the average buying income per family in 1940 was $434. No median figures are listed. The report shows only one county in the entire state of Missouri below Woodland County in effective buying income.

5. U.S. Census of the Population, Vol. II, Part I, U.S. Summary, p. 64.

6. This was an overt manifestation of official hostility to the Extension program. On other occasions the county court has not appropriated the county's share of the funds necessary to sustain the program at maximum efficiency.

7. The first Extension agent was advised to tell people that he was a Republican. His backers thought this would minimize opposition to Extension.

8. The Farm Census for 1954 shows that ninety-two percent of all Woodland County farmers live on their farms.

9. 1945 was the peak year between 1935 and 1955 for number of farms in Woodland County. The Farm Census for that year reports 1,532 farms in the county, an increase of 146 over the number at the time of West's study in 1940. It is significant, however, that the increase came only in units of appreciably small size, mostly under 100 acres. When these figures were made known to one Plainville man, he sarcastically attributed it to "city" Plainvillers who returned to the farm to escape military service.

10. Adapted from the U.S. Bureau of the Census, Agriculture, for years indicated.

11. The 1945 Farm Census reports 232,222 acres of land in farms, whereas the 1954 Farm Census shows 219,733 acres in farms, a drop of 12,489 acres during the ten year period covered.

12. Adapted from the U.S. Bureau of the Census, Agriculture, for years indicated.

13. Adapted from the U.S. Bureau of the Census, Agriculture, for years indicated. The 1954 farm census does not show income earned from crop sales, but because of severe drought money from this source is assumed to be negligible. The bulk of the 1954 farm income was derived from livestock, dairy, and poultry sales.

14. The first lime used on Plainville farms came from another county. Recently lime was discovered in Woodland County, and is being mined and crushed for local use. A few farmers, however, believe that the local lime, which is dark in color, is not as good as the light-colored lime which they are accustomed to buying. Actually, it is a better fertilizer than that which is shipped into the area.

15. West (1945:223) quotes this "conservative farmer," who is now quite progressive in his methods.

16. Adapted from the U.S. Bureau of the Census, Agriculture, for years indicated. It is believed that the 1954 figure would have been considerably less than the 31.4 percent reported were it not for the current drought.

17. Adapted from the files of the State Agricultural Stabilization Conservation Office, for years indicated.

18. See Evon Z. Vogt, *Modern Homesteaders,* for an excellent discussion of water witching and the function of this ritual in another rural American community. For a more complete discussion of water witching see Vogt and Hyman (1959).

19. The 1954 farm census reports only three farmers irrigating a total of only 105 acres.

20. Some local critics believe that artificial rain making interferes with the "handiwork of God." They say "if God wants man to make rain, He'll give 'im the power."

21. During the fifteen-year period under analysis the number of horses and mules declined from 3,272 in 1939 to only 780 in 1954. One young farmer recently "broke a yoke" of steers to work, but he is considered a real oddity by Plainvillers.

22. U.S. Bureau of the Census, Agriculture, for years indicated.

23. U.S. Bureau of the Census, Agriculture, 1954.

24. This conclusion is based on several case studies. One farmer, for example, used a $1,800 tractor only 216 hours, or twenty-seven eight-hour days, during an entire year; another used a $2,100 machine only 112 hours, or fourteen days, during a year's time. See also Missouri Research Bulletin 383 ("The Labor Required and Its Distribution in Missouri Farm Crop Production, 1944"), and Missouri Research Bulletin 399 ("The Operators' Cost of Producing Some Field Crops in Missouri"), for corroborating data.

25. "Some of the modern machines are nonfunctional. Tractors, for example, can be profitably used on only a few of the prairie farms. . . . Some of these are found on hill farms 'with no more land than a man and a mule could farm'."

26. In 1954 Woodland County farmers reported an expenditure of $151,000 for farm machinery fuel, and an estimated $125,000 for machinery repairs. Case studies show that most mechanized farmers plan to spend between $150 and $300 per year for machinery repairs. The basis for the 1954 repair estimate is the data reported in the 1949 census. Exactly comparable figures are not shown in the 1954 farm census. The $125,000 figure seems reasonable when we consider the equipment increase in the county during the past five years.

27. U.S. Bureau of the Census, Agriculture, for years indicated.

28. A few believe that cooperation might work given the sanction of strong ties, such as kinship. However, even under these conditions it is not preferred.

29. A "specialist" is defined as one who earns more than fifty percent of his livelihood from one source.

30. U.S. Bureau of the Census, Agriculture, for years indicated. Figures prior to 1945 are not comparable.

31. These figures are all derived from the U.S. Bureau of the Census, Agriculture, for years indicated.

32. One of many examples of how, during recent years, the function of government assistance to farmers is misinterpreted at the local level.

33. This dairyman, a grade A producer, has $25,000 invested in farm improvements, land, equipment, and productive livestock. In 1954 his gross income from all sources amounted to $6,180. Total deductible operating expenses were $4,420, leaving $1,760 for living and nondeductible expenses. Of this amount, $1,163 was spent for clothing, insurance, electricity, payments on notes other than farm, and groceries. He finished the year with $597 net, out of which he must proportion savings, recreation, and incidentals. His income is not sufficient for him to pay on the principal of his farm debt; therefore, he will pay only the interest obligation.

34. Extension agent's annual report for 1944. This does not mean that this was the first time any county dairyman followed standardized DHIA testing procedures. The first "big-time" dairyman kept DHIA records as early as 1931.

35. Some mechanical traits are common to both grade A and grade C production. For example, milking machines were used by grade C dairymen before grade A production was innovated. In 1950 there were only eleven grade A units in the entire county, but the census figures show that sixty farmers owned milking machines. In 1954, with only forty grade A units in operation,

the census shows milking machines on 131 farms. I should point out, however, that this particular item is required in grade A production but is optional in grade C.

36. The current (1954–55) price for milk stays at about $3.25 per hundred pounds for grade A, and $2.55 for grade C. These prices are actually below the quoted market prices, but are adjusted to the Plainville area by subtracting forty cents per hundredweight for transportation and American Dairy Association dues, expenses common to most dairymen.

37. One conservative farmer in an adjoining community, who owns a dairy herd of thirty cows, "doesn't even own a milking machine." He has several children and says that he doesn't need machinery to be a dairyman. "It would cost too much money for no more than I'd make."

38. Grade A producers take pride in the speed with which they dispatch milking and cleanup chores. One man with twenty cows takes about fifty minutes. Most try to limit the total operation to one hour. A farmer in an adjoining community, with deluxe barn and equipment, holds the reputation for speed—he claims he can milk twenty-seven cows in thirty-two minutes.

39. The drought emergency stock reduction program was violently opposed by most Plainville farmers. However, they probably received better prices for their stock than they would have if they had had to dump them on the market during the height of the drought.

40. The first full-time Extension agent in Woodland County stayed for only two years. Most Plainvillers remember him as "the best agent we ever had," and some now lament that "we were so antagonistic that we made it rough on him . . . because we didn't know any better at the time." This agent has since earned a reputation as one of the best Extension agents in Missouri. Many Plainvillers follow his success with considerable interest.

41. All figures are from the Extension agent's annual narrative reports.

42. This figure includes both beef and dairy animals.

43. Of this number, 738 reactors were discovered.

44. In 1954 ninety-two Woodland County farm units were recorded in the farm census as "general farms." Of this number sixty were defined as "primarily livestock."

45. An ASC field supervisor told me that the State College of Agriculture advocates "no more than one cow for each ten acres

of land such as that found in Woodland County." This estimate is used as a basis for comparing the 1950 and 1954 farm census tabulations of the number of cattle in the county against available pasture resources. In arriving at the "overstock" estimates the only animals considered were cattle. If allowance were made for horses, mules, and sheep, the estimates would be even higher.

46. The number of cattle, beef and dairy, increased from 17,216 in 1950 to 20,481 in 1954. This increase was partially offset by declines in other livestock categories: during this four-year period the number of horses and mules dropped from 2,277 in 1950 to 780 in 1954, and the number of sheep from 3,883 in 1950 to 3,262 in 1954. These figures are all from the U.S. Bureau of the Census, Agriculture, for years indicated.

47. A few of the "big-operator" cattlemen shipped some of their stock to pastures in the northern part of the state during the critical summer months. Many more contemplate it and talk about it, but do not feel that the need justifies the expense.

48. They estimate around $50,000.

49. Three Plainville business owners and operators are prominent cattlemen. Several others say that this type of farming is the "real" way to live.

50. This does not mean that cattlemen do not have work requirements, or that they do not work. Some of them have the best work reputations in the community. The important difference is that seldom do they have work which has to be done at a given place at a specific time, as does that of dairymen and crop farmers. They can schedule work and can pace their labor at their own discretion.

51. The Extension agent during the early 1940s pushed poultry programs so much that he is remembered by many as the "best woman's agent we ever had."

52. In 1945 the federal farm census for Woodland County showed 172,197 chickens, but by 1954 the number was only 83,955.

53. During 1954–55 the price of eggs paid to farmers often dropped as low as nineteen cents per dozen.

54. Three Plainvillers are particularly identified with this venture: the owner of the feed store and two elderly women.

55. West (1945:22) lists thirty-two business establishments. His listing, however, refers only to specific businesses, whereas the present listing is of service institutions and includes churches. If the four churches are subtracted from the list of service insti-

tutions, then the number, although not the kind, of businesses is the same today as in 1940.

56. One merchant laughingly tells of discouraging "winter loafers" who persisted in keeping him up late, "while they talked and spit at the stove," by letting the fire go out. "And you know them fellers was too lazy to offer and go out fer wood." Another facetiously attributes the present small number of loafers who bother him to "padlocking my candy and cigarette cases. Some of them guys was just takin' what they wanted."

57. Spitting is still a notable male gesture. See West (1945: 100, footnote).

58. West (1945:59) discusses children's changing attitudes toward parents. He says that with the advent of the pension some children vied "with each other to 'keep' the parent whose maintenance may bring in from ten to twenty dollars a month." Very few such cases are known today.

59. This does not imply that all or even the majority of Plainville's elderly citizens live in the "rest home." On the contrary, during 1954-55 no more than twenty "pensioners" at any one time were known to live in this and similar homes in the county.

60. Two of the major reasons given by older people who move to the village when they retire are material conveniences and the desire to be around other old people who are now of the same economic status as themselves.

61. The "rest home" features a living ("visiting") room in which residents receive friends and relatives. Various church groups take refreshments to the "home" on holidays and other people occasionally "drop by for a visit."

62. This man feels he has "earned" his right to retirement. He refuses the pension and castigates many for taking it "because they don't deserve it." Like many others who have retired to town on their savings, he believes that only "pensioners" frequent the "rest home," and for this reason residence there has negative status implications for him.

63. School teachers are not considered in this professional category since their incomes are a matter of public record. Furthermore, Plainvillers evaluate their professional status differently from that of the doctor or the undertaker.

64. The undertaker is the only one in the county, and he receives most of the business in this area. The doctor, an osteopath, has no local competition except that of a chiropractor who lives

in an adjoining county and maintains local office hours three days each week. For dental treatment or the services of an M.D. Plainvillers must go outside the community.

65. *County and City Data Book: A Statistical Abstract Supplement* (1949).

66. In 1954 the sale of cream by all the farmers in Woodland County amounted to only $4,402, while that of whole milk totaled $692,587.

67. West (1945:18) indicates that hostility to the mail-order catalogs was diminishing, and that both farmers and merchants ordered many items which local stores did not stock.

68. Such criticism is apt to be more caustic and direct when expressed to a disinterested third party like myself than when Plainvillers are talking to each other.

69. Elementary teachers are "afraid" to agitate for salary increases because "the school board always lets you know that there are some other women just waiting for an opening."

70. There is one exception: one elementary teacher still teaches in a rural school of five grades. Her salary is $2,250 per year.

71. Salary schedules were secured for Plainville school teachers back to 1913–14. Since the establishment of the high school in 1918 salaries of the secondary teachers have always been substantially higher than those paid to elementary teachers. At times the differential has been as much as 100 percent. The factors accounting for this are varied and complex. Central among them, though, is the attitude of most Plainvillers that elementary teachers do not have to be as "smart," or know as much, to teach "them little kids as the big ones." Certainly elementary teachers have less prestige and are considered less professional than secondary teachers. A pertinent factor here is the fact that most of the latter have degrees whereas the former do not. Furthermore, since the high school's beginning, secondary teachers have generally come from outside the community while elementary teachers are usually "locals."

72. The music-English teacher's salary is considerably below that of other secondary teachers. Several people rationalize this discrepancy by noting that her husband also teaches, and because "they are a package deal," one of them must work for less money. To the Plainviller, this logically should be the wife.

73. This man's public status is definitely that of Baptist minister first, followed by politician, then carpenter. In the past he

also worked as a farmer and as a rural school teacher, but none of these statuses assumed priority over that of minister.

74. All preachers receive varying amounts of food as gifts from individual members of their congregations. Most Plainvillers believe that the Holiness preacher receives more of these than do the other preachers. This, in effect, constitutes an economic supplement to cash. However, Plainvillers agree that this type of support is not as widespread as it was fifteen years ago. Preachers augment their regular income by officiating at funerals and weddings, though they usually are not paid for a funeral. They also have many demands on their time for which they are not compensated, such as visiting the sick and paying normal social calls.

75. Many Plainvillers believe that the examinations are "fixed," that "anything the government has a hand in can be fixed to come out any way they want it to."

76. U.S. Bureau of the Census, Agriculture, for years indicated.

77. U.S. Bureau of the Census, Agriculture, 1954. This figure is calculated from sales of livestock and poultry and their products. It does not include money earned from crops which, because of the drought, was negligible in that year.

78. These data were compiled from records in the county welfare office. They are for the month of June, 1955, considered a typical month by the welfare director.

79. The U.S. Bureau of the Census Report on Housing for 1950 lists the median number of rooms in Woodland County houses as 4.5.

80. U.S. Bureau of the Census, for years indicated.

81. The village of Plainville got electricity from a private utility as early as 1926. It was not, however, until after the Second World War that REA service became available to most of the community's farmers.

82. One firm "controls ninety percent of the business in fuel oil" in the village. Its customer load ranges between eighty and eighty-five. A few families buy from another agency, and a few others heat with other fuels.

83. During the period of research there was no home agent in Woodland County. One was hired near the closing phase of the project.

84. Only three people in the village own milk cows. Many more own chickens.

85. The meat market has been open only two years. Other

grocery stores handle meat bought from commercial firms. Two stores sell only frozen meats.

86. Many men carry separate liability insurance on their sporting equipment.

87. Many out-of-state hunting and fishing trips, however, are confined to male members of the family. For example, several men get together and travel to other states to hunt, occasionally even to fish. There are many good fishing spots in other regions of the state; consequently much of this type of recreational activity occurs not more than a few hours', or even a few minutes', drive from Plainville.

88. The importance of participating in these two recreational activities as a basis for certain types of social acceptance is discussed more fully in the section on cliques, in Chapter IV.

4: SOCIAL ORGANIZATION

1. This was discussed with some of the Plainville school teachers. They believe this is a commendable attitude for parents to assume but comment that "they should be a little more conscientious in seeing to it that their children get in some study at home."

2. Many farm boys learn this skill when they are about eleven or twelve. This, however, does not mean that they will necessarily put in a full day plowing.

3. Many parents are aware that technological innovations have eliminated many of the chores which they had as children. For example, oil and gas heating and cooking stoves eliminate, in many families, traditional "youngster chores" of bringing in wood and carrying out ashes. The mechanization of farms also eliminates, or minimizes, the need for sons to assist fathers in certain farm operations. Town families no longer keep hogs or milk cows, and this cuts down on the chores which town boys perform.

4. Many say that a wife should feel obligated to help her husband under such circumstances, that this is definitely one of her role responsibilities. Nevertheless, women should do such work only in emergencies.

5. Plainvillers consider it perfectly normal for town wives to assist in their husbands' businesses, and in a few cases actually to manage them: "That kinda work is different from the fields."

6. A possible exception to this exists in *some* of the farm fam-

ilies in which stock production is the major source of income. The nature of stock production, either beef or pork, is such that wives quite often do not know the details of market transactions, most of which occur outside the community. Again, this is more common among older-aged families than among those who are younger.

7. Major purchases are those other than incidentals for farm or home, or groceries. A few families report that wives do most of the clothing buying, but many more say that such purchases should be discussed by husband and wife, except, perhaps, in the case of clothes for a very small child.

8. Many older men doubt that their wives ever knew how much money they had in the bank. "Wasn't no use fer 'em to. She had butter and egg money, and she bought our groceries out'n that." The same men say that they themselves assumed all major economic responsibility.

9. See also West (1945:175–78) for a discussion of differential treatment accorded boys and girls.

10. That girls often are not satisfied with this conception of ideal role behavior is revealed in interview statements from several adult women who remember being displeased by restrictions during their girlhood. "I always thought boys could do a lot more than we could when we were little kids." "It use to make me mad when mama and papa would let my brothers do things that us girls couldn't do. . . . Boys had a lot more fun."

11. Many Plainvillers, including several teachers, lament that teenagers are expected to show more interest in the high school athletic program than in their studies.

12. In so far as it is possible to determine, "petting" seldom leads to complete sexual intercourse. Premarital sexual relations occur to some extent, however, because occasionally couples "have to get married." Interestingly enough, most informants agree that there is no particular stigma attached to "shot-gun" weddings, although "people shore like to count up on their fingers and talk." Stigma, however, is evident for mother and child alike if birth occurs outside wedlock.

13. Learning to drive the family automobile is a skill normally achieved during this age. In fact, it is not uncommon for Plainville children to drive on country roads, or even on the highways, before the age at which the state legally sanctions their driving.

14. The obvious attraction which high school holds for some lower-status boys is athletic participation. When one of the star

athletes threatened to quit school in 1954, many people commented on the damage that would result to the basketball team, but few were concerned that the boy should complete graduation requirements or, as one interested man said, "learn something while he puts in his time up there."

15. Some teachers are very opposed to the marriage of high school students. They believe that "these marriages could be slowed down" if school authorities would refuse married "kids" the privilege of playing basketball on the school team. They contend that married students are a bad influence on the "moral" behavior of unmarried students. Few Plainville school children marry and continue with their classes.

16. Some say, "If they haven't left here by then, chances are they'll stay."

17. Halloween is a night when teenage boys are permitted extreme liberties. Plainville parents think it "natural" that they should fill the main street with junk, such as advertising signs, wrecked automobiles, and the like. Outdoor toilets are overturned, some to be deposited on the main street; store windows are smeared with soap; and it is great fun to "trick" the school. In 1954, for example, a dead skunk was put on a school radiator to "stink up the place." On other Halloweens live animals have been put in the school building. Some parents caution their children not to bother the toilets of old people, and to stay away from "some of the real old grouches that might hurt 'em." Enough toilets owned by old people are overturned, however, that several young men get together the day after Halloween to go around and set them upright again.

18. There is friction between this husband and wife over the number of children that they should have. The wife wants "more than one or two," but the husband insists that they have no more.

19. Sexual data are not easy to develop with Plainville informants. For most, the topic is embarrassing if conducted on other than a joking level. See also West (1945:166).

20. Most go to an obstetrician in Largetown who is the son of a former general practitioner in Plainville, and consequently is very popular with Plainville women.

21. Many women prefer to have their children in the doctor's office. In order of importance, the following reasons are given: it is cheaper; it is closer to home.

22. Adapted from U.S. Bureau of the Census, Vital Statistics, for the years indicated.

23. West (1945:172) says that infants slept in bed with parents.

24. West (1945:172) notes that people remember cases of children smothering to death while sleeping in bed with parents "in the old days of cord-bottomed beds. . . ."

25. Plainville mothers never accepted the theory of "strict" feeding schedules. See also West (1945:172).

26. See West (1945:178–79) for a detailed account of disciplinary techniques current at the time of his study.

27. Many high-status parents believe that when children from low-status families get into trouble it is "just their background coming out." Some of them also rationalize the disciplinary difficulties of their own offspring as due to the influence of lower-status children upon them "at school."

28. This was a source of difficulty throughout the research. Certain individuals persisted in creating false roles for me by informing old people that I was a government agent checking on inequities of the old age assistance program. Several old people refused to believe otherwise, and consequently would not associate with me or my wife in any capacity.

29. The vocative kinship terms most often used are: (1) Mama, Mom, or Mother; (2) Papa, Dad, or Daddy; (3) Bud, sometimes used for male sibling; (4) Sis, occasionally used for female sibling; (5) Grandma; (6) Grandpa or Granddad; (7) Uncle or Aunt (plus appropriate first name); grownups do not always preface the personal name with "Aunt" or "Uncle." Cousins are called only by their personal names, never prefaced by "Cousin." The most common non-vocative usages are: (1) "My mother" or "My mom"; (2) "My papa" or "My dad"; (3) "My brother Bill" or sometimes "My bud"; (4) "My sister May" or sometimes "My sis"; (5) "My grandma" (followed by surname to indicate ego's parent's side of family); (6) "My uncle Albert" or "My aunt Martha." Cousins are usually referred to as "Albert [surname], a cousin of mine," or something to that effect. Plainvillers seldom differentiate cousins beyond "first." See West (1945:63) for comparable list of terms.

30. A person not born in Plainville can never be really considered a "native." Some people who have lived there for thirty or forty years say that "natives" still, through inference and innuendo, let them know they are "outsiders."

31. This does not mean that kin-groups are territorial groups, because biologically related individuals are scattered over all the community and the county.

32. Some young couples resent "having" to visit so much with

older relatives. Their resentment is intensified by the fact that there are so few couples among their peers with whom they can establish social contact.

33. Many people say that relatives are the last people to whom they should like to lend money, citing as their reason the problems of collection.

34. One prominent kin-group is the subject of current community criticism because they let neighbors care for an aged member of the family who is frequently ill.

35. Some people speak of their "in-laws" as "out-laws."

36. Nor should children marry "kin," "particularly first and second cousins." However, "families around here are so mixed up some of that is bound to happen."

37. See Loomis and Beegle (1950), especially Chapter 5. Also, see Carleton S. Coon, "The Universality of Natural Groupings in Human Societies," *Journal of Educational Sociology,* XX (No. 3, 1946), 162–68.

38. The primary visiting patterns of more than four hundred individuals were recorded. Various techniques were employed to gather these data. For example, every visit listed in the extensive Plainville column of the weekly Discovery *Beacon* during the period of research, and for two years prior to the research, was recorded and cross-filed. In addition, as visiting patterns emerged from interviews or observations, they were recorded and charted. Accessory data, such as reason for visit, kinship affiliation, and the like, were noted whenever possible. This body of information was extensively checked with certain Plainvillers who, by the end of the study, demonstrated excellent channels of communication throughout the community and who were aware of the complex kinship ties connecting various families.

39. "Outsider" in this context refers to several farmers who moved from drought-stricken areas in states farther west to Woodland County in recent years. Some of them bought large land holdings and made extensive improvements. They are Extension-oriented in their farm practices, and call the agent for considerable assistance.

40. Several old people confronted me with the belief that I was really concerned with the past "scandals" of Plainville. Some of them were never convinced to the contrary.

41. An exception is the group of men who are interested in fox hunting. This sport minimizes status differences among those who participate.

42. The significance of these two activities has been discussed in the section on economics.

43. I was advised constantly that I should hunt and fish to be "one of the boys." In this respect, my rapport with many people improved markedly following a boat mishap during a fishing trip. In effect, they assumed the overt attitude that the mishap constituted an initiation. The significance of such fortuitous happenings to the over-all rapport situation is difficult to ascertain. A Plainville friend, however, with obvious exaggeration, said, "The only way in which you could have endeared yourself more to the community would have been to have drowned when the boat went over . . . then they never would have forgotten you."

44. A few people are proud of their knowledge of communicative channels connecting various cliques. One elderly gentleman, a student of local friendship groups, enjoys fabricating rumors, introducing them to key clique individuals, and then tracing their movement as they are disseminated. He made my research role particularly difficult by deliberately misrepresenting the status I was attempting to establish. This was not done with malicious intent, but merely to "get the community riled." When confronted with the seriousness of the situation, he compromised by "tipping" me ahead of time that he was going to start false rumors of this nature.

45. Village dwellers identify residential sections of the village, customarily in geographical terms, one particular section being called "New Town."

46. In the remote past all of the neighborhoods had a greater number of service institutions than existed when either West or I visited Plainville. Fifty years ago, for example, blacksmith shops, grinding mills, and other businesses were common at crossroads settlements, but over the years these have gradually shifted to the village.

47. Since 1939 the Woodland County farm population has declined more than twenty per cent.

48. The effects of these and similar changes on village businesses have been discussed in other contexts.

49. Some activities associated with schools had dysfunctional implications for neighborhood solidarity. Political factions, for example, sometimes split neighborhoods over such issues as hiring teachers, or expenditures.

50. West (1945:221–22) mentions this as one of the objectives of the local agricultural movement in 1939 and 1940.

51. There are a few Independents, some Socialists left from the earlier Populist movement, and a few Progressives in the county. In the 1952 state elections, however, no Socialist votes were cast in Woodland County in any of the races. Prohibition and Progressive party candidates in various state races received a few votes, but never more than eleven for any single candidate of either party. For all practical purposes, Plainvillers consider there are only two parties, the Republican and the Democratic, and most people simply cannot understand anyone who votes outside these two organizations.

52. These, normally all filled by Republicans, are: presiding judge of the county court, clerk of the circuit court, clerk of the county court, county commissioner (3), recorder of deeds, prosecuting attorney, sheriff, collector of revenue, assessor, treasurer, coroner, county surveyor, superintendent of public schools, and representative to the state legislature.

53. This is particularly true of a smaller number who take great interest in local and county elections, but who are extremely covert in their manipulatory activities. Our information shows that one such "covert leader" is one of the strongest men in the Plainville power structure. He succeeds in masking his behavior so successfully that none but the most discerning are aware of it. He attempts to, and often does, manipulate situations in which he has no possible interest other than the knowledge of what he accomplishes. The motivation toward political activity by grass-roots politicians, such as those found in Plainville, is an area of research which deserves much more careful study and analysis than is possible within the limits of the present project.

54. See, for example, West (1945:88–89) for an excellent discussion of the machinations of a local Plainville politician and his manipulation of cliques.

55. A few people, vitally interested in national and international affairs, are outstanding exceptions. They read the popular news media, particularly *Time* and *Life* magazines, and follow favored radio news commentators. Two such men are especially well informed. Their avid interest in extra-regional affairs and their desire to talk about them lead others to classify them as "odd."

56. Interviews with most of these people show they are convinced that state game and fish laws are engineered by "city people" to protect the game for the enjoyment of the latter.

57. There are some who oppose the older value system, and actually advocate greater control by the government. "Like maybe

guaranteeing us an annual wage . . . like them people in the automobile business are getting." Enough farmers favor government interference in their affairs to make parity votes quite close, and crop restrictions and supports are often approved.

58. Meetings are not a characteristic feature of the interest groups focused on dairying. They are, however, prominent in all other groups with the exception of the State Farmers Association cooperative.

59. West (1945:84) says: "The most stable and active of the new organizations formed under outside stimulus are Home Economics Clubs, to which over ten percent of the eligible women already belong."

60. See West (1945:134): "The only farm women who join the Home Economics clubs are securely of the better class. . . ."

61. West (1945:84–85) makes the same point: "The 4-H clubs . . . are less successful than the Home Economics clubs. The children lose interest in their 'projects'; parents ridicule these as useless, time-wasting, or even immoral. . . . The 4-H clubs disband nearly as rapidly as they are formed."

62. Although theoretically the Extension agent develops his annual program from recommendations tendered him by a special board made up of representatives from each of the county's nine townships, there are no binding rules which state that he must follow the recommendations. The fact that agents do not always follow them is a major criticism made by association members. Agents, on the other hand, sometimes believe that the board's recommendations are not realistic, or not worthy of implementation.

63. See Noel P. Gist's study (1940) in which he postulates certain trends in secret fraternal societies. In some respects, certain of these are confirmed in the present analysis.

64. This was one of several guiding hypotheses derived from West's report on Plainville.

65. A more detailed analysis of these changes is presented in Chapter II.

66. See pp. 82–87 for an analysis of the changes which have contributed to new types of leadership roles in the community.

67. The 1950 federal census shows that Woodland County residents twenty-five years of age and over have completed a median of 8.5 years of school.

68. This number was arrived at by recording all of the graduates from the official school records and then laboriously check-

ing the names with informants to determine current addresses of the ex-Plainvillers. The figure includes those graduates who are deceased, in which case residence at time of death was recorded.

69. The majority of those who leave Plainville maintain some ties with relatives or friends who stay in the community. Considering the large number of migrants, it must be assumed that the communicative channels established between them and Plainvillers are important factors in further diminishing the isolation of the latter.

70. The first vocational agriculture teacher was hired in 1933. He found considerable resistance in the community, but by 1940 the program was well integrated into the school system.

71. A few students are exceptions. Furthermore, some who are now attending college, or who have previously gone to college, can easily point out the deficiencies in the Plainville high school program, and can see the need for greater application in high school studies.

72. I was constantly impressed by community interest in school disciplinary matters. Everyone seems concerned as to how well the superintendent controls the children and, even more, as to whether the superintendent or other teachers *can* control them. In severe disciplinary problems the teacher may resort to "spanking" a child, in which case the parent is just as likely to side with the child as with the teacher. Many people say that "most think it's all right to whip the kids in school just so long as it isn't their own."

73. The board is made up of six men, two of whom are elected each year for three-year terms. Since the recent consolidation movement, a "gentlemen's agreement" exists that two members of the board shall come from the northern end of the district, two from the southern, and two from the central sector. There is some prestige associated with board membership, and prominent men are generally selected from their respective districts. It is also possible, however, to create enemies while serving on the board, and for this reason some people "wouldn't touch it with a ten foot pole." Board members are in a position to exert some influence in the community, and some in the past have played local politics, often to the detriment of the school, to achieve personal ends. This was particularly true for a few years following the Second World War, when the situation became so bad that the community threatened to split into factions. The mach-

inations of a few board members during this period are still prominent gossip topics.

74. Individuals interviewed in other communities also believe that high school consolidation is the most logical solution to their educational problems.

75. Seldom do more than twenty people attend P.T.A. meetings. Some of these are not parents but elderly people who come merely for the program.

5: RELIGION IN PLAINVILLE

1. Probably the first question Plainvillers ask a newcomer has to do with his business or his reason for moving to the community. They are also interested in where he has come from. Plainvillers can be, and usually are, very personal about such matters in their conversation with strangers.

2. West (1945:146) indicates this when he notes that Plainvillers, as late as 1939, still remembered the Christian Church fundraising campaign of the 1920s in the following terms: "People remember that men who solicited building funds said, 'Let's build something that'll make that Methodist Church look like a woodshed!' (Instead of 'woodshed,' some said 'backhouse.') At the same time . . . a Christian bank was financed to compete with the Methodist bank."

3. Membership switches such as this, although not unheard of, have never been common. They usually follow marriage, when one spouse wishes to identify with the church of the other, or occasionally are prompted by the desire to affiliate with a higher-status group. Many people are concerned, and a great many more gossip about, the fact that the school superintendent attends the Christian Church and his wife goes to the Baptist. Their behavior is completely inconsistent with Plainville norms, and causes much questioning of and speculation about their motives.

4. The primary visiting patterns of more than four hundred people were recorded and analyzed.

5. "Emotional" is used here to refer to those people who manifest spontaneous verbal or physically energetic behavior in public religious services. This term, not uncommon in the literature, is used by Plainvillers to identify such people.

6. West was undecided as to whether emotional behavior and "religious hysteria" were increasing or decreasing in 1939. He correlated emotional behavior with low status rank.

7. Revival services in all churches are structured very much like regular church meetings. They differ in greater emphasis on being "saved" through extensive prayer at the mourners' bench. The major exception to this pattern is the Christian Church, which does not have a "bench."

8. Of the twenty-eight additions mentioned in the news release, fourteen were conversions, and of this number nine were children of school age or younger. Their behavior at the mourners' bench was a prominent topic of conversation among nonrevivalists.

9. Teachers expressed concern about the aroused group of Baptist children, but for a different reason. Some teachers confidentially complained to me that the excited Baptist kids could not be expected to concentrate on their school work.

10. West (1945:205) indicates some resistance to embalming in 1939. The practice is universally accepted today, though many people cannot explain why they insist on this service.

11. Shortly after we left the field a mimeographed volume of the "tragedies" of Woodland County by three local authors appeared.

6: STATUS RANK IN PLAINVILLE

1. See *Plainville, U.S.A.*, especially pp. 128–33, where West discusses "Differential Attitudes Toward the Class Structure."

2. See *Plainville, U.S.A.*, especially pp. 116–28, and the diagram of "Plainville Social Classes," p. 117.

3. Liston Pope, "Religion and the Class Structure" (1948:84–91), presents a good discussion of this idea.

4. Milton C. Coughenour (1953), in an excellent analysis of social stratification in a northeast Missouri rural community, arrived at similar conclusions regarding presence or absence of a class structure.

5. See especially Ralph Linton's *Study of Man* (1936) and Kingsley Davis's *Human Society* (1949) for basic discussions of ascribed and achieved statuses.

6. Kingsley Davis, *Human Society*, p. 93, distinguishes between prestige and esteem.

7. West does not use the term "status rank," but rather refers to the criteria for class ranking.

8. One of the cases of mobility mentioned by West is the item which Plainvillers dispute most in his report. The case reported involved the marked rise in status of the mail carrier (West,

1945: 137–38). The fact that he rose in status is not disputed by most, but they criticize West's handling of the facts, saying that he implies that the man deliberately and purposefully renounced his kin-group in order to achieve social status. People close to the facts invariably stress mitigating circumstances which they say forced him out of his kin-group, thereby instituting developments which led to the status shift.

7: SUMMARY AND CONCLUSIONS

1. This is "directed culture change" much as Linton (1940: 502) expresses it: "Interference may take the form of stimulating the acceptance of new culture elements, inhibiting the exercise of pre-existing culture patterns or, as seems to be most frequently the case, doing both simultaneously."

2. Urbanization is used here in much the same way as by Bennet and Tumin (1948:432): "the transformation of rural communities within Western society into specialized and dependent communities serving the whole national socio-economic system."

3. "The mass culture is American national culture and also Western technological civilization. It is characterized by science and technology; urbanization; industrialization; an emphasis on secular and materialistic values; mass communications through mass advertising, newspapers, magazines, movies; increasing federal government control and interest in the institutionalized areas of society; belief in the ideals of equality of opportunity and in democracy; and belief in the importance of education to achieve democracy and opportunity" (Rubin, 1951:194). See also Bennet and Tumin (1948) and Odum (1947).

4. The analysis of culture change which follows draws heavily on Homer G. Barnett's *Innovation: The Basis of Cultural Change* (1953).

5. For a complete discussion of the role of "conjunction of differences" in culture change see Barnett (1953:46–56).

6. I should like to echo the sentiments of Charles Hughes (1957:7–14) regarding the applicability of reference group concepts in studying culture contact and culture change situations. I found the concept of "relative deprivation," for example, quite useful in my analysis of the Plainville materials. This concept "centers on the problem of different or shifting standards of adequacy applied to the same events or situation, either by the same group of people at different times, or by different groups"

(Hughes, 1957:11). See also Merton and Rossi (1957:225–81), Merton (1957: 281–387), and Sherif (1953).

7. The shift from subsistence to cash economy is not new in Plainville, but is a process that has been under way for many decades. Plainvillers have become increasingly dependent upon national and international economic trends since about the time of the First World War.

8. See Barnett (1953:156–67) for a full discussion of this variable in culture change situations.

9. Adapted from the U.S. Bureau of the Census, Agriculture, for years indicated.

10. We should note that the buying power of Plainvillers is not so disproportionate as one might think when comparing it with that of urban dwellers. Many Plainville families still produce much of their own food.

11. Mead (1937:16) defines individualism as "behavior in which the individual strives toward his goal without reference to others."

12. Even in this area of behavior some people, particularly businessmen, are reluctant to extend themselves to their fullest through fear of being identified as ostentatious.

13. The specific changes which have occurred in rural society as a whole are summarized in most introductory texts in rural sociology. See especially Bertrand and associates (1958) and Loomis and Beegle (1957) for recent treatments; there are many others.

14. An excellent statement of industrialized agriculture in American society by an anthropologist is Goldschmidt (1947). He offers a plea for a realistic farm policy, not based on a fallacious stereotype (see especially Chapter X).

Bibliography

A major source of reference for this study was, of course, *Plainville, U.S.A.*, by James West (Carl Withers), published in 1945 by Columbia University Press.

Ackerman, Joseph, and Marshall Harris, eds. 1950. *Family Farm Policy*. Chicago, University of Chicago Press.

Arensberg, Conrad. 1954. "The Community Study Method," *American Journal of Sociology*, LX (No. 2):109–24.

—— 1955. "American Communities," *American Anthropologist*, LVII (No. 6):1143–63.

Barnett, Homer G. 1953. *Innovation, the Basis of Cultural Change*. New York, McGraw-Hill Book Co., Inc.

Beaglehole, Ernest. 1957. *Social Change in the South Pacific: Rarotonga and Aituaki*. New York, Macmillan Co.

Beall, Robert T. 1940. "Rural Electrification," in *Farmers in a Changing World* (U.S. Department of Agriculture Yearbook). Washington, D.C., Government Printing Office.

Bell, Earl H. 1934. "Social Stratification in a Small Community," *Scientific Monthly*, XXXVIII:157–64.

—— 1942. *Culture of a Contemporary Rural Community: Sublette, Kansas* (Bureau of Agricultural Economics, U.S. Department of Agriculture, Rural Life Studies, No. 2). Washington, D.C., Government Printing Office.

Bennett, John W. 1944. "Culture Change and Personality in a Rural Society," *Social Forces*, XXIII (No. 2):123–32.

——, and Melvin M. Tumin. 1949. *Social Life: Structure and Function*. New York, Alfred A. Knopf Co.

Benoit-Smullyan, Emil. 1944. "Status, Status Types, and Status Interrelationships," *American Sociological Review*, IX (No. 2):151–61.

Bertrand, Alvin L., and Associates, eds. 1958. *Rural Sociology: An Analysis of Contemporary Rural Life*. New York, McGraw-Hill Book Co., Inc.

Bott, Elizabeth. 1954. "The Concept of Class as a Reference Group," *Human Relations*, VII (No. 2):259–86.

Collier, James E. 1955. *Agricultural Atlas of Missouri* (Missouri AES Bulletin 645). Columbia, University of Missouri Press.

Cooley, Charles H. 1907. *Social Organization: A Study of the Larger Mind.* New York, Charles Scribner's Sons.

Coon, Carleton S. 1946. "The Universality of Natural Groupings in Human Societies," *Journal of Educational Sociology,* XX (No. 3):162–68.

Coughenour, Charles M. 1953. *Social Stratification in a Northeast Missouri Farming Community.* Unpublished Ph.D. dissertation, University of Missouri, Columbia.

———, and Lawrence M. Hepple. 1957. *Religious Groups in Rural Missouri* (Missouri AES Bulletin 633B). Columbia, University of Missouri Press.

Cuber, John F., and William F. Kenkel. 1954. *Social Stratification in the United States.* New York, Appleton-Century-Crofts, Inc.

Davis, Kingsley. 1942. "A Conceptual Analysis of Stratification," *American Sociological Review,* VII (No. 3):309–21.

——— 1949. *Human Society.* New York, Macmillan Co.

———, and Wilbert E. Moore. 1945. "Some Principles of Stratification," *American Sociological Review,* X (No. 2):242–49.

Firth, Raymond. 1959. *Social Change in Tikopia: Re-Study of a Polynesian Community After a Generation.* New York, Macmillan Co.

Gist, Noel P. 1940. *Secret Societies* (University of Missouri Studies, XV, No. 4). Columbia, University of Missouri Press.

Goldschmidt, Walter. 1947. *As You Sow.* New York, Harcourt Brace Co.

——— 1955. "Social Class and the Dynamics of Status," *American Anthropologist,* VII (No. 6):1209–17.

Gordon, Milton. 1949. "Social Class in American Sociology," *American Journal of Sociology,* LV (No. 3):262–68.

Gross, Llewellyn. 1949. "The Use of Class Concepts in Sociological Research," *American Journal of Sociology,* LIV (No. 5):409–21.

Hatch, David L. 1948. *Changes in the Structure and Function of a Rural New England Community.* Unpublished Ph.D. dissertation, Harvard University, Cambridge.

History of Missouri. 1889. Chicago, Goodspeed Publishing Co.

Hoebel, E. Adamson. 1949. *Man in the Primitive World: An Introduction to Anthropology.* New York, McGraw-Hill Book Co.

Holik, John S., and Lawrence M. Hepple. 1959. *Index of Religious Group Action* (Missouri AES Bulletin 633D). Columbia, University of Missouri Press.

Hughes, Charles Campbell. 1957. "Reference Group Concepts in the Study of a Changing Eskimo Culture," in *Cultural Stability and Cultural Change,* Proceedings of the 1957 Annual Spring Meeting of the American Ethnological Society, edited by Verne F. Ray, Seattle, Washington.

Hughes, Everett C. 1945. "Dilemmas and Contradictions of Status," *American Journal of Sociology,* L (No. 5):353–59.

Hollingshead, August B. 1952. "Trends in Social Stratification: A Case Study," *American Sociological Review,* XVII (No. 6):679–85.

Kahl, Joseph A. 1957. *The American Class Structure.* New York, Rinehart and Company, Inc.

Kaufman, Harold F., *et al.* 1953. "Problems of Theory and Method in the Study of Social Stratification in Rural Society," *Rural Sociology,* XVIII (No. 1):12–24.

Kimball, Solon T. 1955. "Problems of Studying American Culture," *American Anthropologist,* LVII (No. 6, Pt. 1):1131–43.

Kluckhohn, Florence R. 1950. "Dominant and Substitute Profiles of Cultural Orientations: Their Significance for the Analysis of Stratification," *Social Forces,* XXVIII (No. 4):376–93.

Landis, Paul H. 1948. *Rural Life in Process.* New York, McGraw-Hill Book Co., Inc.

Lenski, Gerhard E. 1952. "American Social Classes: Statistical Strata or Social Groups," *American Journal of Sociology,* LVIII (No. 2):139–45.

Lewis, Oscar. 1951. *Life in a Mexican Village: Tepoztlán Restudied.* Urbana, University of Illinois Press.

———— 1953. "Controls and Experiments in Field Work," in *Anthropology Today,* by A. L. Kroeber *et al.* Chicago, University of Chicago Press.

Linton, Ralph. 1936. *The Study of Man.* New York, Appleton-Century-Crofts, Inc.

————, ed. 1940. *Acculturation in Seven American Indian Tribes.* New York, Columbia University Press.

Lipset, Seymour, and Reinhard Bendix. 1951. "Social Status and Social Structure: A Reexamination of Data and Interpretations," *The British Journal of Sociology,* II (No. 2):150–68, 230–54.

Longmore, Wilson T. 1953. "Special Agencies Within the Department of Agriculture," in Loomis, *et al., Rural Social Systems and Adult Education.* East Lansing, Michigan State College Press.

Loomis, Charles P., *et al.* 1953. *Rural Social Systems and Adult Education.* East Lansing, Michigan State College Press.

———, and J. Allan Beegle. 1950. *Rural Social Systems.* New York, Prentice-Hall, Inc.

———, and J. Allan Beegle, 1957. *Rural Sociology: The Strategy of Change.* Englewood Cliffs, N.J., Prentice-Hall, Inc.

Lynd, Robert S., and Helen M. 1929. *Middletown: A Study in Contemporary American Culture.* New York, Harcourt Brace Co.

———, and Helen M. 1937. *Middletown in Transition.* New York, Harcourt Brace Co.

MacIver, R. M., and Charles H. Page. 1949. *Society, An Introductory Analysis.* New York, Rinehart and Company, Inc.

MacLeish, Kenneth, and Kimball Young. 1942. *Landaff, New Hampshire* (Bureau of Agricultural Economics, U.S. Department of Agriculture, Rural Life Studies, No. 3). Washington, D.C., Government Printing Office.

Mead, Margaret. 1937. *Cooperation and Competition among Primitive Peoples.* New York, McGraw-Hill Book Co., Inc.

——— 1956. *New Lives for Old: Cultural Transformation-Manus, 1928–1953.* New York, William Morrow and Co.

Merton, Robert K. 1957. "Continuities in the Theory of Reference Groups and Social Structure," in *Social Theory and Social Structure* (rev. ed.). Glencoe, Free Press.

———, and Alice S. Rossi. 1957. "Contributions to the Theory of Reference Group Behavior," in *Social Theory and Social Structure* (rev. ed.). Glencoe, Free Press.

Miner, Horace. 1949. *Culture and Agriculture: An Anthropological Study of a Corn Belt County.* Ann Arbor, University of Michigan Press.

Moe, Edward O., and Carl C. Taylor. 1942. *Irwin, Iowa* (Bureau of Agricultural Economics, U.S. Department of Agriculture, Rural Life Studies, No. 5). Washington, D.C., Government Printing Office.

Murdock, George P., *et al.* 1950. *Outline of Cultural Materials.* (3d rev.) New Haven, Yale University Press.

Nadel, S. F. 1951. *The Foundations of Social Anthropology.* Glencoe, Free Press.

Nadel, S. F. 1957. *The Theory of Social Structure*. Glencoe, Free Press.

Odum, Howard. 1947. *Understanding Society*. New York, Macmillan Co.

Parsons, Talcott. 1949. *Essays in Sociological Theory: Pure and Applied*. Glencoe, Free Press.

Pfautz, Harold W. 1953. "The Current Literature on Social Stratification: Critique and Bibliography," *American Journal of Sociology*, LVIII (No. 4):391–418.

Raper, Carl. 1949. "Rural Social Differentials," in *Rural Life in the United States*, ed. by Carl Taylor. New York, Alfred A. Knopf Co.

Redfield, Robert. 1950. *A Village that Chose Progress*. Chicago, University of Chicago Press.

—— 1955. *The Little Community*. Chicago, University of Chicago Press.

—— 1956. *Peasant Society and Culture*. Chicago, University of Chicago Press.

Rubin, Morton. 1951. *Plantation County*. Chapel Hill, University of North Carolina Press.

Sales Management, Inc. 1941. "The 1941 Study of Effective Buying Income for 1940, in Sales Management," April 10, 1941. Missouri County Data, p. 228.

Schmidt, C. T. 1941. *American Farmers in the World Crisis*. New York, Oxford University Press.

Sherif, Muzafer. 1953. "The Concept of Reference Groups in Human Relations," in *Group Relations at the Crossroads*, ed. by M. Sherif and M. O. Wilson. New York, Harper and Brothers.

Smith, T. Lynn. 1940. "Trends in Community Organization and Life," *American Sociological Review*, V (No. 3):325–34.

Spicer, E. H., ed. 1952. *Human Problems in Technological Change: a Casebook*. New York, Russell Sage Foundation.

—— 1958. "Social Structure and the Acculturation Process," *American Anthropologist*, LX (No. 3):433–41.

Steward, Julian H. 1951. "Levels of Sociocultural Integration: An Operational Concept," *Southwestern Journal of Anthropology*, VII (No. 4):374–91.

Taylor, Carl C. 1942. "Rural Life," *American Journal of Sociology*, XLVII (No. 6):841–53.

——, ed. 1949. *Rural Life in the United States*. New York, Alfred A. Knopf Co.

Tolley, Howard. 1941. *Material Bearing on Parity Prices: Presentation by Howard Tolley, Chief of the Bureau of Agricultural Economics at a Hearing on Parity Prices and Income for Agriculture before a Subcommittee of the Committee on Agriculture and Forestry, U.S. Senate, July 1941.* Washington, D.C. (Mimeographed.)

United States Bureau of the Census. 1932. *Fifteenth Census of the United States: 1930, Vol. III, Population.* Washington, D.C., Government Printing Office.

———— 1935. *Census of Agriculture: Statistics for Counties.* Washington, D.C., Government Printing Office.

———— 1939–40. *Vital Statistics of the United States.* Washington, D.C., Government Printing Office.

———— 1940. *Census of Agriculture: Statistics for Counties.* Washington, D.C., Government Printing Office.

———— 1943a. *Sixteenth Census of the United States: 1940, Vol. III, Housing.* Washington, D.C., Government Printing Office.

———— 1943b. *Sixteenth Census of the United States: 1940, Vol. III, Population.* Washington, D.C., Government Printing Office.

———— 1945. *Census of Agriculture: Statistics for Counties.* Washington, D.C., Government Printing Office.

———— 1947. *County Data Book: A Supplement to the Statistical Abstract of the United States.* Washington, D.C., Government Printing Office.

———— 1950. *Census of Agriculture: Statistics for Counties.* Washington, D.C., Government Printing Office.

———— 1952. *Seventeenth Census of the United States: 1950, Vol. II, Characteristics of the Population.* Washington, D.C., Government Printing Office.

———— 1953. *Seventeenth Census of the United States: 1950, Vol. I, General Characteristics.* Washington, D.C., Government Printing Office.

———— 1954. *Census of Agriculture: Statistics for Counties.* Washington, D.C., Government Printing Office.

United States Department of Agriculture. 1937–54. *Missouri Agricultural Stabilization Conservation Program, Statistical Reports by Counties.* (Mimeographed.)

———— 1951–54. *Woodland County Agricultural Stabilization Conservation Program, County Statistical Report, Annual.* (Mimeographed.)

———— 1954. *Agricultural Conservation Program: Missouri,*

Handbook for 1955. Washington, D.C., Government Printing Office.

———— 1955. *Development of Agriculture's Human Resources: A Report on Problems of Low-Income Farmers.* Washington, D.C., Government Printing Office.

Useem, John, Pierre Tangent, and Ruth Useem. 1942. "Stratification in a Prairie Town," *American Sociological Review,* VII (No. 3):331–42.

Vidich, Arthur J., and Joseph Bensman. 1958. *Small Town in Mass Society: Class, Power and Religion in a Rural Community.* Princeton, Princeton University Press.

Vogt, Evon Z. 1947. "Social Stratification in the Rural Middle-West: a Structural Analysis," *Rural Sociology,* XII (No. 4):364–75.

———— 1955. *Modern Homesteaders.* Cambridge, The Belknap Press of the Harvard University Press.

————, and Ray Hyman. 1959. *Water Witching, U.S.A.* Chicago, University of Chicago Press.

Warner, W. Lloyd, and Paul S. Lunt. 1941. *The Social Life of a Modern Community.* New Haven, Yale University Press.

————, and Associates. 1949. *Democracy in Jonesville: A Study in Quality and Inequality.* New York, Harper and Brothers.

Warriner, Charles K. 1955. "Leadership in the Small Group," *American Journal of Sociology,* LX (No. 4):361–70.

Watson, James B. 1952. "Cayuá Culture Change: A Study in Acculturation and Methodology," *American Anthropologist,* LIV (No. 2, Part 2), Memoir Number 73.

Wheeler, Wayne. 1949. *Social Stratification in a Plains Community.* Minneapolis, privately published.

Williams, Robin M. Jr. 1952. *American Society: A Sociological Interpretation.* New York, Alfred A. Knopf Co.

Wilson, Marion. 1907. *Wilson's History of [Woodland County].* [Discovery,] Herald Press.

Wolf, Eric R. 1955. "Types of Latin American Peasantry: A Preliminary Discussion," *American Anthropologist,* LVII (No. 3): 452–72.

Woodland County Agricultural Extension Office. 1938–54. *Woodland County Rural Program: Extension Agents' Annual Narrative Report.* (Mimeographed.)

Index

Baptist Church, 169-72, 279 n. 9; attitude toward Ladies' Bridge Club, 159; attitude toward TV, 27; disapproval of pool hall, 79; minister of, 87-88, 171, 267 n. 73; national Baptist movement and, 246; revival meeting, 177-81
Barbers, 16
Barite, 11
Barnett, Homer G., cited, 226-58 *passim*, 280 nn. 4, 5, 281 n. 8; quoted, 253
Bathrooms, modern, 96; *see also* Plumbing
Beef, 71, 235; *see also* Livestock
Beef specialists, prestige of, 196, 207-9
Beef specialization, 44, 48, 50-54, 60, 229, 230-31
Beegle, J. Allan, quoted, 134-35, 139, 281 n. 13
Behavior, individual and group, 107-67, 192, 193-94
Bennett, John W., cited, 198, 280 n. 2
Bertrand, Alvin L., quoted, 3, 281 n. 13
Birth control, 117
Births, 19-20
Blackleg, 68
Book clubs, 30
Borrowing, 140, 241
Bottom land, 44
Boys: career objectives of, 162-63; dress of, 103-4; economic roles considered appropriate for, 108; West on differential treatment accorded, 270 n. 9; *see also* Children; Teenagers
Boy Scouts, 7, 152, 159
Bridge Club, *see* Ladies' Bridge Club
Bull cooperatives, 61
Burials, *see* Funerals
Business buildings, 14-15, 77, 241
Businessmen, 16; attitude toward belonging to cliques, 136; attitude toward changed shopping patterns, 234; dress of, 102; efforts to revive consumer interest, 86-87; new role of, 234; *see also* Service establishments
Businessmen's organization, 7, 148,

159-60; *see also* Commercial Club
Butchering, 240
Butter and egg money, 67, 270 n. 8; *see also* Dairying; Poultry

Cardplaying, 212
Career objectives of Plainville's high school students, 162-63
Cash economy, 229, 231; *see also* Economic system
Cash income, 200, 225; *see also* Income
Catholic families, 169
Cattlemen, 44, 73-74, 234, 265 nn. 47-50; *see also* Beef specialists; Dairymen
CCC, 227
Census data, use of, 6, 9
Census tabulations (1950s), 19-21
Census of Housing, U.S., 93
Census on incomes, 32-33
Change, process of, 1-2; *see also* Cultural change; Social change
Cheese plant, 60
Childbirth care, 118-19, 271 nn. 20, 21
Children: on farms, 66-67 (*see also* Farm families); friction between husband and wife over number of, 271 n. 18; population figures, 1940–50, 21 (*tab.*); relationship with grandparents, 126-27; training and education of, 121-25, 269 nn. 1-3, 272 nn. 23-27
Christian Church, 7, 169-70, 173-75, 278 nn. 2, 3, 279 n. 7; Commercial Club monthly meetings in the basement of, 160; minister of, 87, 174; relationship of Ladies' Bridge Club to, 159; religious behavior in, 177
Christmas program, children's, 159, 176
Churches: attendance, 184-88; attitudes on revelation of grace or conversion, 181-82; attitudes toward training of ministers, 182-83; in class system, 190-91, 193-94; competition among, 112-13, 180-81; cooperative endeavors, 174-75; doctrinal issues, 175-76; effect of mechanization on, 141-44; mem-

families, 261 n. 4; on care of infants, 119-20; on clothing, 102; on differential treatment accorded boys and girls, 270 n. 9; on division of labor, 66; on dysfunctional consumer patterns, 56-57; on electric power use, 94; on embalming, 279 n. 10; on emigration, 18, 163; on external influences, 247; on farmer-merchant relationship, 85; on fidelity, 116; on funeral practices, 189, 279 n. 10; on grandparents-grandchildren relationship, 126; on Home Economics clubs, 276 nn. 59, 61; on hostility to mail-order catalogs, 267 n. 67; on influence and prestige, 250-51; on interest groups, 154, 156, 157; on kin-groups, 132; on loafing groups, 78; on magical practices, 53; on mail carrier, 279 n. 8; on money system of farmers, 260 n. 2; on neighborhoods, 139-40; on New Deal reforms, 255; on old age pensions, 266 n. 58; on politics, 145, 146, 275 n. 54; on radio ownership, 25; on rearing of children, 121-23, 270 n. 9, 272 nn. 23-26; on religion, 168-72 *passim*, 184, 185, 278 n. 2; on retail business, 81; on sex differences, 107; on size of family, 117; on social mobility, 218-19; on social planning, 258; on soil depletion, 46; on threshing, 240
Wheat, 47, 48, 229
Wildlife, 12, 102
Willingness to work, 212, 213-14
Wilson, Marion, quoted, 13
Withers, Carl, *see* West, James
Wolf, Eric, cited, 222
Women: attitude toward role responsibilities, 269-70 nn. 4-8; decreasing role in dairying, 229-30; desire for more leisure time, 237; dress of, 102-3; on farms, 66-67; food savings from garden cultivation by, 100-1; gossip and, 138; management and care of poultry, 74-76; role of, as mother and wife, 108-9; working outside home, 89; *see also* Ladies' Bridge Club
Wood, 240; *see also* Fuel; Timber

Woodland County, 2-3; birth and death rates: 1940-49, 20 (*tab.*); births by attendance, 1938-52, 119 (*tab.*); comparative age levels, 1940-1950, 21 (*tab.*); comparative populations for, 1930-1940-1950, 19 (*tab.*); farm population, 274 n. 47; farms by acreage class, 1945-1954, 43 (*tab.*); farms by ownership class, 45 (*tab.*); feed expenditures in, 50 (*tab.*); geographical setting of, 10-31; incomes from all sources, 47 (*tab.*), 68, 75, 231, 232, 281 n. 10; money circulated in, in 1954 from federal programs, 90; owner-occupied dwellings in, 94 (*tab.*); participants in improved pasture program, 42 (*tab.*); population changes, farm and nonfarm, 20 (*tab.*); retail business in, 80-81; sale of milk to plants by farmers, 60-61; settlement of, 12-13; tractors on farms, 55; use of electric power on farms, 95
Woodland County Agricultural Extension Association, 38, 152-56, 246, 249
Woodland County Dairy Festival, 67
Woodland County Dairy Herd Improvement Association, *see* Dairy Herd Improvement Association
Woodland County Extension Service, *see* Extension Service
Woodland County Farm Bureau, 152, 153, 230, 246
Woodland County Welfare Office, 90, 245, 268 n. 78
Woodmen, 156
"Work swapping," 58, 133, 140, 240, 241-42; *see also* Cooperative behavior
World War, Second, effects of, 18-21, 132, 159, 227
WPA, criticism of, 151, 255

Young people's organizations in churches, 174
Youth, *see* Teenagers

Zinc, 11